DOG *of* GOD:

The Novel

a wild romp through magical worlds

Dear Rickard O; thank you for coming into my life & bringing so much light right when I needed it so much. You're my light angel. Blessings on ya! Cher

Cher Slater-Barlevi, MA

BALBOA PRESS
A DIVISION OF HAY HOUSE

Library of Congress Control Number: 2012910229

Balboa Press books may be ordered through booksellers or by contacting:

Balboa Press
A Division of Hay House
1663 Liberty Drive
Bloomington, IN 47403
www.balboapress.com
1-(877) 407-4847

Printed in the United States of America

ISBN: 978-1-4525-5348-1 (sc)
ISBN: 978-1-4525-5349-8 (hc)
ISBN: 978-1-4525-5347-4 (e)

Balboa Press rev. date: 12/21/2012

For my husband "Stev",
and for our loving dog family:
Jim Bob, Evian, Vittel
Squiggi
Bear, Bijou, Boo Boo, Bambo

ACKNOWLEDGMENTS

Through the 8 years it took me to finish my novel, I had great positive and joyful support from my fine editors:

Toni Jenkins, Mary Worthington, Debbie Williams, Geoff Bain, plus Nurse Pam Gruber for medical advice.

As I was getting my Masters at the University of Santa Monica, I was so brilliantly encouraged by Mary and Ron Hulnick, the staff, and my class of 2011. I completed this novel as my Masters project.

Additional thanks to my life-long dear friends who went with me to Brazil and took me to places I would have never ventured, both on this earth and within myself: Dale Bach, Dr. Suzy London. I want to include Dr. Cleia Mara Fernandes Barradas and her husband Carlos Barradas for teaching me hands-on Spiritist healing protocol. I also owe many thanks to Dr. Debrah Sirmans, Heather Cumming, Martin Mosqueira, Bob Dinga, Inely Cesesna & Michael Murphy for teaching me the ways of Brazil.

I am so beholden to all my writing teachers and fellow classmates at UCLA and a particular teacher at Media Bistro: David Israel, for helping me find Xico's voice. Special thanks for holding my hand as my writing coach for all my years as a screenwriter : Ken Rotcop.

And lastly:

The distinct honor of being in the presence of the amazing work of Medium Joao Teixerira de Faria (John of God) and all of the 32 spirits who work through him in loving for the brave enlightened souls here on Earth having a human experience.

My heart is full.

INTRODUCTION

It was 1973. There I was, standing outside my car in the middle of the Pacific Coast Highway, while the man who had just smashed into the front of my classic Alfa Romeo was screaming at me incoherently. Under the din, a little inner voice was directing me to "Move! Someone is going to hit the accident." But too late. I heard a Mercedes screeching its tires—the noise coming from behind me—smashing my legs between her bumper and mine and throwing the accident 10 feet ahead.

In surgery, I actually died and chose to come back. From that time forward, my life changed drastically in many ways. I noticed I had become very sensitive to the seeing of other dimensions.

After 30 years of hearing the Western doctors' evaluation of the X-rays, all telling me "Oh what a mess, nothing we can do", and giving me no hope but to just suffer as a cripple in pain for the rest of my life, I said to myself, Nope, that's not okay with me. As my last hope, I flew to Brazil—hobbling on 2 canes—to be worked on by the infamous psychic surgeon, Medium John of God. His reputation reported 40 years of serving miracles to millions of people.

My accident turned out to be an immense Blessing . . . a gift.

After the accident and the experience of life after death, I developed a heightened awareness. During the next 30 years, I trained to become a medium. When I was in Brazil, while Medium John of God was on stage doing surgery on people standing in an energetic anesthesia trance, I was able to see how all the miracles were happening around me and to me. There were hundreds of humans who had come from places all over the Earth seeking hope and healing. And behind them was a light show of thousands upon thousands of "Entities" helping him with his work from the Otherworldly Dimensions. This truly was a place of the miraculous.

Eight years later, still walking without canes, I traveled back to Abadiania, Brazil to see John of God to ask for a blessing for my nearly completed novel. Nearly everything in the book was based on the true stories I had heard and experiences I had witnessed, while I was there during my four return trips, weeks at a time. It was in the moment of requesting the blessing for my novel that the doctor entities, speaking in spirit through John of God, requested that I change all the names and places because it was "factitiously" told through the eyes of Xico. (This was an actual healing dog I befriended when he had come to my room many nights to help in the healing of my legs.)

This was all fine with me. Again, I chose to see it only as a blessing.

For some readers, this story will appear as pure fantasy (and what a wonderful way to journey), while other readers will just know, and embrace and celebrate the Infinite Laws of the Universe and the magnificence of it all.

Cher Slater-Barlevi, M.A.

"For those who believe, no words are necessary. For those who do not believe, no words are possible."

Medium Joao De Deus

A scientist journeyed to Mexico, where he had been told he would find a very loud-sounding bat: if human beings could hear this bat it would have the decibels comparable to the roar of a jet taking off in close proximity.

The scientist brought very sensitive equipment with him. This kind of equipment, for example, could detect and record the energetic, screeching sounds coming from the electric wiring on telephone poles, as well as coins clinking in someone's pocket while they walked down the street fifty feet away.

Upon finding this particular bat, he marveled at what was most certainly true, for the roar was deafening. Along with the bat, he heard a multitude of sounds coming from other sources he was never even aware of. He contemplated the relationship the dog has to noise hypersensitivity.

Can you imagine? The scientist would have missed out on this extraordinary experience if he had closed his mind, saying: "Because I cannot hear or see this phenomenon with my human ears, it doesn't exist, and therefore, what I'm hearing from this sensitive equipment means absolutely nothing."

Mediumship is merely sensitive equipment.

MONTREAL, CANADA
THE LAST OF A HARD WINTER, 2004

CHAPTER 1

A police car moves slowly down a quiet residential street. Due to the short winter days, the evening cold is already crusting the snow, making the roads slippery, making it difficult for the officers to find the house number in the dimness.

The patrol car finally slides next to the curb and the drone of the motor dies. The officers inside wipe the fogged windshield, straining to see the small clapboard house just up the shoveled walkway. Its one lit window shines across the soft-mounded yard.

The two police officers exit and head for the house, sliding and slipping with every step. Tramping up the stairs to the porch, they pound on the red front door. As they wait, cold puffs billow from their nostrils. A woman peers through the curtain, then jerks it closed.

The wait seems interminable for the two officers as they hit themselves for circulation under their jackets, stamping and blowing against the cold.

Yes? . . . the door opens a crack.

Lillian Fleur?

Yes . . .

Do you mind if we come in?

What is this about, officers?

May we enter and discuss our reason, it's very cold . . .

She makes no indication of being hospitable.

Madam Fleur, we have evidence that you are harboring a small dog confiscated from Paramanguaia (Para-mon-gee-a), Brazil.

I have no dog, officers, so if you'll excuse me . . . The door starts to close.

We've just interviewed your neighbors, and they have verified that you indeed have a dog on your premises answering to the description we have on file.

The door shuts and remains shut. The officers knock again, wait, knock louder, then pound the door. Still no movement. The larger officer yells through the door, This animal is in your possession illegally, Madam. Open up now, or we will have to take more forceful measures!

The woman opens the door, her arms folded across her body, but she says nothing. She is noticeably nervous, with little beads of sweat on her upper lip, even in the winter's cold. The officer continues in a normal tone, Madam, According to Canadian Law 13789 of the penal code, you are in possession of stolen property—a dog from Brazil.

Tears well up in the woman's eyes. Please leave me alone! I have no dog, I-I don't know what you're talking about.

We see that indeed you have just returned from a trip to Brazil transporting a dog. Sergeant Fernando Oswego Rodrigues, a high ranking official from Brazil has personally contacted us for verification so this dog must be very important. . .

She slams the door and the police hear the lock clicking into place—along with a dog barking somewhere inside.

ZEEEP & EEEOO
THE DOLPHINS
IN THE OCEAN OFF THE PACIFIC COAST

CHAPTER 2

Away out in the blue of the waters and away down in the black of the Ocean depths-an event is going on. Two lovers are about to partake in their daily race that starts very early in the morning and goes until one or both are too exhausted and can go no further. Today will be a great race because it is the beginning of the currents of warm; the dolphins have been traveling a long way together to elude the northern waterways of the cold . . .

Twofeetcubittimesfifteenraisedtothefifthpower—got it! Go now! Go-go-go!

WHOOSH—up,up,up, dark to light—major tail kick, FA-WAP . . . AIR. Breathe, in-out, in-out, fill lungs, sheebit first time it always burns, get over it, thankgawd cooling: in-out-in-out, she's in front of me, tilt head down-WHOOOOHUMPPT—water: faster with more thrust, com'on, com'on, com'on, thankgawd she's falling back, yahahaha ye-ssss always faster underwater, feeeeels sooo good.

SONAR READING: object ten feet head.

TRACKING: moving sideways, moving upward: thick, thin, thick, thin; strings together, strings out = lunch!

My fave! Squid . . . ahhhh.

Race canceled.

Lookit her fizzzt past, damn she's fast. So glad to have her back—I'm smiling, I'm smiling, she always makes me smile. That's why I love her. But my tummy calls.

Squid.

Two feet, ten inches north by northeast—go!

YES! STRIKE! Ahh, yessss—yumyumyum, whooooo tickleeey; struggling, squirmin' little tasty squididy squid: numnumnum, ahhhhh sooo satisfiyin', ahhhh.

Uh oh.

She was back. She was puffin'. She was mad.

Hey, you can't do that, nose head! she was sayin'.

Gawd, it always drove her crazy when I changed my mind so fast. Couldn't help it, though. Always said, Opportunity shows itself—ATTACK!—or it just passes right on by looozer.

Besides, I just happened to be a teeny-bit hungry after a whole morning of racing. Gotta give it to her though, man, she's got it—fast as hezzop—great competitor. Keeps my torso tight. That's my girl, Eeeoo. You might think Eeeoo's her name, it's not. It's her frequency—Eeeeeooo—think about it.

Me? I'm Zeeep: also fizzzz fast, dikdik impatient, love to race, always racing . . . but it's not my finest talent. My finest? Well, take a guess . . . heh, heh. And my next finest attribute? I am an aquatic acrobatic artist. I excel at: back-falling, breaching, three-quarter body breaching, half-body lobtailing, flips of all kinds: somersaults, twists: right turns, left, sqeezzzzipper. I am, however, still working on the spin. Whoa! Now that's a beebo-a-ramma. Saw it demonstrated off the coast of Santa Barbara, whole pods of these pinstriped jobs executing with the finest precision, all the hezzop over miles-and-miles of territory—greatest thing I'd ever seen. Dikdik!

I admit I'm a show-off. Most dolphins are.

Take Eeeoo, now she's . . . she's to the extreme. She was famous once, ya know. Truth. Was a main feature in some kind of Aquatic Zoo. Kinda sad story. Whadda life, workin' with the humans. Not somethin' I'd a chose. The stories? Gaaaawd.

Now, some of those human folks were good, loving, devoted—even stellar—but man, some of 'em—sick! Sick to the core. Nasty, nasty bunch. So much so, they fitzbing un-did all the good.

How'd Eeeoo ever get into a situation like that? Well, we were young, just teenagers. We were each other's first love. Outta control. Sheebit like that always leads to trouble. Eeeoo got addicted. Yeah, strung out on tour boats cuisine that would chug up and down the coast. She was hooked on the amazing eats they'd throw off the side of those boats—prize fish, delicacies not from around here. Not so tasty, I thought. Not fresh from the ocean, I could tell. But a farm pond (I later found out.) But not Eeeoo, no,no,no, she became fanatical to the prestige of foreign dining. I guess. I dunno. Women.

I gotta confess though, that for a while I even got hooked, heh, heh, heh. Yep. What was addicting was free food, heck yesss—more time for fun. Now that I think of it I'm still addicted. I'm addicted to fun . . . and again with the confessions: that's why it was so hard to go through all the stuff that happened to us because of it.

SABRINA
MONTREAL, CANADA
WINTER, 1998

CHAPTER 3

The nurse's eyes turned to her. Squinched way down to a hard line, her eyebrows grew together and two worry lines popped up between them. Sabrina could feel her whole body tense up.

Because we have vaccinations, the nurse replied. I need to review your records, young lady . . .

What was she talking about? She remembered the whole month of looking into the mirror and seeing all the big red welts all over her body along with a thick, fat neck, not to mention the feeling someone had scraped her throat raw with a knife when she swallowed. She'd looked like a . . . like a . . . well, Snooker, the boy that lived next door, had called her a *holymoly freak-o-zoid*. He'd pointed at her, scrunched up his face real ugly-like and said she looked like she was growing . . . *volcanoes!* She agreed. Her face was a barren wasteland: the likes of the man-in-the-moon.

She found this a fascinating landscape. If she picked at them, they'd bleed and all kinds of pus would run out and after a day the mountainous obtrusions would cap themselves in black. She couldn't help *not* picking them, heck they itched like crazy. Her mother would reprimand her. Stop it!

she'd say, while safety-pinning the cuffs closed on Sabrina's pajama sleeves to restrict her criminal fingers from their adventures. She'd ask over and over, Do you want scars for the rest of your life?

Her mother's attempt was futile. Sabrina always found a hole-way for at least one of her fingers to wriggle out of both sleeves—if not, she'd make one by chewing, pulling, and biting down hard with her back teeth then grinding them together on the spit-wet, thread-barren fabric. Two fingers were all she needed for anything, especially *a victory over the boils.*

The pus fascinated her: all warm and so sticky that when she put her fingers together they'd stick. Maybe she could use it for glue on something—so she tried to stick two pieces of Kleenex together. She found it was best to let the pus dry before it would stick together really good.

The boredom always drove her even crazier.

She wasn't allowed to read because the doctor had said that her eyes would be ruined and hers was the only family she knew that didn't own a TV in the whole wide world. Her mother said that it ruined people's brains and made children stupid and fat. *What about crazy, Mom!,* she thought to herself, grunting hard as she ripped her doll's arm from its body.

Of course, it was also taboo to go out to play. She was sure she was *quarantined* with something deadly. No one had told her yet (who would?). She had just figured it out herself. Her older sister had been *quarantined* when she was little. She was the only kid in ages that had contracted polio. Most unusual they'd said, a freakish happening. She was moved to the back of the house, closed off from everyone for at least a year. Well, maybe it wasn't a year, Sabrina wasn't quite sure, because it happened when she was really young. She does remember, however, the doctor and her mother wearing masks that bandits wore in cartoons, when they went in to tend to her. What Sabrina couldn't figure out was how Patti hadn't gone stark-raving mad having to stay in her room for so long. Maybe that's why she's such a weird duck . . . Sabrina had shivered over this realization. Was she the next to be infected with the same mental disorder?

Sabrina loved being outdoors. One day, against her mother's wishes, she scooted her bed right up against the window. Because she was on the second floor, if she got real close to the glass she could pretend she was flying like a bird over the trees outside—that—and she loved huffing real hard on the cold glass with her hot breath so she could print her name with her pointer finger and make little pictures all around it. When the finger drawings would fade, she could make them come back magically by hot-breathing all over the window again. It made her a little light headed, but she liked the feeling—this too, was another adventure she could go on if she kept it up—she noticed the room would change colors and little stars would appear.

Cool.

There were some perks in being sick, as her sister had pointed out. One, you never had to make your bed—heck, you could *eat food* in it if you wanted to. Two, you never had to clean up your room. Three, you could draw until your hand fell off if you wanted to. Sabrina loved to draw. Someday she was going to be a . . . *let's see, what could you be if you were old and could draw. I could fly a plane . . . and draw in the sky.* She sighed. That'd be great. Then she'd have all this money by then, as much as she could find and throw it out the window for all the poor children who didn't have food and a nice place to live. And the kids would catch it and they'd buy mansions for their parents to live in. And they could buy horses to ride to school and then they wouldn't get picked on by the other kids because they'd be so much taller and bigger on top of a horse . . .

She looked out her window and noticed Snooker was tramping around in the snow in the yard next door—his snowsuit two-times larger than he was. He'd seen her now and was making all kinds of faces at her. Snooker was given that name for a very good reason. What a brat, she thinks. He threw a few snowballs and one actually hit the window and made her jump, and he laughed and laughed and pointed up at her and then he fell down in the snow and rolled around.

He calls me a dork! she thinks.

Feelings of jealousy made her grind her teeth. If only she could go outside. If only she could go outside . . . she'd go skiing again . . . with her father. Not her sister.

Just her father and her—alone—this time.

The last time she went skiing was with her father and her sister, just a few weeks before she got sick. She usually does anything sporty quite easily. At school she's called *Tomboy-Tommy-Tom*. She was proud of it. She's always hated frou-frous, except Grandmère's French stuff—that she loved. She hated dresses of any kind. Hated skinny models, thought they looked kind of sickly, kind of like what she looked like now, but without all the splotches and protruding neck glands.

Anyway, she'd never been skiing before so she had been giving her father a hard time the whole trip, whining about this and that. Her older sister was a teenager so she wasn't talking to either one of them the whole way. She had plugged herself into a space in between her headphones, her body gyrating to an irritating beat, which sounded like sh-sh-shhhhhh sh-sh-shhhhhh to everyone else. Once, Sabrina had to talk to her when they'd pulled in for gas and she'd jerked out one of Patti's headphones and screamed, you have to take me to the bathroom! and Patti had gotten all P-O'd because Sabrina had ripped out a lock of her hair tangled in the headphone and had yelled back, Go yourself, you're not a stupid baby! and then both of them had shrieked, Dad-dee! right together at the very same time and Dad had bellowed, Quiet! Am I going to have to whoop both of you? . . . Huh?

Oh, it was a long, hard drive.

Sabrina had been so worried. Was she going to die if she didn't know how to ski? It was possible, she was sure. The ache in her stomach made her think so. She'd tried to imagine standing on top of those long boards that she'd seen Dad clamp between the ski rack pinchers. In her mind, she'd step into the bindings (how that worked she couldn't imagine), take off, and head straight down the mountain. She knew there had to be a way to turn those things, to make them stop, but for the life of her she couldn't figure out how and the more she thought about it, the more it made her nervous feet hit the back of the seat and made her chew her gum faster. And the more and more butterflies were flapping all around in her stomach, the more she'd make up silly songs and sing as loud as she could, which was getting everyone mad. She didn't care, she couldn't help it.

By the time they had arrived at the Ski Area, of course, she was an utter nervous wreck. As her father was unpacking the gear from the trunk of their Peugeot, the first thing out of her mouth was, Dad, I have to pee, I have to pee, and after that, of course, came, I'm hungry! and after that Daddy? I don't want to ski! You can't make me.

Her dad had joked with her saying, Ah, my little cherry blossom, me thinks wee are a leettle scar-red ahhhh, perchance, ma chérie?

He always used a fake French accent in a funny voice, his charming tactic to get her to smile. Then he released two skis from the ski rack and presented her with the ungainly package she was to carry. She promptly fell to the ground and refused to budge.

The quad chair was a breeze to get on. Benjamin had requested the attendant stop the chair completely so Sabrina could sit right down and scoot over to the side at the far end. Benjamin sat very close and put his protective arm around his kids but Patti wouldn't have it. She made a teenage stink over it and moved herself with a pout to the furthest end of the chair.

Other than that, the ride up was a success. Sabrina had marveled at the flight over the white embroidered treetops. She'd pointed at the jutting mountain that had shown gold above the valley they were leaving behind. She'd transformed her nervousness into excitement and exploration. Benjamin was in awe over how a child could do that. He wished he had retained that characteristic from his own childhood. His obstinate ego, he realized, had become his nemesis.

Just as they were to dismount, he was careful to remind Sabrina to hold her skis in a point and to bend her legs and to lean in the directions she wanted to go and that would help her to turn—this was going to give her the control she needed.

Sabrina stood up, holding onto her poles, hearing in her mind all the instructions from her father. She saw her father skiing ahead, pulling her from the tips of her poles and the chair continuing on and her sister streaking past like a shot, never to be heard or seen again all day long.

Away from the chair's path, her father let go of her poles. She was still moving, pointing her skis in a triangle like her dad had said, and she had to focus real hard now because she was all on her own. For some reason, she was breathing shallow but she wasn't in a panic...yet. Not until she started moving faster. Her legs were sure, her feet pointed inward, she leaned to the right—she turned right! Wow. She ventured to lean to the left—she was turning left! Good! Now what? Okay, try leaning right. Okay, that worked again. She heard herself sigh for a breath, she wasn't breathing, she must breathe! Okay, I'm making myself breathe. I'm turning again, whew...

I'm skiing! It hit her, she was skiing... ohmygod, she was skiing. She yelled out at her father who had suddenly appeared in front of her, skiing backwards, beaming like the brightest sun in the heavens. I'm skiing, Daddy! I'm skiing! she yelled to him.

That's it! You got it, ma chérie. Follow me, he instructed.

In her revelry, Sabrina hadn't noticed her father had moved behind her, and was straddling the outsides of her skis and was gently edging them closer together. She could feel his strong legs to the sides of her, his torso behind her, and his hands under her armpits. She looked down and the hill was coming faster and faster. She heard her father's voice say, now step down hard on your right foot and lift up your left and lean forward. Wow, she was turning quicker. Good! Good! Keep your legs bent...Now put your left ski as close as you can to your right ski... good! Their movements were following the rhythm of the slope and she felt like she was dancing. What a glorious feeling! A great bond was forming and their hearts were beating to the music of the laughter between them. They were the only souls on the slope, the only angels in heaven. The warmth of trust and love flooded their union, and the chasm they'd created in the past closed forever.

And as she blinked, she was back in her room seeing herself in the mirror with the pink polka-dot robe and the quilt Grandmère made and her face in the mirror full of splotches. Looking out the window, across the yard furrowed and bumpy with the memory of Snooker's inane snowball-play, she could feel a flush of warm anticipation mixed with the pain of deep yearning to see her father walk up the snow path to their front door—finally coming home from work.

ZEEEP, THE DOLPHIN
OCEAN OFF THE PACIFIC COAST

CHAPTER 4

I bet at this point you're wondering, how the heck do we two dolphins, Eeeoo and Zeeep, know all our hip language? You know—clichés, slang, computer lingo, dialect from all over the world—and just how the hell do we even know the English language? Easy: that I owe to Eeeoo. She's amazing. Figured out how to download from the brains of all the hundreds and hundreds of tourists floatin' up and down the shore—tapped in and accessed everything. Brilliant. She can even download and transmit on many different esoteric levels: the physical, astral, causal, mental, etheric, and super etheric—she's one talented cetacean.

So then, you see, I was able to get a download off of her, easy—got everything hologram quality. My only problem is I get it all mixed around, I don't know Hillbilly from Valley girl, Western Cowpoke from New England proper, little kid from old lady and then there's my dolphin language muddled in there, too.

Bear with me, until Eeeoo can get around to downloading it with a little beeborama—I'm dealing with an un-shuffled deck.

She did assure me the download was totally safe, though, 'cause we've got bigger brains than the humans (and they only use three to five percent anyway) so not-to-worry, no danger of overload. However, after rifling through all the garbage I got a little concerned. Man-oh-man, I've never seen such a slushy pile. The things they've collected—appalling! Not all of it though—about ninety percent I'd trash—but I found some good stuff, too.

Don't know why they don't use a lot of it—they'd be brilliant. They could completely turn this earth around, clean it up, be happy, never have crime or war, feed everyone. I don't get humans.

One day there was this boat, kinda looked funny to me, I told her so.

Hey, I told Eeeoo, I don't see any tourists. No jovial energy was coming from it. No little kids' laughter like always—just this cracked up kinda vibe. I had this weird feeling but try to tell someone who's strung-out they shouldn't do something, they can't hear you no matter how loud you yell.

So the stupid ego-driven-teenager that I'd become, from being overloaded with spam, got all peeezonked at her. Just left her there—zipped on outta there to hang out with my boys.

Unbeknownst to me, that day they were throwing out this amazing array of delicacies, a smorgasbord like no other, musta been laced with something cause she got all groggy and started floatin' to the surface, layin' on her side and that's when it happened—WHAMO—before she knew it, she was all caught up in this net thingy and her dikdik lifeless body was being hoisted onto the deck of that fitzbingbongin' boat.

Now, I'm off racing, but I'm feeling really guilty. So's when I show up, the boat's takin' off like a shark outta hezzop—and I sensed they were absconding with my sweetheart. Well, I was right. I must have followed them for at least an hour before total exhaustion set in and I lost them.

Man, I was torn-up for weeks! Searched every inch of coast, must have gone over a hundred miles past our pod territory. I was sendin' out sonar: two miles—then ten—then hundreds in all directions, calculating echo-locations: ten-to-the-forth. Doin' E-equals-Pi-r-squared 'til I thought my forehead would explode.

Just as I was about to give up, I picked up her sonar scanning for me. The frequency: zeeep, zeeep— zeeep, zeeep — zeeep, zeeep was coming from just a little past the shoreline an eighteenth of a mile in. I was so elated, my heart was racing—tears, the whole bit. Eeeoo—eeeeeoo—eeeeoo, I answered, until I figured out there was no way I could walk on land—Jesus. Ya know, there was a time way, way back, when we dolphins did walk on earth, had hair, everything. Hey, that's why they called us mammals. I didn't know this, not a clue, 'til one day I just stumbled upon a stray download: I'd tapped into some history in my memory banks. (It's a dolphin thing that happens now and then, I found out later.) Yep, we were called Archaeocetes fifty-million years ago, had bodies anywhere from six-and-half feet to sixty-nine feet long. Of course there were these huge guys too; whales, believe it or not.

We all lived on land for a little bit, hung out in swamps and some shallow seas, had a good time 'til we figured, hey, let's get with the times, go modern, get buff, take to the oceans for good. Of course this took eons, but those four paddles we had for limbs evolved into two little front fins and those big long tails we had, well, they got trimmed down to what we got now. Add a few bells and whistles like, you know, sonar, infrasound and echolocation equipment a-n-n-n-d whah- lah!

But I digress.

Anyway, I'm running around like an octopus without legs, and I'm shriveling up from the stress of having to deal with so much guilt. I've lost at least 100 pounds, my skin, cracked and wrinkled, barnacles were growing over my eyes, I was a mess. What was happening to my baby? My love? I was so lonely, how could I possibly go on? Then the day came when I actually heard Eeeoo's clicks in my travels near San Diego. She too had been compulsively trying to find me. She sonared me to follow her. She was being moved to an Aquatic Zoo way down in Mexico.

Okay! I'm jazzed, but I'm so tired. I really didn't know for sure just how far away she was, I just kept following her signals. I'm swimmin' along draggin' my bones, when all of the sudden, I get this whacked-out signal. At first I thought it was me finally cracking up from exhaustion, but it was Eeeoo's clicking and it was coming in so strong, I knew she had to be right on top of me. I looked up and I could see a vague shadowy form way up on the surface. It took all I had to push to the top, but by then a new surge of energy had started whamwhamwhamming through my body. Whooooooh. I got to the surface, started deep-breathing air for the first time in ages, and boy was that a painful rush. And I see the boat and pick up Eeeoo's sending zeeep,zeeeep,zeeep 'cause she senses I'm right there close to the boat and I'm eeeeeeooo-eeeooo-eeeeoooing like crazy, 'cause at the point—lo and behold, as sure as I'm a dolphin, and I'm not sure how it happened—but Eeeoo comes flying right over the edge of the boat like an angel on a rampage, into the ocean, right into my flippers!

I don't know, I don't know to this day how it happened, I mean, Eeeoo said that she was just transported, lifted by some kind of light-beings or something, but whew, how do you believe that stuff? Guess I have to after seeing it with my own two eyes, ya know? Anyway, I gotta tell you I think it happened as a prelude to what was going to happen to us later, because that was <u>nothing</u> in comparison.

But there she was . . . looked great . . . felt incredible. We circled and rubbed and slid all over each other and except for her dorsal fin that was flopped to the side and sadness in her eyes and the gash in her lip and the wound that ran down the side of her body—she still had that sleek girlish body and the heart of my true love and all in all, it didn't matter, it was like time had never passed. We looked into each other's eyes, zeeeped and eeeooed until we had made amazing love—gentle and slow and present (hezzop, we weren't really in any shape for the rough stuff we were used to) but . . . I was healing her and she was healing me and I looked around and our pod had circled us and they were sending us healing and it was mind-blowing to be in all that energy . . . no . . . it was fitzbingbong awesome!

I was so happy—there was my lady looking into my eyes, crying (yeah, dolphins cry) and we're making vows until the Manatees come home. And I promised her there was no way possible, ever, that I would ever leave her side again . . . ever. And at the time, I meant it with all my heart.

DR. ABRAHAM LATHAM
NEW YORK, NY 1998

CHAPTER 5

Ahhh, coffee and cigarettes—the perfect breakfast—fast and effective.

Dr. Abraham Latham, Abe to some, breathed in the fragrant steam curling up from his coffee. Peering into the darkness of his fine brew, he drank deep and slow, savoring the taste. He leaned back in his leather desk chair and slung his feet up to rest them on his desk. He ran his hand through his dark hair and stretched as he yawned hard, setting off a fit of coughing.

It was six AM and damn he was tired, he thought, as he watched the winter morning glow slowly creep over the sides of the cold metal buildings standing as silent, colorless sentinels outside his office window. Silence in this city was an anomaly, he was thinking, as he was running his fingers over the prickly stubble on his chin and watching the sunlight splash across the windows, harsh enough to make his eyes tear up and remind him of the headache waiting in the back of his eyes.

He blinked down at the paperwork spread out before him and found he had to fight to focus his eyes. He let out another deep yawn and gulped down the rest of his coffee. He noticed it bit like acid. He lit a cigarette and looked forward to its calming satisfaction flowing through his muscles, but nausea hit him hard for an instant, then disappeared. Standing, his heart pounded in his ears. A wave of panic coursed through him. He bent forward to brace himself on his desk. Was he going to faint? Taking a deep breath he righted himself. Must be the late hours, he thought. Or was 45 getting old?

He had fallen asleep on his papers the night before, only to awaken with a noisy snort. He must have groped his way over to the couch to finish the night. Everything was just a blur now, but he realized it had happened a lot lately with this damn book deadline looming over my damn head like a damn hangman's noose. Abe rubbed the ache in his shoulder, knowing there was no one but the cat back at the apartment who would care if he came home—not the wife he didn't have or the children or even a girlfriend. It occurred to him that the cat probably didn't care either. She had her litter box—getting a little rank by now, he was sure—and the two upside down gallon bottles that released any amount of food or water at any time. No, he thought, there is no one at my apartment who would give a damn. And when it came down to it, what did he care anyway — he really had all that he needed at the office: workout shorts, T-shirt and a change of clothes, and cigarettes—everything, really.

He stifled his yawn, remembering, with a flash of dread, the big day ahead, wrestling with the best publishers in town. He found himself wondering if they really were the best. He wanted only the best. Nothing less would do for this Dr. Abraham Latham, ever.

After his morning cough subsided, he smashed his vile-tasting cigarette in a drinking glass and loosened the belt on his slacks and let them drop. He grabbed up a worn pair of workout shorts draped over the sofa, snapped them in the air and stepped in, removed his rumpled Armani silk fitted shirt, then replaced it with his ragged workout T-shirt pulled from the same pile.

* * *

Echo of the squash ball smacking walls, smacking floor, smacking paddles, squeak and squeal of tennis shoes pounding wooden floor boards, laughter and cursing, sweat spraying the air, the breathing and the grunting. Abe felt a pain coursing through his arm. He grabbed his knees trying to brace himself from a fall and all while his best friend, Bob, was too busy lobbing a serve to notice that his friend was about to collapse to the floor.

Taste this sucker! Bob whooped while his ball smashed hard up against the back wall, returning low and out of range. Then, as he turned in celebration he saw Abe's splayed body - face ashen, eyes tortured.

What the ...Abe! You okay, dude?

Through labored breath, Abe answered, Yeah, yeah ... fuck!

Bob ran over to Abe, hitting his thigh repeatedly with his paddle, breathing hard trying to speak, No...you're...not, shit head. You're white... as Snow White on a ski-slope, asshole. Don't shit me.

Just gimme a minute here...damn.

Abe got up and limped over to a bench and grabbed a towel. He felt the warmth of it, dry against his icy face and saw the room move and grow greenish. It felt like a huge rubber band wrapped around his chest. He put his head between his legs and waited for warm blood to fill it, waited for his breathing to slow, waited to quell the panic that threatened to overwhelm him.

Bob's voice was going in and out: Abe, hey man...you...no that's...take another deep breath now, Abe...breathe, goddamn asshole!

I'm okay. Green flashes of light danced before his eyes. Leave me alone, said Abe—finding it helped to breathe deeply. The balls of light faded as the pain subsided. His whole body was wet, clammy cold. But it was over. He could feel a warm calm come through his body now. The buzz in his ears cleared. He took a relieved breath and stood up.

Sit the fuck back down! Bob demanded.

Abe tried to remain standing but couldn't any longer—ice pulsed through him again.

Oh gawd damn, Abe said, woozy as hell. Bob helped him to the floor.

What's your name? yelled Bob.

What are you yelling about? You know my name.

What is it? Say it.

You're a fuck head.

Abe, raise your arms.

What for?

Just do it, dammit. I'm trying to find out if you're having a stroke or a heart attack or what. Stick out your tongue Abe, stick it out.

Abe finally stuck out his tongue like a bratty kid.

Bob's face relaxed as he released a nervous laugh.

I think you're okay, he said, you're okay, right? They say look for a crooked tongue-

You'm speak with crooked tongue, Big Chief Trying-To-Be-Smartass-Doctor. Abe toweled the sweat on off his face.

Hey, you wouldn't have a sense of humor if you were having a heart attack would you?

Abe's fingers raked his soaked hair, Oh you <u>are</u> a brilliant doctor, Chief. You have missed your calling, Tonto.

Yeah? Ya think?

No.

Abe looked up at the clock. Oh damn, *Doctor Smartass,* he said, help me up. I've got a meeting in an hour.

Bob shouldered Abe to his feet. I'm coming with you, he said.

No, you're not.

Yes, I am, and we're heading straight to the ER and have you checked out. So call your meeting and tell 'em you won't be able to make it.

No we are not. I've got major meetings today with my publishers. This is not a day for a picnic out in some ER waiting room.

Look at you. You're shaking like Elvis, and sweating like Mike Tyson, and you think you're going to walk into a meeting and impress anyone?

The two stood stiff, eye to eye, chins set hard.

You my mother, Chief? Abe said, his eyes slitted.

Today, I am your mother from hell.

* * *

Machines ticked and whirred everywhere. The smell reminded Bob of something that turned his stomach—something in his memory—maybe it was his tonsils being removed when he was six, maybe it was watching his mother die of cancer when he was ten. To Abe, it didn't even register—you hardly ever can smell your own house odor, or body odor, or where you work everyday.

Abe was lying on a gurney in the ER with people in blue scrubs swarming around him. Even before he had been recognized, from the moment the words "chest pains" were out of Bob's mouth, things had moved fast. Now that a growing circle of people knew they were working on the great Dr. Abraham Latham, the action was swift and sure. He was given aspirin and nitroglycerin. An oxygen mask was slapped on his face, his arm jabbed for an IV, leads to an electrocardiogram pasted on his body, and blood was being drawn.

After about half an hour, there was a lull in the action, then the ER chief appeared, looking grave. Looks like a mild MI, doctor...who's your cardiologist...absolutely no smoking...stand to lose some weight...diet... none of anything Abe was even listening to.

The ER doc insisted that Abe stay where he was and rest while they ran further tests. He charged Bob with the responisibility of making the patient behave.

An uncomfortable exchange of glances followed as Abe lay back impatiently. Hey, you want to tell me where you've been for the last three weeks?

Brazil.

Brazil. Without me? You shit. You know I love Brazilian women...legs, the most beautiful long legs—

True. True. But that's not why I went.

Abe smiled, You going Homo now?

Yeah, you interested?

Give me a break.

No, I was down there with Dr. Sirmans and my film crew observing a Brazilian shaman.

What in the hell are you doing with a Brazilian shaman?

This guy is a famous healer, a psychic surgeon—

Abe let out a sarcastic laugh, looking long at his friend: blond and tan, dressed in white cotton, looking like he hung out with a crowd from LA or Florida—New York liked black. Is this some more of your woo-woo stuff? Abe asked.

Not woo-woo, genuine—tried and true stuff, man.

Abe's lip curled up on one side and he shook his head. I'd kill to go outside and smoke.

I'm the only one around here you'd have to kill.

I could, you know, for dragging me here. So you saw this witch doctor?

Yeah, a witch doctor that had all his victims stand on this stage, their eyes closed in trance—under energetic anesthesia.

Never heard of an energetic anesthesia...woo-woo shit.

Just listen, I'm telling you. He picks one man, turns him around—the guy can't feel anything and instead of being unconscious, he's fully awake-lifts his shirt and proceeds to make a very clean surgical incision right down the back of this guy who has his huge ugly hump. The guy's still standing and I see maybe just a little bit of blood—a trickle. And what's really amazing, the whole time the guy doesn't register any pain whatsoever, even when the shaman puts his hand right into the guy's body up to his wrist and removes this gross pound-and-a-half wad of gook. He lays the glob in the tray his nurse is holding, then stitches the guy up with only one tiny stitch—*one*. This now humpless guy kinda falls and gets carried off by these big burly men—they him take to the infirmary for twenty-four hour observation. And we got it all on film.

Abe shook his head and rolled his eyes.

We interviewed the guy a few days later, shot it on tape, said he was awake the whole time, felt the knife but no pain. Said he'd been born with the hump and it felt so strange to be standing straight up for the first time in his life. Bob laughed out loud. Said, he had to learn a whole new perspective on life . . . so to speak. Hard to imagine what that would be like, walkin' around lookin' at the ground all the time then—

Abe broke in. Yeah, I've read about those guys—bunch of crooks. The patient turns out to be an actor, the surgery is all sleight of hand, the gook gets switched when they've got a diversion going on, the rest of the people get bilked for scads of money, then they die anyway. This stuff happens only in developing countries for a reason, Bob.

Oh you're so hard, hard, hardheaded. But I have to tell you, I saw it up close and so did every one of the doctors I was with. And, Abe, how could anyone fake a hump anyway?

Easy.

Bob reached for his brief case, riffled through his files and pulled out a letter. He leaned forward, his eyes intense on Abe and presented it as though on a platter.

Abe grinned at his friend's determination to try to convince him.

Five decades, Bob said, this man has given his life for people who have no hope and he has *never,* not *once* asked for money. He's known as Seu Miguel and there is plenty of research done on him. Books. Websites. And he encourages anyone to try to find him a fraud. He was born into extreme poverty, so he wants to make sure *everyone* has the opportunity to be healed. The man works on a thousand people a day.

Oh, come on.

True. And I personally have read hundreds of riveting testimonials. Seu Miguel has been under hundreds of investigations and gone through some horrible beatings. High-ranking officials have tried to rip him up in court, everything you can imagine has been done to this guy . . . and they *can't* prove a thing.

Okay. I believe you.

No, you don't.

You're right.

Bob waved the letter again.

How about a testimonial written by one of your best friends, Dr. Franklin Sirmans – want me to read it?

Abe ripped the letter out of Bob's hand while he mumbled something about hating being read to . . .

Sirmans went with you? Not a word to me. Sure . . . let's see what Frank's got to say. He's probably had voodoo done on him, too.

That happens in Africa or the south, not Brazil.

Oh don't try so hard.

Abe reached for his jacket. Damn these hospital gowns are breezy. He pulled out his reading glasses, flipped them open and tried a few stabs at his face before they slid into place, then read silently to himself:

Miracles in Brazil

Moradia de Dom José de Barros is a unique hospital located in a small village centrally located in Brazil, helping the rich and the poor alike for no payment. People come from all over the world to experience "The Man of Miracles," Seu Miguel dos Milagres, a medium healer, a surgeon who has been practicing without a medical license for nearly four decades. He is sometimes referred to as "the surgeon with a kitchen knife." With what is identified as a spiritual anesthetic—because the patient experiences no pain even without any allopathic drug administered—Seu Miguel's body is said to be animated by entity doctors who incise the patients while they stand, then suture the wound with a single stitch using a simple sewing needle and thread. The wound will have little to no blood loss and is nearly healed by the time he has finished.

On occasion, Seu Miguel dos Milagres inserts a long-nosed scissor into the patient's nose and by twisting it, a frozen spine becomes animated, and the patient will walk on his own instantaneously, releasing the crutches he came in with. When treating leprosy or other severe skin disorders, Seu Miguel dos Milagres applies Holy Water on the lesion then briskly rubs the area, adding more and more water. Within a few days, the oozing red lesion will start to turn to healthy pink and continue on to complete recovery.

There has never been a case of infection due to any of these procedures.

Abe quit reading and looked out over his glasses. This is all very interesting Bob, he said.

Ah c'mon man, that's your friend's testimony straight from his own lips.

Even if he is an MD and one of my best friends, he still quacks like a duck. Who the hell knows why Frank would want to squander twelve years of university and his reputation by publishing such drivel?

Abe, with all due respect...I just have to say: all those twelve years, *plus*, you doctors have put a lot of time into your education, being supported by fat-cat drug companies I might add—beaten to death by their propaganda, becoming pushers of what: Percoset, Tramadol, Codeine, Morphine—whatever. But what they *don't* cram down your friggin' gullets is—what happens if those drugs don't work? Where do people turn if, God forbid, you have to tell them 'I don't know' or 'pack it in, chum, because you're outta here?' Answer me that.

You got a point, Abe's smirk giving him away.

Yes, I do. Miracles do happen. You should come with me next time I go...

Don't even think about it my friend—

So I see our friendly medical profession *has* washed the hell out of your brain, said Bob. You haven't heard a word I've said.

Maybe not. Abe stood up, grabbed his cigarettes while gathering the gap in the back of his gown and going to the slit in the curtain to look out. Shit, isn't anyone coming? I gotta go pollute something fierce.

ZEEEP, THE DOLPHIN
OCEAN OFF THE PACIFIC COAST

CHAPTER 6

Which brings us to now, a few years later.

We've just come off of a race, me and my boys, oh, and Eeeoo of course - our token female. Hah, hah...joke! Token, hezzop, after her time in that aquatic slammer: she's back, she's big, she's love-alicious and she can make most of us-guys and girls alike look like sittin' pond scum. Amazing how some creatures can go through life-altering experiences and come out changing their biggest fears into amazing accomplishments. Yeah. Face your fears buddy, and ya get free of 'em, yep. That's what I think.

Oh,oh. Oh,oh. Here it comes. Right now, I'm lookin' into a creepy-crawly fear of mine just where the hell am I gonna catch my next snatch? I'm horny as hell and I gotta do something about it and Eeeoo's headed off for some class she has to teach. You're right, Eeeoo and I have vowed mono... something. But what's a guy gonna do if his mate is off being goody-goody all the time? She's off teaching a bunch of little ones to download a bunch of information in their petite brains making all these cute, dainty holograms- then trying to send them off psychically to some humans on some research boat somewhere. She claims they're communicating. Crap, I call it. Humans don't need or want the truth, that's what I think. Give up on those scumbags is what I say. Shebit, yeah. Leave 'em alone and come take care of your man. YEEEEEEIIIIIIKKKK! Phooey.

Sorry.

I guess that doing without gets one just a little uptight, a little cranky. So I'm going to just calm down now, then when I'm calm, I'm going to go find my Eeeoo, squelch my carnal needs temporarily and ask her if she'll dine with me after work.

MEMO TO SELF: Act civilized... okay, bratto?

So, that's what I did.

I swam on over to her school and moseyed over real sweet like and set down in her cute little school circle and listened to what she was telling the teens, pretty cool stuff after all, about love, about me, about how I'm her best friend as well as her husband—so blame sweet. Said, that was the best relationship to have. If it's based on sex it doesn't always hold up under the heavy pressures of life blah,blah,blah. She's busy, but yes, so sweetly she tells me in a hushed voice soft like an angel's breath—that she'd just love to meet me after. Whoopee! Says, she has a hankering for those tiny, shiny silver, twitchy fishies. Yeh, yeh! Heard they were great aphrodisiacs! That's what I heard. I am soooooo looking forward to our date ravaged in blissful orgasms one right after the other—after our squirmy hors d'oeuvre, of course. Man, try as I may to squelch my urges, even the <u>*thought*</u> *sends me thrills. Soooo hot am I! Hot-hot-hot! Man! what am I gonna do until then? Gotta work it off!*

I look around and get a reading of a schooner off to my right, a half-a-mile or so. I promise Eeeoo I'll meet her later, that I wouldn't be late ...again ... like I do sometimes, no, most times. No big deal to me. To her —huge.

So I'm off. It sounds like the vessel's drifting right now (to my advantage), but my intuition tells me there's a good puff of wind coming up and there's something I've been wanting to try— like crazy— ever since I heard that something magic is supposed to happen when you can get yourself riding the wake of a fast moving boat. All the guys are talkin' about it, but they won't let on what the magic is—something they say I have to experience myself.

So always game to any challenge, I head out.

I was right; I arrived in the nick of time: the ship's magnificent sails were puffed up like a huge Double D-cup (learned that tasty little term from a bunch of crusty ol' fishermen). The vessel had a good clip going so I applied all my well- honed racing skills, moved up past the front of the ship and managed to maneuver onto the apex of the bow. I had to fight a real heavy pull to the right, trying for balance... and. hot damn! Guess what folks? It <u>*was*</u> *magic! Ta-da, I not only reached the center of pure balance but I was just floatin' there on that wake, doing a little steering now... a little steering then, remembering to breathe, and man, I was on a freaking free-ride, going faster than I'd ever experienced before in my whole entire life—and I'm doin' nothin'.*

Hezzop, I could go hundreds and hundreds of miles like that and never have to lift a fin, flap a fluke or tip a dorsal. Life was soooo bitchin'! EEEEE-WHOOOOOOO! I even got creative: flipped over on my back and swam upside down—whadda rush!

Oh Shit! What time is it?

The thought hit me like a fast moving bullet flattening out hittin' metal on contact. All my instincts were up flying red flags yelling, yew-whoo . . . yew- whooo . . . DUMBHEAD!

I quickly flipped over there and then, man, I knew she was waiting—I could feel her anger. Remembering back, I had told her to head-out to where the tuna were camped and I promised I'd meet her there. (Gotta tell you, want the best eats, go where the tuna hang out.)

Now I face a bigger problem: how was I gonna get off of that sucking machine? That thought brought what felt like swarms of bubbles popping around crazily in my stomach. Shebit! I thought, Oh,well—heeeere goes. I leaned heavily to my right, my point of entry, so I knew it best, and WHAM! I caught a wallop up the side of my head that felt like I'd been slammed to kingdom-come and now was getting beaten to death in a jet-speed current off the side of the hull.

I'm good, I'm good, I said to convince myself as I was being sucked dramatically downward, sliding down, down, rubbing against every cotton-pickin' razor toothed barnacle on the way. Sharp as hezzop those little buggers. I'm bleeding, I'm bleeding! I'm dying, I'm dying! I'm screaming!

Man, I was losing consciousness big time . . . then I hear this . . . voice in my head, (where the hell that came from I have no idea.)

*It was saying, **You're not falling backward, the boat is only moving forward, bank to the right again, as hard as you can and you <u>will</u> get free.***

*Instead, I went left—more pain than God—then I heard the voice yell, **RIGHT!***

I exaggerated curling my body to the right and instantly I was floating in the huge, quiet-blue expanses, watching above me—as I took in a deep, calming breath—the smooth, pointed shadow slip silently through the water like a hot, sleek surfboard chiseling a wave, then disappearing into the murk—where the hell did that Voice come from?—man, I must have really taken a good whack to the brain.

THE WIFE OF SEU MIGUEL DOS MILAGRES A THIRD WORLD VILLAGE IN BRAZIL 1998

CHAPTER 7

It lay on the metal tray beside the needle and a spool of cat-gut thread. The sunlight sometimes flickered across it, but beyond that, it just looked very ordinary.

Yesterday morning, Seu Miguel dos Milagres had asked his wife to be the one to select it. She had been very nervous, who was *she* to carry such accountability? Sometimes she hated being the wife of a world famous psychic surgeon.

She went looking for it throughout the day: was this one too broad, too big; that one too dull, another not sharp enough on its point? She'd ended up making her assignment much too important and lunch had been missed, dinner would be neglected as well. She was just a housewife, these were the tasks she was comfortable with, the ones she knew—not what he had wanted her to do today.

She ended up driving an hour and a half clear over to Brasileia but realized half-way there she couldn't just go to her own doctor, it would have to be a stranger.

The new doctor had asked her many questions: Why such an unusual request? What was it to be used for? She'd broken out in a sweat and covered it with an excuse of a menopausal attack. She told him she was an artist and needed precision on a piece she was cutting; a thick plastic and it was to be as detailed as fine lace. No, she did not let on in any way she was the wife of one of Brazil's famous psychic surgeons. Many medical doctors did not approve, and she couldn't take that chance. Seu Miguel would need it by tomorrow: hundreds were coming for the *invisible* surgery, but 25 people were to be operated on and he needed to make a clean, professional looking cut.

The doctor handed his choice to her from his own cabinet under lock and key. Would he be invited to her showing? Yes of course, she had said and wrapped it in her scarf, thanking him.

Later, as she proudly presented it to Seu Miguel, he seemed impressed she could come up with something so professional, but added all he had really needed was a kitchen knife.

THE DOLPHINS
PACIFIC OCEAN

CHAPTER 8

So here I am, slithering sloppily through the deep-dark depths of the ocean, knowing I'm late as hell, trying to find my way, blame obsessive thoughts are flyin' around bangin' in my head, repelling off the sides: fap-fap-fap! and somewhere way in the back of my mind I'm pickin' up on this real creepy feeling . . . like when you have a head-cold and your sonar goes on the bleep . . . more in your belly than your head—but the more I think about it, it's something like Eeeoo would say, psychic intuition, I guess, yeah maybe more like that, 'cause I was pickin' up that somethin' was really stressin' Eeeoo. I mean if there were hair on my back, it'd be stickin' up, I swear!

I actually shuddered when the distress signals came: EZZZZZIP SOUMP—EZZZZZZIP SOUMP confirming my fears, and in the muddle I could vaguely hear Eeeoo's voice, Zeeep! Help, Zeeep! I had to do some calculating so I could try and get my bearings, but my ecolocating was coming in fuzzy or maybe the sounds I sent out weren't strong enough for them to return because of splitting of electromagnetic waves in water caused by dispersion. Everyone knows the electromagnetic wave leaving the surface of the half space, directed into the half space and with an assigned f, is split in a number of waves with different velocities; if n is a function of the position the paths of the waves are different and reach a given depth at different points and times. Since the medium was water the dielectric parameter containing a rational power of if and the parameter values of

Hasted and I finally estimated that the measurement of a length of 1 km, using a frequency of 10 MHz, had to be effected by an uncertainty of 38 ns or 1.22 m.

Realizing this, I re-evaluated my calculations. They were familiar—familiar enough that I barely could make out what probably was a herd of tuna—at least fifty, maybe a hundred. That surely was where Eeeoo wanted to dine, but now there were distress signals from not only Eeeoo but also the tuna! Didn't make sense. Then I detected two eco-readings. Changing my distance evaluations, I calculated: fourtyfivecubitsbyseventyfiveminusfifty-tothefifthpower, the mass was huge, translating to at least 50 feet long . . . hell, that could be a Humpback. If so, why the panic? If it were a shark pack or a killer whale then we could talk, but it was way too big. Then I measured the elevations on the bottom of the ocean to the underside of the object: it was coming up as an uneven undersurface, not something organic. I knew I had to keep going, enter the beehive so to speak. As I headed toward the surface a bit, using my eyes as my last resort, I could finally make out something: sharp, straight, fish bodies streaking through shafts of light that stabbed down through the murk—they were swimming radically: fast forward, quickly backward, turn around—something very fishy was definitely going on.

Then came the soft bump . . . a familiar rubbing that sent goose-pimples all over me. I turned to see Eeeoo and nearly shed my skin right there. I forget how much I miss her until I see her. All I wanted to do was crawl right into her body and become one. She was not about the romance; she was clicking for me to stay focused. She pointed out that the tuna were swimming very close to us, they don't usually do that, freaks them out too much—very protective of their personal space.

She was right. They were near us now—the waters were thick with tuna. I felt panicked again, Eeeoo follow me!

I rapid clicked, and burrowed: poking, bumping, slamming against tuna bodies as hard as I could, making enough space for her to follow. When we thought we had finally reached the edge of the masses, we rammed headlong into something webbed: strong and stringy, tied in square shapes. Memories of racing alongside great expanses of netting; trying to find a way to release Eeeoo's body from her incarceration, came flooding back . . . only this time, I was inside this net <u>with</u> her. I wanted to say, What's up with you and nets? 'cause when I'm scared, I always joke to release the tension, but it didn't seem like a good idea . . . instead I was realizing we had been down for too long and it was time for us to surface to restore air reserves or we'd surely drown.

At that moment, unable to move, feeling bodies on top, under, to the right side, I looked out my left eye, into Eeeoo's right—feeling her soft, sweet body touching mine, and all panic left. Our breathing together was soon indistinguishable. Our love was growing and expanding out into the Universe where we were soon to be delivered, where we had originally come from.

She tucked her chin under mine—we closed our eyes and listened to the music of our heartbeats fading—pa-dum, pa-dum, pa-dum, pa-dum....

THE VOICE
THE INNER SPACES OF ZEEEP'S SOUL

CHAPTER 9

In the space where there are no words—I am.
Although I understand every language ever created.

I dwell here also without "time" to lead me astray.
I know no "space" to make me large or small.

I only know what . . . Is.
Is-ness exists only in my knowing, yet I can know
All at one time. Because that is all there is.

I love intensely.
I only know Love.
I am Love.

I look for humor everywhere
and look upon humor as the greatest healer.
But what is healing?
Healing is returning to our innate perfection.
Healing is the perfect teacher of Souls.
I am the caretaker of Souls.
They are the caretakers of me.

We are one.

I speak softly most often.
Sometimes I need to yell.
I am THE VOICE

ZEEEP, THE DOLPHIN
PACIFIC OCEAN

CHAPTER 10

. . . and there is a point when animals know they are to let go of their physical bodies—when their bodies are no longer able to serve them, they leave them behind for another's food, clothing or compost—

What the hell is he saying? AND just who's speaking? I thought, as I listened to this humongous voice that sounded like it had come out of the depths of the sea or somewhere—

Most times when they are being devoured alive by a predator that's got them in a death hold, their bodies seemingly becomes paralyzed. At that point, the spirit gives up the struggle and leaves long before the body dies. This is, in a sense, a sacrifice, something innate to all animals. Knowing, truly, that there is no death, only rebirth, they move on easily: experiencing no pain, entering instead, into a euphoria. The human is the only animal that struggles and fights with death—

HELLO? WHO ARE YOU? I yelled. WHAT ARE YOU TALKING ABOUT AND WHO ARE YOU TALKING TO? CAN YOU TELL ME WHAT THE DIKSNIK IS GOING ON?

. . . .

Nothing.

More questions raced through my head. Where am I? 'Cause I'm floating or something. Whisshing down this swirling light shaped like a . . . like a . . . tunnel, yeah that's it, somekinda tunnel and going lickity-slpit toward something bright

. . . shebit it was bright, and somekind of light is coming toward me getting bigger and BIGGER AND BIGGER! Shhhhissh, so . . . bright!

ARE WE DEAD? I ask.

. . . .

Nothing. No sound was unlike any I'd ever heard . . . it had dimensions of nothing.

. . . .

WHERE'S EEEOO? I'm thinking as I'm full on panicking now!

I'm . . . right . . . here . . . nosehead . . . hey . . . open unto your new eyes, silly.

It was Eeooo's voice, so I trusted her . . . I trusted her and I opened them and—WHAM, SWIIIIISH—I slammed them shut! Tooo much brightness! YIIIIK it's <u>really</u> bad for a dolphin's eyes; we can't squint, no-no-no-no-no.

Hey, super-silly, Eeooo's voice comin' ever so super-soft, You've got new eyes, open'em!

I can't!

You can.

It's gonna hurt . . .

No it's not.

I take a wee-little peep outta my left one . . . and I'm looking deep into Eeeoo's eyes, and I mean deep, so deep I actually <u>can</u> swim around in them. I can see right through her body—it glows. I open both eyes and I look down at mine—it glows too.

I look around, still in some kind of water-like substance—kinda thick like, kinda syrupy like—I see everything like a magnifying glass, amazingly clear, intensely detailed: all the tuna we were packed in with are now swimming around freely, doing acrobatics like a dolphin, acting crazy, some even sprouted wings and flew out of the water—now that was too much!

What the hell is going on? The landscape is . . . seeable! No murkiness anywhere; this was something I didn't get to do much—see with my eyes, and I can't get over it—everything being so <u>super</u> crystal clear, schools of all kinds of fish: blues, greens, chartreuse, magenta, gold, silver, pearlish purples—colors I've never seen on earth. Sculpted coral-hillsides are radiating these indescribably brilliant colors; floating out-out-out in waves that merge with everything they come in contact with. Hey, whooooo. I just got hit with a wave of golden lightning—and it shimmered <u>me</u> . . . yeah, I actually wiggled like Jell-O . . . and I felt . . . there's no words for this but suddenly I'm aware of an infinite knowledge with unspeakable words . . . and a lotta good <u>that</u> is gonna to do me—I'm thinkin' to myself—I'm supposed to be telling my story here. Whatz-up-wit-dat? Who do I gotta talk to about this?

Then I hear that Voice again, off my left ear, ***Someone will be along soon, son. Have patience, you cannot push the river.***

Wadda smart ass, I think . . . to myself.

At that point, I'd come to the conclusion that Eeeoo and I had entered into this dream we've been in a thousand times before . . . kinda like a h-u-u-u-u-ge deja-vu, man. I mean, everything is glowing from <u>*within*</u> *and we're slithering through iridescent and gleaming subterranean mountains, meadowy bottoms of electric, waving and dancing sea-grasses, gliding by shimmering walls of tiny, silver fish, sparkles of plankton and invertebrates, snapping electric eels throwing off intense coruscations like amazing works of art. We're taking a trip through a friggen aquatic art gallery and it all feels familiar but still . . . I'm bummin' out.*

I gotta tell you, I'm just a little disappointed that the transition wasn't more . . you know—eventful. Heck, no crashing symbols, no angelic musicals, no earthquake . . I know we're not superstars but heck, we did a lot of philanthropic work, you know . . . well at least Eeeoo did and don't we as a married couple . . . ? Uh-oh . . . Eeeoo's giving me that, shut up you ingrate, look. Okay, geeesh.

She's coming at me countin' the blessings, like: there's no more pain . . . no need, or desire for sleep . . . no need to constantly hunt for food . . . no constant demanding sex driving you koo-koo . . . no more having to put up a fight for anything . . .

HOLD ON! NO MORE SEX? She'd just lost me big time! Now I'm reeeeeeally, reeeeeeally bummed.

She slapped her side in a huff and left me—she needed her space.

An octopus came floating by, stopped, and gave me a wink.

You winkin' at me, I ask?

Yeah, he says.

So?

So, this sex thing? I got some good news.

Whatzat?

Here? Here you can go back to Earth astrally and have sex anytime, anywhere, with anyyyyone.

No shit?

Fact.

How do ya do that?

Think it.

Think it, what good is that?

Same results.

No shit?

Try it. Now that you're over here, you got no earthly monogamous anything, anymore.

No shit?

Fact.

Thanks, man.

No problem, any other questions, see me. The Octopus waved goodbye with all his arms as he jetted away.

Cool.

I turned around and came face to face with none other than . . . Eeeoo. I smiled, she didn't. I was talkin' reeal fasssst telling her that I had no intention of ever cheating on her, she was the love of all my lives but she didn't seem to be listening, instead she was fading—fading-fading away, telling me that she had to go check in with her spirit guides. They needed to get her ready for her next life right away, that she would love me for as long as it took for us to be together again then POP she was gone, a small orb of blue light—intricate, radiant, geometric patterns moving within a pattern—was in her place then that thing took off like a flash and POOF just vanished.

No Eeooo! COME BACK! COME BACK! I screamed. I was telling the truth now. I mean it. I would always be true to her, no matter what!

She was gone . . . I freeeeeaked. Looking up and down and sideways and backwards . . . she was friggin GONE, man!

I was flapp-favol-flooped! I couldn't breathe, I couldn't speak—never NEVER in my wildest dreams DID I THINK this would EVER EVER EVER EVERRRRRR happen again! It was all my fault, I just knew it! I felt so bad I wanted to kill myself but I was already dead . . . or not . . . shebit. What was I going to do now? She was the other half of me and now I felt . . . HALVED.

Incomplete.

Alone.

I felt like I had gas in my stomach and I couldn't ever belch. I felt like a whole entire whale had fallen on me.

Where was my Eeooo?

Where . . . ?

SEU MIGUEL DOS MILAGRES (MEDIUM MIGUEL OF MIRACLES) PARAMANGUAIA, BRAZIL 1998

CHAPTER 11

He hadn't been thinking straight all day long. Since morning, his world had felt like a floating fog, while the dream that he had awakened from was still sharp with feelings and slippery recollections of ghostly voices whispering something that left vague hints of an impending doom.

When he woke up that morning, medium Seu Miguel Sousa da Silva *(See-u Meeg-el Su-za da Seel-va)* untangled himself from the comforter's cocoon. He sat straight up and stared at nothing for a good five minutes before he was able to shake off his dream. It left abruptly with the shudder that filled his lungs when his feet touched down on the stone-cold floor. He grabbed the robe slung over the chair and found he longed for the warmth of his simple home in Tupani, Mato Grosso do Norte *(To-panni Mau-do Groz- zah du Nort),* where his sweet wife Inely *(E-nel-lee)* breathed softly onto his cheek while she slept.

He shuffled to the bathroom, feeling hung over from the intense healing work that had lasted far into the night and early morning. The Entities had kept his body on the Moradia de Dom José's de Barros *(Mod-o-shee Dome shJo-say day Ba-hoose)* grounds, for they would be using it early this morning—there was someone coming for a healing, they had said, or did they say something had to be attended to?—something of grave importance.

Seu Miguel cradled the weight of his throbbing head in his cool fingers knowing they would also remove this pain from his over-worked frame and cranky muscles—this was a perk that went with the job. The Entities have always looked out for him in a timely way—except for that time—the one and only incident where he could remember feeling betrayed.

He shook off his unsettled memories and stumbled over to his desk and let out a deep sigh as he sat down in his Brazilian-redwood meditation lounge chair. He took note of the deep gratitude he felt. He no longer shuffled when he walked. He no longer had that one-sided paralyzed body. He smiled as he raised his arm in the air and moved his fingers—something that had been impossible just a month ago.

Memories of that night flooded his mind—the excruciating pain that clutched his heart during the gathering for thousands of people at Hospital de Bela Aurora *(Hose-peet-tal Bel-woo Ad-roar-da),* a wretched feeling he'd never before experienced, the feeling of falling into helplessness, becoming extremely nauseated and nearly falling face-forward to the floor . . . and the frantic race to the hospital.

Pressa, por favor! This is the famous Seu Miguel dos Milagres, give him only the best, they had demanded. Machines wheeled in one after the other: X-ray, CT scans, MRI, electronic measure of the brain waves, blood and brain fluid testing—then panic erupted—every single machine had to be wheeled out because somehow all the electrical mechanisms had fused together.

More machines. More damaged backups rejected. The electric grid all over the hospital was malfunctioning—panels of lighting shutting down or imparting an irritating flicker. Hours of waiting while technicians were flown in, more machines from Brasilia, from Rio, from anywhere they could find them, only to have more electrical failures or machines that had actually blown up.

The hospital staff was in frenzy—this had never happened before—but Seu Miguel knew what was going on, the Entities were trying to heal him but the energy was being negated. So while they kept preparing for surgery, Seu Miguel got up (with the help of the Entities) and shuffled out of Hospital de Bela Aurora, gownand all, where he was met by his wife waiting in their car to take him home.

Looking at himself in the mirror, he saw that the stroke had left him leaning and paralyzed on one side of his body, his hands were stiff and he was blind in one eye. During the day it was just . . . something to deal with. However, at night when he was trying to drop into sleep, he was often wild with rage. Why couldn't the Entities work on him when they were able to heal everyone else? He fought intermittent anger and feelings of betrayal. He went through months of arriving for work with only one side of his body functioning while the other hung as a dumb, dead weight. Some healer he was, he thought. Resentment took over his anger when the Entities were able to animate his entire body, each side working normally and accomplishing their healing, but the minute they were done with their visitation, his body returned to its crippled state.

Seu Miguel was losing his enthusiasm for being the spokesman for the Otherworld. The betrayal he felt was showing up as anger. He no longer wanted to serve. He entertained going back to the tailoring he did with his father, or maybe he'd just sell cars from now on and step aside for the next healer to come aboard.

One night, The Council of Entities awoke Seu Miguel in the middle of the night with a new idea—Seu Miguel would operate on himself. The next morning he told Inely the plan: she was to be his nurse and doctor, she was to be the one that would guide his shaking hand if need be, she would be the one that he would entrust with his life. Looking straight into his eyes, not hesitating for a second, she accepted the task. She had filled his heart with her loving devotion—even though she was trembling inside, overwhelmed with such a responsibility.

That day, his wife Inely had gathered the staff, making sure they knew how important this healing was: the prayers had to be just right, the highest and most efficient Mediums needed to be collected and seated close to Seu Miguel. Which of the Entities would be doing the surgery today, she wondered? She told her husband she hoped it was King Solomon—the most intensely powerful. On the other hand, she thought maybe it would be Dom José de Barros *(Dome shJo-say day Ba-hoose)*—a gentle and compassionate energy—a powerful energy Seu Miguel had known the longest, the very first Entity to incorporate in Seu Miguel's body at the age of 14.

Seu Miguel watched his wife remove the surgery utensils from their antique, glass-fronted cabinet. She selected the scalpel she'd found in Brasileia and put it on the stainless steel surgery tray. It was the sharpest and newest. If the Entities were to ask her to do the surgery, she would never trust herself with a simple kitchen knife. She would use only the best.

* * *

Seu Miguel and Inely walked into the Great Hall of The Moradia Dom José de Barros *(The Home of Bishop Jose de Barros)* named after the revered Dom José de Barros, where the chair was—the one he always sat in when in trance. The room had been prepared. All was in place. They could feel the intense energy flow from the large audience of Mediums who had miraculously shown up with very little notice. The media had also somehow gotten word of the event and had blown in like an inexplicable wind.

Inely cradled the steel tray as Seu Miguel was seated after being put into trance. She lifted his shirt and felt the entity move from Seu Miguel, coolly enveloping her as well, then she felt as though she was being lifted up—and that was the last she'd remembered.

The audience had watched as Seu Miguel positioned his hand over the scalpel in the hand of his wife and made the incision—in truth, it was the Entities who were animating her work. A small stream of blood was seen, but looking up at Seu Miguel they could see he was actually smiling as he reached inside his own body and removed a large blood clot and laid it on the tray—then his wife helped him suture himself up. After the surgery, Seu Miguel had returned to his normal consciousness, walked out amongst his clapping fellow workers and as he passed, they could see that all signs of paralysis had completely disappeared—never to return.

* * *

Seu Miguel shook off the distant memories and remembered the day ahead. He walked across the courtyard and pulled open the door in the brick wall that he'd laid himself. He walked through a room filled with tables covered with rainbow-colored and uncut quartz crystals and emeralds mined from his very own caves. The Entities had shown him where to find the caves when The Moradia Dom José de Barros was in need of financial support. Stopping to look closer at the newest arrivals, lifting them to the light, as always Seu Miguel was entranced by the colors and geometric structures that formed such perpetual beauty.

Suddenly the jarring memory of that morning's dream called back its horror: those feelings of burning urgency, the blurred images, the voices that yammered: *caution . . . large man . . . officer . . Brazilian embassy . . . trouble*—a scratched record playing in the back of his mind. His feelings reminded him of all the times that he had been thrown in jail because of others' jealousy. He had been denounced by medical professionals and by people who believed that he had been possessed by the devil.

By the time Seu Miguel arrived at the stage and the throngs of waiting people, he was so shaken that he summoned Armando and his crew to retire with him to his meditation room. There they called forth the Entities to assist Seu Miguel in understanding the prophesied disaster that awaited him that day.

THE DOLPHINS IN THE GARDEN OF TRANQUILITY

CHAPTER 12

Be not afraid, my son. You and Eeeoo are now being integrated into The Garden of Tranquility*, and POP, I too was transformed into an orb of iridescent light. I scoped the area all around me. Whaaaaa? I had been encased in a bubble of some kind and there was nothing else of me, nada, my body had evaporated or something!*

I was spinning around in this orb all discombobulated.

Extremely agitated and forgetting Eeeoo for a millisecond I screamed in to the void, WHOOOOO AR E YOU? And <u>*what*</u> *has happened to my EXTREMELY fine dolphin body? Huh? Huh? While I kept twirling around, looking for anything that would answer my questions, I was becoming exhausted. But that didn't stop me from yelling at whoever and wherever that guy was.*

Hey! I worked hard on that body—only 10% fat, tight glutes, abs that pack a ten, strongest racing tail around, ask anybody . . . HEY!

Man, I was pezzonked! and I whipped out maybe a few more unanswerable questions—I can't remember—'cause I realized I was totally caught up in just looking at all the amazing stuff around me . . .

Whoa . . . there was magnificence . . . everywhere. Golden light shards, brilliant flickering bubbles filled with light, reminding me of . . . well, kinda like being under water with thousands and thousands of bubbles but these bubbles zipped around, little packets of energy . . . zip zip zip little zippers. Then I figured it out. They <u>*were*</u> *like me. We little zippers, zippin' around all glittery, like raindrops full of rainbows in the sun, sparkling diamonds on velvet grass, shimmering, gleaming like the ring around Saturn . . . and hey! I was tripping through all these images and . . . it was freaky . . . at the same time I was connecting to something huge. And all of a sudden,*

I knew everything. I swear, everything! Ev-ery-thing. A friggin computer I had become. I had indisputable knowledge these bubbles were referred to as Orbs—I was a friggin' ORB and we Orbs contained all the elements that had ever existed in all of time or space or whatever.

Then I looked up and I saw thousands and billions and gillions of numbers all around me, some would change places, some would disappear. I dunno, was I looking at THE Big Kahuna in the Almighty Omnipresent Sky? All I knew was that I had somehow tapped into this friggin' giant computer—layers and layers of knowing all, sitting right there right in front of me all at the same time. How could that possibly be? Yeoooooweeee! My brain was going a mile-a-friggin-minute completely freaking out with all the info I could ever want to access—NOT a good place to be for someone with a compulsion disorder—HELLO!

Bu-bu-but it was like maybe HEAVEN . . . and I was getting hotter and hotter and hotter—and filling up—felt like I was ready to explode with so much Joy.

Could I handle all this info? I'm askin' myself. Heezzop, YESSSSSSS. Bring. It. More! More! It felt so GRRRRRREAT!

But . . . then.

HEY! I yelled, 'cause I was getting so high—higher and higher—and it wasn't gonna stop!

Whoooooo I'm gonna blow a circuit here! I'm yelling to the cosmos—thought the powers that be might want to know. Hey waaaaah . . . ! I'M GONNA BLOW A CIRCUIT HERE . . . don' t think anyone is listening so . . . HEY, HEY, HEY! I—JUST—MIGHT—BE—GONNA—BLOW—A—CIRCUIT—HEEERE . . .

But . . . hey! No one was listening?

It suddenly dawned on me that who cares who's listening? I DON'T CARE . . . WHAAAA-WHOOOOO-WHO-WHooooo. RIDE 'EM, COWBOY! Man, I could hear my voice ricocheting throughout the Cosmos. And then dikdik . . . suddenly . . . .

Nada.

Nothin'.

Notta peeep.

I was missing my munificent high, bigtime.

. . . .

HEEEEEEEEY. . . . is anybody out there?

More nothing. . .

Nada . . .

Just all these . . . Orbs zipping zip-zip silently around . . . like me, orbiting around in a black void of some kind, made for . . . waiting. I was thinking . . . waiting (something I had no talent for as yet.) . . .

Maybe I had blown a circuit . . ..

Then . . . I heard that deeeep, slumberous voice, a voice like a river rolling along in a cavernous valley, the voice I' d heard before many times but never appreciated so much as this moment.

Don't you remember The Garden of Tranquility, my son?

Who are you and why do you always call me . . . son? I asked.

I am The Voice . . . The Voice of Spirit, of Knowing, of Benevolence, of Loving, of Serenity, of Compassion, of Munificence, Largesse, Generosity, Philanthropy, Bounty—

HEY! (I had to butt in on His Eminence, like I said, not real good in the patience arena.) I GOT IT ALREADY, FELLA . . . I yelled, yeah I was yellin' this, then shut up real fast 'cause I suddenly felt like a real boob.

But The Voice wasn't the least bit put off, ***Open the eyes of your soul and you will see . . .*** *I heard him say.*

Didn't know where my soul's eyes were, so I opened the ones I knew how to open. Okay, eyes open. Eyes lookin', things are SWISSSSSHing around so fast everything got completely blurred—and I got a lit-tle dizzzzy—but suddenly my vision cleared. I was able to see from all levels: high-low, out-over, over-under, through, then beyond through.

The Voice was right, this was a special space. Whadda transport. Better than any ride back at the pond. And I was taking some time trying to get use to this sleek, new compact orb body. (I was still used to my tubular body, with the appendages, and my pesky undisciplined sexual organs popping out at the most inopportune and opportune times.) But this new vehicle couldn't have been better designed for this strange and fascinating place I was traveling through—a place with no black or shades of gray because there were no shadows. There was no sun, which had to mean there were no stars, no moon. Was there only day and no night? I had to think so. The light came from within all the organic structures— me included. Gardens of glorious beauty: trees the height of mountains, greens of all possible shades, magnificent flowers that bloomed and re-bloomed in a matter of minutes.

The Voice spoke, ***This garden was where all animal souls and elementals originally sourced from—that was, until the day I created a new animal of sorts—the human. It was an experiment I was particularly excited about at the time. I gave this human animal the power of choice and freedom, let it loose to roam and create artistic things like the god-apprentices they were meant to be.***

You mean you gave them that kinda power? You crazy, man? I said.

Should have had you on my team at the time, son. Help me see what was coming.

Why? Wha' happened?

Well, let's just say they got . . . a little too creative.

How?

Theoretically, in the beginning the humans just wanted to see if they could re-create my garden. They renamed their creation Earth, and it was okay for a while until they started choosing greed and power over everything—including the elementals—as well as one another.

But what happened to your garden?

Well son, that's when separation from my garden was created. Before that moment, no separation had ever existed because my garden was only created in Love.

Because Love . . . can't be separated, right?

And my son, the fact is that, separation really doesn't exist. It's just an illusion created by those souls wanting to be their own god, disconnected from me.

So you really didn't create the Earth? Man did?

Not only that, they were able to create a whole second Universe, a false Universe, one disconnected from the Light within (like my creations). So they created a Sun to light the Earth and then some stars and other planets.

Wow, I hate to admit, but that's pretty impressive, don't you think?

Not really, Zeeep. Remember, it was created only in the mind. It was only an illusion.

Oh right. I get it.

Where they came from was the Truth.

Gotcha.

Yes . . . and the humans were so proud of what they'd done, they developed Ego to keep them from Me and the All Knowing Truth that was their original Home.

Then The Voice got a little tickle in it, it wavered and cleared itself and I definitely could feel its sadness . . .

No sadness, son. Because they're still here with Me. Just a part of them are in the illusion—the dream. And their dream is teaching them what it is really like to be a creator.

Yeah, but whatta huge pain in the butt it is for you, I said. I mean, look what they're creating!

I was really feeling sorry for this Voice guy. I mean, The Voice was pretty cool—laid back cool and I absolutely could feel His heart filled with Love for his humans . . . and His patience . . . I mean, how long has this been going on—for how many eons? And thinking a stitch further, I guess I really didn't understand. Why don't humans just choose to go back Home to be with the Infinite All Knowing. Ya know? Give up this fake stuff—just confess they made a mistake, eat some humble pie and go back Home. Hezzop, why keep making the same stupid mistakes over and over again . . . 'cause of this Ego?

And The Voice actually was reading my thoughts 'cause He tells me, ***Well, it's gotten pretty complicated, after so long the humans started to forget—so now they have to go back to the beginning of their creation, look at it carefully, re-live it, and forgive themselves for making their illusions their Truth and finally release the ego attached to it—before they can totally come back to the Truth.***

I don't get it. Why do they have to do all that? Why can't they figure out everything is all fake and c'mon home?

Because everything is energy—with different vibrations. And because they're so used to thinking in illusion, their thinking doesn't have a frequency

high enough anymore. So, when they try to come Home . . . thinking the way they do—

I get it, they fade away—

Exactly. They can't stay Home. Every thought they think here has to be a very high frequency and if there is fear or guilt or hate or any illusion attached to their thinking . . .

Which is a much lower frequency, right?

Right—

So how can you stay Home, if you don't match the frequency of Home, right?

You got it, son.

It was making so much sense to me as I looked out over that gorgeous landscape rolled out in front of me and I was feeling pretty good about everything I was learning . . . until . . . I realized, what the hezzop was I doing here? Returning as a half or a whole? Was I just something those humans created? Was I the real thing or was I dreaming? I suddenly got the heeby-jeebies—knowing that my thinking is full of all kinds of junk.

What was really in store for me?

SABRINA
MONTREAL, CANADA
WINTER, 1998

CHAPTER 13

Sabrina's finger traced tiny delicate crystals etched in the car's frosted window glass beside her. They reminded her of the lace doilies Grandmère embroidered to protect the antique, lemon-scented, mahogany table that she brought over from the old country. One of her favorite things to do at Grandmère's was to see her reflection in the old blood-red wood. She loved how it always made her reflection look spooky when she moved her face to different parts of the table.

She smiled as she thought of the birthday cake that Grandmère would have baked when they arrived, ready and waiting: Chocolate, through-and-through. Eight birthday candles on top, all of them brown, (so they, too, would look like chocolate.) The whole house would smell like chocolate. Her smile got bigger; she could actually smell it now in her mind.

She could hear her Grandmère's soft voice telling her—when she could no longer resist running her finger through the deep, thick icing—tah-tah, *ma chère,* only after you have blown out zee candles and made yeeur weeesh. After the silly French Birthday Song, she would be tasting that first gooey bite on her tongue, the coolness of the whipped cream and the m-m-m-m-m would tickle her lips. Grandmère, this is the best Birthday cake you ever made, she would say, even though her mouth would be way too full to talk.

She giggled to herself and sank deeper in the warm musk of the Cadillac's backseat, snuggling under the softness of the fake-fur blanket she'd pulled up under her chin.

What are you giggling about, sweetie? her mother asked, looking over her shoulder.

Her excitement spilled out. Mom? Dad . . . ? Is Grandmère going to make me a birthday cake?

Hummm, what's that, Sabrina? Her dad had seemed far away in thought and from over the blanket she could barely see the back of her father's head in the driver's seat.

Is Grandmère going to make me a birthday cake?

Yes dear, of course, he said.

Chocolate?

Chocolate, through-and-through . . . And candles?

Hmmm, I don't know about that . . .

Why?

You're too old, Pumpkin. Eight is way too many candles. Sabrina laughed hard, Oh Daddy . . .

She was happy with the silence that followed until she felt the sleepiness come creeping—she had to keep talking to stay awake. Mommy? . . . Is eight too many candles?

She saw her mother's face peering over the front seat, her face wasn't happy.

Sabrina, go to sleep. We'll get there faster if you go to sleep.

But I don't wanna go to sleep! she exclaimed, followed by the biggest yawn she'd ever yawned.

Go to sleep, dear. You know you want to.

No, I don't wanna go to sleep . . . she said in a whiney voice because she was getting very, very tired now and the backseat of the Cadillac was warm and snuggly. She truly felt like she was at Grandmère's house already, all safe and tucked in. But she was too excited about her birthday, what presents awaited? And what was in the trunk just behind her seat that Mommy got her . . . what did Daddy get her? She pulled out her crayons and pad and drew a picture of her dad and her skiing—her favorite time with him. Maybe he got her some skis for her birthday, wouldn't he just be amazed if she had drawn a picture of them skiing and when he turned around and saw the picture, he'd be amazed that she'd figured it out before he gave them to her, wouldn't it be great?

. . . Daddeeee?

What, Sabrina?

Look! I drew you a picture.

Her mother turned around ready to snap at her to go to sleep, but her face softened when she saw what Sabrina was holding up.

Ben, this is so sweet. You should see.

Dadeeee, look! Turn around.

That's enough Sabrina. Go. To. Sleep! Now! he said.

She knew she was in trouble because his voice had an angry tone and the slap-slap of the tire chains in the snow was also begging her to fall asleep.

Sabrina sometimes felt uncomfortable around her dad. She didn't know why but sometimes it repulsed her to hug his big belly that hung slightly over his belt. Sometimes it was something else. Sometimes it was because he hugged too hard. She would swear she could feel her bones pop and split under his viselike grip. But she knew she loved him intensely. Maybe too much. She could tear up just thinking about him and when he was not at home, she would find herself always looking for him, waiting for his return and it was always such a painful wait, seeming like it was forever and ever. But when he came home she would know it, she could feel him coming, and she would always be the first one at the door and yell Dadeeee and jump up and down and wait for him to hug her, which didn't happen when he was too tired. But she'd wait and it was always so painful, the waiting.

One of her favorite things was to look at her mother and dad's wedding pictures—that's when he was very handsome and her mother was—as Snooker said, she was *gee-or-jee-us* while he had winked and made licking noises, which had made Sabrina's stomach turn. Her parents didn't look anything like they did now. They dressed differently, wore their hair differently. Even their smiles were different. What had happened?

She wished she had known them in the picture. Her mother's dress was the most beautiful she had ever seen. Not in real life. It was an angel's dress. Tiny white flowers nestled in her long, golden hair, glowing like a halo. Looking closer, Sabrina could make out her mother's delicate heart-shaped smile—her eyes were full of . . . of happy-ever-after.

Her dad looked like the perfect prince dressed in his uniform: a stuffy, high collar and a double-breasted coat with gold buttons on each side and equally stuffy pants with a stripe and a . . . sword. Why did he have to have a sword at his wedding? Was he that unsure of mom? Afraid she just might not marry him and he'd have to resort to some kind of violent tactic? Adults. Sabrina had double-triple trouble trying to figure them out, so very often.

Then there was Grandpère standing next to her dad. He was dad's dad. A General of some sort, mom said, with lots of colored badges, almost as many as the guys in the *Castors* and the *Louveteaux* Troops at school. Some of those boys had so many badges they would clink when they walked down the hall—put a pack of those boys together and walk them down the hallway—what a racket it made.

In the picture, Grandmère was standing next to her mother. Sabrina could see Grandmère hadn't changed much—she still had her kind eyes and forever-sweet smile. She could feel her heart fill up with so much love for her when she looked into those photo eyes. She was so easy to love, so easy to touch. Her skin was softer than anything she'd ever felt before. She couldn't think of anything softer, except her kittie's fur. But that was fur. Her Grandmère would tell her anything she ever wanted to know. She knew what she'd ask her the next time she saw her . . . like, whatever happened to Grandpère? Why hadn't Sabrina ever met him? Dad said he was still alive, but that was it. Nothing was ever said about Grandpère.

Daddy? She was still holding up the picture and she waited a long time for an answer that did not come, and her thoughts flowed into how it would be magical to wake up and instantly be at Grandmère's house rather than the three hours it took to get there and . . . but daddy? . . . da-deee . . . da . . . her eyelids were too heavy and her picture too heavy and the last thing Sabrina remembered was looking at her mother in the front seat and the wave in her red hair and hearing her soft voice singing to the radio, the musty smell of the upholstery, and a vague feeling that her father was going to turn around to see her picture and right now he was mad but when he saw it he wouldn't be any longer but she was tired now . .

Slipping away into sleep, she never remembered hearing the thundering crash of the ten-ton truck smashing into their Cadillac.

ZEEEP IN THE OTHERWORLD

CHAPTER 14

I was really captivated with this place wherever it was. I was checkin' out the gargantuan difference between where we had come from on Earth and this place on the Otherside. I mean now everything on Earth seemed like a darkened dream of flatness. Here it was vibrant and unbelievably . . . well, if I could find words, I'd use them but there were none in Earth's vast vocabulary. So whatever I say will not even come close to what I'm seein'.

And through all this—spectacularity—we were flying over, I was scopin' out all this super-dooper eloquent architecture: a whole buncha huge buildings and every one of them had hundreds of steps out front and gardens that went forever. I knew these were Temples of some kind 'cause I remember something like that in the oceans back on Earth buried in seaweed and barnacles while Eeeoo and I were playing hide-n-seek and outta the green and blue electric space—whamo—thoughts of Eeeoo started running through my head like a speeding train through a tunnel—Eeeoo, my Eeeooo, how I missed my Eeeoooooooo.

I bumped into a tree. A big huge tree, a tree taller than I ever thought possible.

You okay? *The Voice was back nosin' round.*

Yeah. I said. I wasn't though. I was mad. My heart hurt and it wasn't from the bump. But then it kinda shocked me to see what I was seeing . . . suddenly humans appeared everywhere. But they weren't walking around like they do on Earth, I mean some of them where, but most of them were . . . flying! Like birds they were flying. But they really didn't have wings or anything. They could just transport themselves in the air from one place to the other. And I noticed they were all about thirty years old, no kids, no old people and they were totally beautiful specimens—yeah, great bodies, great hair, all Greek Gods these humans . . . or were they really humans? Maybe they were something else. Human they weren't I decided, couldn't be. Humans came in packages that were too fat or too thin, ugly and hairy and some had good looks but most . . . blaaaah. Naw, they had to be something else.

What are you rambling on about? *The Voice asked.*

Hey, Voice? Are those ya know human-being type people hanging around down there?

Yes, son.

What? Naaaaw, can't be.

Why not?

Well, because they're so . . . hot lookin'.

Like I said, they come Home between lifetimes.

How come so . . .

Perfect?

Yeah, how come?

Well, when they come in as children, they're perfect . . . ever seen an ugly child?

Then what happens?

The saying: you are what you think, comes into fruition.

You're kidding. They actually become the way they look, by what they think?

Quite so.

So they actually are in their perfection here and if they were to maintain what they think here they would never grow old or get ugly or anything?

That's true, son. And imagine what a beautiful Earth it would be, too.

You mean they create what the Earth looks like by how they think?

Yes indeed. Look around. If they can do it here they can, and eventually will, do it on Earth. But by that time, the two will become One and there will be no more separation.

Wow, you have a great imagination, Voice.

I just see what Is, my son.

But here they float around in their bodies, they can do that on Earth if they had a mind too?

Some already have.

How about orbs like I have?

They can use bodies, they can use orbs too—

Yeah, I choose orbs, they're much faster.

Bodies are nice. They do go slower because sometimes it's just nice to take a leisurely walk somewhere . . .

Must be a human thing—loving to walk . . . Seems borrrring to me. Slow is not in my vocabulary.

That's so true.

Orbs do me fine . . .

And sometimes orbs are used for information or energy packets—but you'll learn all about that later.

Yeah, and why am I gonna need to know about this?

You'll see.

You'll see, naaa-naaaa, You'll see. I swear, sometimes His Voiceness can be a little irritating with all the mystery stuff.

You notice there are very few roads or walkways going and coming on this Side? The Voice said.

So? What's so strange about that? Nothing like that ever exists underwater.

Right, other than a walk now and then, there's really no need for these things because here at Home—

You call this Home all the time. Why is this Home and Earth is not?

Because this is the reality. The other is only a dream.

Okay, tell me more about Home.

Here everything is possible by merely thinking of it, *The Voice went on . . .*

Wouldn't that: one, be dangerous? And two, after a while, get boring?

Well, you're jumping ahead of the game . . . I'll just let you think about that for awhile. But just remember, as long as you ponder these questions you will be attached to Earth and it will keep you having to return and return until you understand that it has nothing to do with anything Here

Well, The Voice was talking way over my head but I was into the architecture anyway—I couldn't believe all the mansions everywhere.

Man, who lives in these shacks? They must be rich! I asked.

There's no need for money here. Everyone has everything they ever need. Everyone knows they are one with everything. However, these buildings we see here are not used for housing but for purpose and knowledge—they are Temples holding certain frequencies of information—

And . . . whazup with all those steps?

Very good, son. You're using your intuition. I was about to say that the steps indicate what frequency the Temple will hold. The more steps, the higher the frequency.

I was so glad we were past the talking and into the action as we flew top speed through a bunch of beautiful gardens and raced up some 500 stairs spiraling up this hill leading into a very large Temple of Wisdom.

We went in. It was indescribable, but I'll try. Up, up, up way up, the ceilings were so high you couldn't really be certain there was a roof (I could have sworn I saw clouds floating around up there.) And what I thought was a lobby was only a magnificent hallway—the kind that kids are told exists only in fairy tales. (Ya think?) The place really had a thing for columns—hundreds of columns—as far as my puny eyes could see. Whooo I understand why, whadda power statement. And the hallway was puny compared to the huge marble domed room with enormous windows overlooking the hillside and the gardens we'd just buzzed up from.

The Voice had us popping into another Temple that kinda was a downer in size compared to what came before. It only had seven steps but it's the concept that made this place such a big deal. This place called The Akashic Records had recorded every single thought that had ever been thought or will ever be thought—and there it would remain for all eternity. Whew, think about it. I don't know what the hezzop The Voice would ever do with all this information stuff, but he seemed to think it was extremely vital. This room was awesome once we were deep into it because it seemed to go on forever and ever: like a library, every stack, had another stack, ad infinitum.

Then there was this other room—records of every creation that has been created or would be created in the future, then another room where every lifetime ever lived had been recorded, past and future. And you could watch it on a surround screen with surround sound—surround everything.

And this can all be here at once because in this dimension: there's no time or space, no past or future, only what Is-ness—

Okay all very interesting but again, still a little over my head. And I was playing along but I noticed my reactions were comin' off a little snooty, because I was getting leery, I mean, why was I being shown carte-blanche all this stuff? Just who the hessop was I, a lonely little ex-dolphin in an orb body? All I wanted was to find Eeeoo but the more we did this, I mean, just think about it, what the heck was this little excursion about anyway . . . and being followed by The Almighty Voice? I started hanging back taking my time. Was I acting suspicious? I-think-sooooo.

Reading my mind again, The Voice said, ***Don't dawdle, son. There is a reason for this. Come with me.***

Fiiiit! Like where else would I go? Duh. I followed. Ho-hum. More trees, flowers, valleys, hills, a lake here and there, all 3-D beautiful, it was like flying like a bird which can be a little boring after . . . I had no idea how long we'd been, cause the Voice was right there was no time and space. But suddenly my attention peaked when I wanted to go through something rather than around, I could. It was so cool. All I'd hear was a little pop-pop when I did it.

We pop-popped through the next Temple . . . The Temple of Research. Soooo beautiful! Lotsa columns as usual, but tall! Musta been at least 600 feet tall (who knew because there was no space) and surrounding this was a big open area made of intense pink marble with bright blue streaks running through. Never before had I seen something so beeda-badda-butiful. I gotta say—exploring all this cool stuff I really started missing Eeeeoo something fierce. She would have really dug seeing this stuff.

Then, think it and there it is . . . Eeeeoo was right there in front to me—in orb form. How did I know it was her? Who the frickfrack knows? I just knew. Besides I thought I could see her face right there in that bubble . . . well, eyes, yesssss the eyes I'd know anywhere even if she were in an orb.

Eeeeoo! I freaked. You're here! Where have you been? I'm zippin' and zottin' around her like a lightning bolt I'm so excited to see her and she's just floating there in her little perfect Orb. My love was here with me again and I was so excited.

Where have you been? But, like ramming into an iceberg, it hit me. Eeeeoo was there, but she wasn't seeing me! EEEEOO IT'S ME! I screamed. Talk to me.

I changed position. I looked right into her soul. Eeeeoo it's me! Talk to me.

Eeeeoo blinked a few times, but moved on down the hallways as though she was looking for something. I chased after her. She stopped before a lit panel, and I was so close I pop-popped right through her. I turned around in time to see: out of the panel floated a light in a big balloon. It moved over her like it was eating her up. I freaked again. But it wasn't eating her after all, I just couldn't see her but she was actually absorbing it—slurped it right up into her Orb.

The Voice explained, ***You see, she was teaching her healing class, she's dropping in to research some information, then she'll pop out.***

I yelled at The Voice, WHY? WHY DOESN'T SHE SEE ME OR HEAR ME?

She can't. She's in another dimension.

Another dimension?

Yes, she is at a much higher frequency or vibration.

Why? Why can't I be in her vibration? I miss her. She's my other half! We're one!

Not quite.

Beeezopsheebit you gongeromeeba. She's my wife! We are married for eternity, so give her back. NOW!

I didn't take her.

Then it hit me. You mean, she doesn't want to see me?

Oh yes. She loves you dearly and holds you deep in her heart.

You sure?

***Well, son** . . . The Voice said. Going for that son stuff again and again was beginning to rub me a little itchy but I swallowed that insinuation 'cause I thought he was a good guy and I didn't really want to punch him like I did some shark-type punks I knew back in the pond.*

I digress.

*The Voice continued, **She's coming through what highly-evolved dolphins know as The Window in Time. We'll be teaching you this, when we think you're ready.***

I'm ready. Teach me now.

When you let go of being Zeeep we can teach you.

Suddenly, I had this creepy feeling crawl right over me. A creepy feeling that everything was going to change. I was never going to be Zeeep again and if that was what I had to do to be with Eeeeoo, I would be anything. I was never going to be champeeeeen racer of the blue, leader of the pack? I was chilled to the bone and I didn't even have them. If He wanted me to be a lowly slug in a pile of slime so that I could be with Eeeeoo, I'd do it.

But just before Eeeeoo faded away, I felt it. I filled up with so much love I thought I was going to explode . . . again. I knew . . . I just knew, that moment, that Eeeeoo was thinking of me and knew I was there.

I love you Zeeep, I could hear her say. I will look for you when you come. We will be together if you do your work, she said, please look for me. And as she faded away I could feel a soft tear, a tear she had shed, just before she faded away for good.

I was crushed and, at the same time, empowered. She loved me with all her heart and soul and we could never be separated because of our Love. I just knew, but even so, all my insecurities had just come spilling out!

DR. ABRAHAM LATHAM
NEW YORK, USA
WINTER, 1998

CHAPTER 15

The ocean was lazy today.

Flat water was not the best for sailing, so Abe had borrowed Bob's motor yacht. He appreciated Bob's taste in décor: no tiny paper and string replicas of schooners, or stuffed ocean kill, no sea shell soap dish cradling a little gold star-fish guest soap, none of that. All was high tech and sleek: polished chrome, deep cherry wood polished to a high-shine, and soft leather upholstery stretching over the sleek furniture.

It wasn't until he was way out in the liquid expanse of what seemed a floating eternity that he realized how much he'd needed time away from dead concrete and the clang of the city. Settling in the captain's chair on the highest deck, he set before him his makeshift office: a laptop and portable printer. He took a few sips of his cherry martini and set to work on a rewrite of his fourteenth chapter. Digging deep into his briefcase he felt for the stack of crisp, tightly squared papers under his fingers. He was always surprised with a slight thrill of excitement when he connected with this particular document. If he were a woman, this would be his pregnancy: a birth waiting on the horizon of time without inkling as to when the happy event would dawn. A female had the advantage of knowing nine months was the magic deadline, but the book had been gestating for nearly two years. He ran his hand over the cover page, his eyes lit on his name: Abraham Latham, MD, and it swelled his heart. This was not a novel with the heart beating throughout, no not at all. This book contained *just the facts, ma'am*. A book of charts, graphs and figures could seem soulless—but this one was not. This was his work. Years of research and interviews. A textbook so carefully composed to a precise beat, it portrayed a . . . simplicity—a Topo map for the physician, charting a concise explanation—sparing patients from thinking they were victims of their spinal cord injuries. God knows they had enough already to deal with. No, this book had merit. Had purpose.

It was his service to others. His compassion flowed toward these unfortunate souls—a single mistake or trick of fate had thrown them into a life with no thread to lead them back to anything familiar. Born again, as it were. And if there were such a thing as reincarnation, a spinal cord injury would be it: to be awakened into a broken, worthless, unmovable body. A soul incarcerated in hell. And in many instances, without a voice to speak.

Why had he chosen spinal cord injuries as his field of study? He didn't know. He just felt an unfathomable connection that had held him all through his stay at Duke. All the years of training, then years of teaching: sermonizing like a wild gospel preacher, *If the doctor were to fall into the patient's ocean of misery in order to save him, they would surely both be drowned*. That was the purpose of this book, to help keep the mind in charge over the frailty of the heart.

He made his last correction and slapped the manuscript on the table with a marked pop. He hated the title—he'd have to work on that. Then he'd put together the table of contents, should it have a glossary? It was for the lay public, so yes. And a bibliography and after that, who knows . . . be done?

From down in the main cabin, he heard a scratchy voice being transmitted. He triple-timed the boat's steep, descending steps to the decks below.

Whiskey-Charles-Mike-5225 . . . Whiskey-Charles-Mike-5225. This is US Coastguard calling 'Desert Sailor', come in 'Desert Sailor'—over.

Abe ripped the handheld mike from its holster on the VHF radio and breathlessly spoke, Come in. This is 'Desert Sailor'—over.

The gravelly voice continued, Hail to signal, this is the Coast Guard Marine Operator, we have an emergency landline connection, will you receive?—over.

That's a 'Positive', operator, please transmit—over.

His heart pounded.

As he waited for the transmission, his mind raced over the possibilities: was this for Bob? and how would he be able to redirect them? He had no idea where Bob was—Turkey, he guessed. If it were for himself, how did they know to contact him here? His stomach twisted into a tighter knot.

This is the Coast Guard operator, we have your call, go ahead caller.

A weak, tear-driven woman's voice crackled through. Hello . . . Abe? Abe?

End your relay with an "over" ma'am, the operator's voice crackled.

Over . . .

Lilly? Is that you? . . . over.

Yes . . . it's me, Abe. I-I-I have horrible news. We were on our way to mother's and we've been in an accident . . . Ben was killed . . . outright . . . Over.

A long pause followed. Abe knew his sister was trying not to cry. I'm sorry Sis, so very sorry. Is Sabrina okay . . . how are you? . . . Over.

I'm okay, I'm okay . . . no I'm not. A stupid broken arm and my right leg is a mess, some lacerations, nothing that can't heal, but . . . b-b-but Sabrina—Oh God, Abe, they say she's broken . . . her back! She's in a coma and they can't . . . wake her up! Lillian burst into deep sobbing but managed to add, o-ver.

Oh God, this is terrible, I'm so sorry . . . Sis? Try to remain calm, Lillian, don't make any decisions until I can talk to one of the doctors. I'll fly out as soon as I can. Which hospital? Over.

Her voice temporarily faded, . . . Where the hell are we? Abe could hear an unintelligible voice answering somewhere in the room.

Montreal General, her voice coming in strong again. We're in Emergency. Please hurry, Abe. Over.

Have your doctor radio me here on the boat for the next half hour. I'm about 25 miles out from Long Island. I'll have a Coast Guard helicopter fly me to you. Over.

Abe? Thank you, thank you so very much. Over.

Sis. Be brave. Over—and out.

The line went quiet.

Abe stared out at the placid ocean; his breathing came in shallow pants, his hands gripped the cold metal railing hard as he realized he was slipping, without reserve, into feelings a doctor wasn't allowed. Professional or not, this was his family and all of his damn training would just have to go to hell. Flashes of the car accident from his childhood came to him—vivid—along with a long buried stabbing pain: there before his child eyes he was witnessing his own parents being smashed between screaming metal. He knew what Sabrina saw. And he remembered that the horror of being the one to survive had been harder than dying that day right along with his family. His heart ached for Sabrina's soul and a question burned within—had she taken this coma on, rather than live out the pain he knew so well? along with the horrible and tremendous guilt . . . Oh, Sabrina—poor small, innocent Sabrina. His head was pounding.

He grabbed his stomach and let foul curses directed toward the heavens go straight at God and was finally able to break the dam of tears he'd held back for years and years.

The yacht rocked silently on the water, a man doubled over holding onto the side of the boat with dead eyes staring out, and a flock of sea gulls whispered across the sky. Then the man stood and went below, and with a mighty roar, the yacht sped for shore.

ZEEEP IN THE OTHERWORLD

CHAPTER 16

Why the Hezzop can't I be with Eeeoo?

Patience, my son.

I'm not your son! Don't call me your son. I know who you are, you . . . are a mean guy. A really mean guy, that's who you are! EEEEErrrrrk. I got sooo pizzonked that I started flying around out of control, yelling, gimme my Eeeoo back right now! A regular tantrum was in full swing and I was so mad I popped my orb right through a bunch of columns one right after the other, pop, pop, pop, pop but I stopped and stayed right in the middle of one of them and didn't come out because I learned my lesson (I was paying attention), if I thought I could, I could.

There, that'll show that fatassbigshot.

Son? Come on out - we have to talk.

No, not until you tell me where she is and what you've done with her? I can't do anything until you tell me why we can't be together? My chest was beating like a tom-tom and I was breathing fast. I'm not going anywhere with you or doing anything until you tell me right now—how can I be with Eeeeoo again?

I heard a big sigh that must have been The Voice's, 'cause it sounded like all the waves in the ocean exhaling. ***Son? I'm sorry. I guess what you are not understanding is, all of this you're experiencing has nothing to do with you or Me or Eeeeooo. It has to do with purpose. It has to do with learning and getting a job done and patiently letting it unfold so you can go on to a higher frequency.***

No. I don't understand.

You know what frequencies are—you were a master at frequencies my boy, back at what you call the pond.

Yes, yes I was.

You know what they are and you use them, but you don't have the discipline to raise your own frequency. You stay locked in the same frequencies by thinking thoughts that kept you stuck there.

Okay. How'd I do that?

Think back, remember what you were thinking when you were with Eeeoo fighting the nets before your transition?

Yeah, I was dikdik pizzonked. I hated everything in sight. Hate-hate-hate was all I thought—pure and simple.

Pushing and bumping and that famous tail-slap of yours that can be lethal if you're not careful.

I had to get me and Eeeoo outta there, we were gonna die!

You were very angry.

Yeah! So?

Anger doesn't allow clear thinking—the frequency is too low and too uneven.

Anger gave me a lot of energy to get things done, man.

True. But there was a different choice, a much faster, more even frequency you could have used that would support your Highest Good and others as well.

But I wasn't responsible for others, just Eeeoo and me.

Ahh, but you didn't have to hurt others to get what you wanted. That functioned as a low anger.

I got it, okay? And my anger was torrid at this point.

When you get it without being defensive, then you get it.

You are being tough on me, man, and I'm not appreciating it right now. I did the best I could at the time.

Just making a point, my son. Please put your EGO away. There is no reason to defend yourself. I'm on your side, my boy.

Okayokayokaysheesh.

Take a deep breath, relax. Open your mind to all possibilities.

I closed my eyes, took a deep breath and started to shake like mad. All the memories of Eeeoo and me at the bottom of the ocean, fighting like mad not to die, came flooding in. All the anger I was holding in my belly came running up through me and I found myself crying from way down deep for a good long time . . . but then it was gone, as fast as it had come . . .

I felt serenely calm.

You want to come out now?

Sure. And I popped through the column side and started flying upside down. I flipped myself rightside-up and opened my eyes and smiled. Whaaaaat just happened? I said. I feel so much lighter.

Grace. By fully emerging yourself in your pain and letting it go, by changing your mind about not holding on to your anger any longer, you changed your frequency. And you'll never go back.

Well, that was easy.

He laughed. ***This time you got it, my son.*** *Then he got serious again.* ***Now, remember when you gave up the impossible fight at the nets with Eeeoo?***

Yeah.

Remember that time?

Yeah.

Remember her eyes . . . just looked into Eeeoo's eyes . . .

Yeah.

What did you see in her eyes?

Pupils?

No . . . what did you feel?

Oh, Looove man, I felt nothing but deep, Unconditional Love. (Whew, now I was fightin' back the tears again.)

Now Love, my son, is the highest frequency there is and as soon as you can learn to be in that frequency at all times, even when looking at what looks like death to you, then you can go where Eeeoo is and be with her forever and ever.

This bit of information took its place in my throat and grew to a golf ball size—I tried to swallow and couldn't—I realized the tears this time were of pure Joy, pure magnificent Joy. Guess I finally understood the truth.

Okay, I said, then that's what I'll do. What do I have to do? Just name it. Anything.

We'll have to find you another life where you'll have to go through all your darkness and all the decisions you've made, decisions that still keep you in the lower frequencies.

Okay okay okay, no prob—

You'll relive all those decisions, learn the lessons, and change your thinking so it supports you and your gift.

Gift? Gift? What gift?

You'll see, it is a Great gift.

Oh good, I love presents.

No, my son, this is an innate talent you'll need to hone. It's not going to be easy. But in this life you'll be helping a lot of people while you learn about yourself.

People? You mean . . . people as in humans?

Yes, son.

. . .

Zeeep?

I don't care! Bring it on! I said,
And
I really meant it.

LILLIAN FLEUR
NEW YORK COUNTRYSIDE,
WINTER, 1998

CHAPTER 17

She stood on the front porch of a large house, its lit windows against the black of night hinted at its elegant mass. Mounds of snow had been cleared that afternoon, but now new snow was painting the driveway white again.

The woman, looking through silent falling flakes of white, could see at the bottom of the stairs tiny spots of daffodil yellow and crocus lavender peeping through shades of grey. On the horizon, trees dipped and bowed and scatters of wild geese dotted the blue steel sky.

The early evening chill was downright piercing, but it was a relief from the scorching argument she'd left inside the house just now. Moments before, realizing that her blood was at boiling point, she had stamped to the front door, threw on her wraps and slammed the door behind her. She let out a scream that had been instantly swallowed by the quiet that comes with new snow.

Six months ago, Lillian Fleur had medi-helicoptered Grandmère and Sabrina from Grandmère's simple house in Canada to her brother's lavish New York estate. Then she'd packed all their meager possessions into her ancient VW bus and driven it down from Montreal. She'd sold her house and handed all of her hopes and dreams over to her brother—virtually sighing a gigantic breath of relief. Little did she know that she'd be ensnared by his egomania.

How dare he ask her to trust him—bequeath her whole life to him—then callously bludgeon her with harsh judgments as he had done tonight! Where was he when she had driven every day through sleet and black ice in that drafty chariot-of-clanking-bolts, to sit by the side of her youngest daughter in that . . . that stale-aired, disgusting New York hospital, with . . . with its faded dirt-lime green walls . . . everything in it made of . . . of . . . plastic and metal . . . including the damn staff working there!

She was becoming aware of the pain of her teeth grinding. Her tears, however, weren't coming—hell, she was still just too *damn* mad. Every bit of her optimism had been caked and corroded with her brother's life-sucking medical jargon.

She'd heard her brother's hateful words, said without any care or delicacy: Lillie . . . there's just *nothing* more you or anybody can do for her, give it up, and the quicker you come to accept this the better.

How could a man give up on his own flesh and blood? A woman would never . . . never in a . . . her next thoughts had walked off down some lonely trail headed to somewhere unknown—what the hell was the use? She was so fucking tired of being strong all the time. She actually was envying her daughter at the moment—imagine that? What she wouldn't give to pull up the covers, climb inside her useless body with her and live happily ever after, right there. At this juncture, having someone taking care of *her* seemed optimal.

She turned to go back into the house, but her anger still wouldn't let her. She pulled up the shawl over her coat, rewrapped it tighter around her neck and took off down the stairs and into the night. She could hear in the distance a bevy of coyotes yip-yip-yipping off in the next dale. She didn't care, she just needed to move, to scream and yell and talk to herself and curse, yes curse, and puff and sweat and get this rancid anger venom moving around in her body, up and out. She listened to her boots crunch the snow in between her breaths and her cursing had run itself raw, so now there was no yelling, only a sore throat and the breathing and the uncontrolled ranting in her mind, retracing every word Abe had said—and all her retorts. The anger exhausted her until it finally dissipated into an empty fatigue.

As she started feeling better, she ran pictures in her mind of the places she and her VW had gone together. Ah, to be free again to travel wherever that old bus wanted to take her, such a loyal and dependable friend. Her road family had lovingly named the bus, *The Egg-Beater.* She never had looked at herself as a hippy because she'd never done the drug scene, but she had been a young orphaned fugitive in those days, always running from the establishment.

* * *

It started in 1967, when her husband, Benjamin, returned from Vietnam on furlough on her sixteenth birthday, stole her *Egg-Beater* in the middle of the night, drove it up into Canada and disappeared. That was when she found out she was pregnant with Barbara. She was a woman now, holding within her the beginning of a new family—and crying out to *be* held, to *be* needed, to *be* with the man she loved.

When the Army knocked on her door with nasty innuendoes and threats for the umpteenth time, Lillie packed her bags, took the next bus to Canada and looked for Grandmère Fleur. She'd never met her and had no idea what kind of woman she was, but what did she have to lose? Grandmère was the only family she could give to her baby and all she knew was Benidicte Rachelle Soules Fleur lived somewhere in Montreal. Luckily she found the name and address in the phone book.

She remembered lugging her suitcase as she walked ten miles from the bus depot and she was in her eight month and at every step she took the baby would kick under her ribs until she felt like she was bruised on the inside. She remembered finally seeing Grandmère's house and thinking it looked just like *the little French cottage down-the-lane* in her children's picture book and she felt everything was to make a turn for the better. She was amazed and then delighted when she and her unborn baby had been affectionately welcomed by that wonderful old woman and as she walked through her warm house, cooking smells wafting from the kitchen, she had stopped to look closely at the photos on the walls while Grand-mère'd had begun to tell her about her hard life. Grandmère had been a war-bride, married to US Army Major General Huxley Fleur, who raised his five sons with strict rules and harsh discipline. All became soldiers; all but Ben were killed in Vietnam. After her third son's death, Grandmère mustered the courage to leave her husband and join her French family who had immigrated to Montreal.

Within the month, Lillian and Grandmère had managed to track down Ben—he had joined a network of draft evaders and deserters. Lillian joined him briefly, then returned to Grandmère's house where she gave birth to their first daughter, Barbara. After the war, Ben and Lillian settled in Canada, where she watched helplessly as Ben was tormented with illnesses and flashbacks. Teenaged Barbara succumbed to depression and suicide.

Patti Anne, their second daughter, was sickly most of her life. Times were very harsh.

Lillian researched Agent Orange, the herbicide used in Vietnam, and began to believe that her family's tragedies had been caused by its effects.

* * *

As all the past memories filled her mind, a cold chill ran though her; it truly seemed as though they were cursed. Lillian hiked, puffing hard, to the crest of a knoll that looked over distant hills. Strangely, a new calm had moved in, most likely because of the aerobic endorphins flooding her body. She took deep breaths, gulping in the crisp air and smiled as she remembered the beautiful ray of sunshine that lit up her and Ben's and Grandmère's years of darkness. It was when little Sabrina entered into their lives. She was a delight: cheerful and inventive—a gift for all they had suffered—untouched by any genetic mutation. Life was so much more meaningful when there was a little one filled to the brim with laughter. Lillian's tears came welling up, not for the pain, but for the *joy* she felt for her daughter, and she didn't wipe them away. They didn't sting with the cold, they felt warm and comforting and refreshing. Sabrina was worth everything she had gone through . . . even Abe's shortsightedness.

She turned and ran back through the night, back to the mighty house on the hill, and she hoped Abe hadn't gone up to bed yet because she had to thank her brother for everything he was doing for Sabrina and herself, and she would tell him that they would find a way after all because Sabrina was a blessing . . . and a blessed child.

ZEEEP, THE ORB
PARAMANGUAIA, BRAZIL

CHAPTER 18

Fissstbishh kerrrash! Ouch!

The Voice was watching me flip around running smack into myself. Hey, I said after the third time . . . back off! He finally admitted the he may have punched in too much info while downloading all at once without a training period or reference points. Duh. I said . . . ya think?

He thought about it for a while then proceeded to let me know he was thinking about a different tactic: ***Sorry son, now that I've made my changes, I will now subtly and gently download more information from the cosmos, this is sure to support my new intention.***

So nice to have been re-considered, I was a little irate I must admit.

He thought maybe I had been slugging along way too slow for my dolphin intellect for me to understand a human consciousness, so He decided to rev it all up big time to make it easy for me to rip through more facts/figures and your typical insights therefore trying to curtail my freaking-out badly . . . Then The Voice told me he was starting the download again about human development but I swear on my mother's dorsal it felt kinda like an octopus was massaging my head. Nice . . . I totally turned into something I'm definitely not—a big mushy wuss. This wave of luscious relaxation turned all my bright spiky red colors I had goin' on, into this swishy, velvety-green slush . . . ahhhhh. I tried but I just couldn't fight it, I was becoming addicted to the download:
1151957982131010984085870983486091898674815130829564225

07703987980209848708791781††† ϟ *ßß‡€Ω‰‰Æ*☯ ØÛ⊠ 🖼 ϟ
🌎 ♈※✷⊙⊙↑↓↖ϟ ↗↙↘⇥⇤⇞⇞⇟⇟↯↯ϟ ♑♐ℯ𝓉∧∧∇∇∇⊄¬¬¬
√√√ ϟ ∭ŸŸ◊◊◊◊ΔΔΔ ϟ = ☯ = ***999666333 =.0***

Watching my brain computer run a bunch of numbers that turned into weird symbols crossing my mind's eye, I became kinda confused with the results . . . Point Zero? Was this a typo in the Universe I had stumbled over? I was feeling all silly and lightheaded and full of myself but I found words just kinda fell out of my mouth anyway.

Hey, your Eminence, sir, I said, Maybe—just maybe—the Universe isn't perfect after all . . . 'cause your High Holy, I found a little teeny—tiny blooper, no, in the scheme of things it could be a super duper blooper .

He let me rattle on to the place of total embarrassment, but The Voice mostly knew what was going on and got all laidback just letting my loopi-doopiness be okay. Even after scanning my vast expanse of dolphin knowledge, I was always amazed how He had access to facts I had never even considered.

No, son, Point Zero is the point of perfection that exists on the Otherside. Everything on Earth is comprised of molecules of DNA that has preserved in its memory banks, Point Zero, the absolute point of perfection. For instance if your body experiences an accident and, say a fin is badly damaged, your body will still have the memory of its perfect state. Point Zero is very important to healing . . . for if your fin remembers its perfect state, then it can repair itself.

Wow, do humans know this?

You'll find ancient scrolls of holy writings telling of an Infinite Perfect Plan—an organic perfect memory. But it wasn't until recently that one of the human's renowned living scientists put a name to this factor. He calls it Point Zero.

Man, that is so cool. I was starting to really get into the particulars of this healing stuff and it was exciting.

May we resume our download, now?

Oh yeah, yeah, resume . . . resume away—

The Voice thought maybe I should have access to a little more sophistication for the English language, but hey, he can download until he drains the whole cosmos, but if I don't wanna use—sophistication—I'm not gonna. Know what I mean? I am boss of my own downloads, and he better know it. With that, the words zip—flashed by: BRAZIL/ LAND/ TOWNS/ CULTURE/ RELIGION/ INHABITANTS . . . and a whole bunch of those symbols which didn't make sense and I had a sneaking suspicion that what was goin' on was:

On the other dorsal, this was the Earth lesson, second part of my studies and I gotta tell ya I really was diggin' on my new earthly-modified, spacey-out-there, orb body I was hot-doggin' around in: it cornered with the ease of a jet ski and swooped down right over the top of lush green hills and zigzagged through the little puffed trees scattered all over their backs, faster than sheebit.

The thing that was making me a little wacky, though, was seeing land for the first time in what must have been eons. (I've had hundreds of lifetimes as an aquatic species of some kind.) But the lifetimes I did live on land, I don't recall anything that even looked close to what I was hovering over this part of South America called Brazil now: there, sprinkled all over the hills were scads of huge dirt-red-brown mounds—four-to-five feet tall.

Whazzat? I asked, while dropping and hovering over the dirt pile to get a closer look.

That's where Brazilian termites live, son.

Termites! The download must have been successful. I instantly knew what termites were and why I knew what termites were: It stemmed back to my past life as a big wooly bear living in the woods of Alaska. Wow, I was thinking, what kinda termite would build a whole hill like that? Then I saw pictures in my imagination—horrors of me as a bear, being attacked by monster termites while I was prowling around innocently for a harmless in-between meal snack. Huge winged three-tiered bodies, bright red, with these gargantuan pinchers that were stabbing into my skin, plummeting my body to the earth like a felled tree and tearing me to shreds for their fajita dinner that night....

I shot back to the sky while I shook off this image and the frightened feelings that were causing my orb to misfire and threatening to thin its walls. The Voice redirected my thoughts to appreciating the afternoon rain shower we were flying through: all misty and warm.

Feeling much better and seeing that my orb colors were back to their optimum glowing, I got back into the travels through black and white clouds—none like I'd ever observed before. These billows of white vapors were piled high on each other like a buncha huge ice cream cones floating by, so dense I could have jumped on top of one and slid all the way to the bottom and then pinged over and landed on the black one and then had a slow tickle descent while enjoying a quick snooze on the lovely pinkish one. It was sure tempting to maneuver a cloud diversion tactic, but The Voice was pushing me somewhere fast and furious, zipping along, faster and faster, until I saw down below a teeny-tiny little village practically sitting smack-dab on what looked like a path sprinkled with fast moving bugs.

As we dropped closer in I could see these bugs were huge (bigger than huge termites even.) The Voice eventually told me they were cars—cars? . . . cars . .

. cars—download CARS: VEHICLES FOR TRANSPORT/OTHERWISE KNOWN AS MACHINERY. Oh. But then, there were these thingies, even bigger thingies, reminded me kinda of a big whale, but square: no grace, no speed, come to think of it . . . naw, not even close to a whale . . . forget that. And these guys were ugly as your worst nightmare: puke black canisters spewing out gunky clouds as they made this humming-puffing-screeching noise all the way to the tops of the hills they were trying to climb—and . . . once again, a (late) download: TRUCKS/ USED FOR TRANSPORTING GOODS. The silver ones however, were buses (yeah I got a late download on that too: BUSES/ USED FOR TRANSPORTING HUMANS).

As we moved along, I got tinkering at the back of my mind: what the hell was The Voice relating to earlier about humans being God's apprentices? I really don't think so, ya know? Looking down at those creations on the road, these humans had created some pretty ugly machines so far as I could see. I was not impressed. Nope. Humans had a long way to go as far as I was concerned, and it got worse as we continued our journey, down and over this little town.

Up close, I saw a bunch of beat-up corrugated metal all tossed like a salad; pieces of discarded wood mixed in with a bunch of trash—brilliant colors of dull-brown, tan brown and dirty brown: HOUSES/ HABITATS FOR HUMANS. People actually lived here, I asked? The Voice downloaded: POVERTY AND POLITICAL GREED, so I could understand better, but I still couldn't. I watched big people, little people and teeny sized people running around trying to live under a pile of boards. Memories of the ocean filled my brain—where any place was home and it was beautiful and peaceful—and it suddenly dawned on me . . . <u>Was this place Hell</u>?

Depends how you look at it**—said The Voice, **let's just say, there are fewer choices here than the ocean.** The Voice sounded strained. **Let's just say most of the people you see here manage to be happy, no matter what. Humans always have choices. That is a golden rule—choice.

Okay, unfortunately this concept was a little over my head at the time, Whoa, I thought to myself, I'll try to figure that one out later.

However, once we had buzzed over to the otherside of the highway, the terrain had improved a bit. Buildings seemed to have some form to them—bright orange boxes—looking the very same color as the straight dirt roads that ran like a grid through what The Voice said was a village. A large sign spelled out: PARAMANGUAIA.

Why's everything orange? I ask.

The buildings are made of brick from the dirt you see.

Hah! Then I figured out something so very brilliantly: termites eat wood, they don't eat brick. Right? Right? Am I right?

And . . . I, the orb in training , made another astute observation—that suddenly at the end of the village the terrain had changed—I saw white boxes with blue bottoms and patches of green and beautiful colors. Whazat all about? I wanted to know.

That my dear son is—Moradia de Dom José de Barros: : (Mod-o-shee dee Dome shJo-say day Ba-hoose) The Home of Bishop Jose de Barros, where we will find the famous healer Medium Seu Miguel dos Milagres: *(Sa Mee-gale dos Meel-log-gres)* **Medium Miguel of Miracles—our destination.**

I was excited as the always-late readout came through:

GREEN is Lawn. COLORS are flowers and flowering trees. The BUILDINGS are painted white-stucco edged with bright blue. COURTYARD: a large grassy and brightly flowered yard, appreciated by and created by humans.

I sighed, directing my thoughts to His Highness. I said, Look, readouts need to come a little earlier. You think you could get that together sometime soon? I know I have an attitude but . . . this new stuff is very confusing. And if the equipment is faulty, The Voice uses, it tends to drive one mad!

But, I thought I was confused until we buzzed over the last building and lo-and-behold I saw ten huge silver buses looking as though they were out sunbathing or something in this parking lot—then I really was confused. I swear there were hundreds and hundreds of humans swarming around them like these little white mealy bugs; they were moving out in formation in these straight lines that fanned out like a spider web through the courtyards and sitting areas. It was creepy.

I hovered my orb down over tops of heads, following some pretty vile smelling bodies, Pop! (I swished through a wall when I wasn't looking.) Inside the hall, I heard a single voice straining through what The Voice told me was a microphone after I'd rocketed about a couple-a-feet straight up from fright from just the sound of it. The Voice said the man was saying the Lord's Prayer in Portuguese, which I had to wait again for my readout before I found out what that was.

We ended up hovering before this guy, dressed all in white, standing on the stage doing all this yama-yama over a sea of bowed heads. Gliding closer, hesitant as hesop, I hovered face-to-face with the guy on the stage. He was a tall, strong-looking man—

The Voice said, ***Made in Brazil.***

Shock! I realized the Voice had made a joke.

It looked as though years and years of hard work were all meshed-up in his eyes, and when I entered into his eyes, I could see his soul way back behind there.

I could feel with my sonar instincts: he was wise and strong; a little stern, but tons and tons of kindness was there, too. Suddenly I got all these chills running up and down the backside of my orb body.

I had to ask The Voice, Whoa, just who is this guy? But before He could answer, I felt all this wild electrical energy flowing out from him. It took me straight back to the sonar scans days in the pond when we dolphins would use that energy on each other for healing. I shimmered in this splendiferous feeling for a moment, then asked, Whoa, is this a dolphin man or something? I was pretty impressed.

This, my son, is Seu Miguel dos Milagres,** The Voice instructed, **known to people as Medium Miguel of Miracles.

No sheebit?

Shhhh. Can you watch your mouth, please?** The Voice whispered, wiggling my orb like jelly. **If you look closely there are some mighty Holy Entities helping him out here today, and it is customary to show respect.

I was so excited, looking around, wondering what Entities looked like, it just slipped out, No sheebit? . . . Oopssorry . . .

***Eh-hem,** The Voice cleared his throat.*

Sorry. Bad habit.

*The Voice continued, **Today, son, Seu Miguel will be healing at least a thousand people—as he does each and every day that he works.***

Whoa, pal. Hold on. You think I'm gonna believe that? One thousand? I'm good at healing, and I couldn't do more than fifty a day back in my ocean days. Eeeoo was the best healer and her top was two-fifty a day. A thousand—pretty steep there bud. Suspicious, I was on to him like a leech on warm skin—thinkin', not gonna believe nothin' for an instant, 'till I see it—that's for sure.

Are these people all sick? I asked, hiding my suspicious attitude, as I swished out through the crowds, doing a head count, then triumphantly took my stand, Hey, there's not even a thousand people in this room.

Yes, but if you take a closer notice, there are people carrying photographs, some have come with hundreds for Seu Miguel to view and attend to, not to mention stacks and stacks of letters with prayers asking for healing. You see, not everyone is well enough to travel from clear across the world, let alone from a nearby village. Healing, however, knows no space, or time, it can happen anywhere.

Yeah, but I see there are a bunch of people in the audience who aren't sick, I said, bouncing from head to head, Here's one . . . Here's one . . . One over here, two sitting together . . . A whole row of them over here—I was so sure I'd finally outsmarted the Big Poobah.

Those talented people have come to help because they are here to serve the others—these too are Mediums—dedicated to Seu Miguel's work. Just their presence helps to hold the energies around Seu Miguel's body while he is doing his Medium work. It also helps the doctor Entities on the Otherside to have the energy to occupy Medium Seu Miguel's physical body and do the surgery. Without their help, the miracles cannot manifest as quickly and succinctly. It's all team work here. The meditators, Seu Miguel, and the Entities—

—and the sickies too, I added.

People come from all over this world to experience what happens so rarely anywhere else on Earth.

Still not completely satisfied, I swished up to the front of the stage and looked out over the audience again, and WHOA MAN! The energy was . . . It's . . . it's . . ., I couldn't spew out a word, or any set of words to explain this powerful river-rush of . . . of . . . Ecstasy. Better than any sex back at the pond I'd experienced as yet!

Hey dude? I said as I was hovering over the audience's heads, Did you slip me a mickey or something? My mind was shot like a cannon out into the Universe. I . . . I . . . I think I'm due for another download or something, I think I've blown my circuits . . . I can't find any words . . .

Nor will you, the language of love is a language without words.

Give me a break here. There's something wrong with my equipment, I swear.

Okay, let's do a test: think of a word—or even half a word.

I couldn't, I swear, and another shot of Ecstasy ran through my orb's follicles, Whoooow-hoooow-hooo, this stuff izzz amazing . . . Hey . . . whoooo . . . I believe! And who in the hezzzop even cares!

This, my son, is the energy the Entities use to heal these people. Pure, unadulterated, unconditional L-O-V-E straight from the Omnipresence.

That's powerful sheebit man . . . wadda kick.

Eh-hem.

Sorry.

Strangely, I suddenly knew what The Voice was talking about. I don't know how I knew, maybe a download catch-up or a universal understanding that is the core of each one of us—asshole or saint.

My curiosity was peaking like crazy as I glided over the audience to get a closer look at various bodies in the audience: some didn't look sick at all but I could see and feel this sticky blackness, yucky all around and through their hearts and other organs. Others, however, were so crippled that it tore my ticker out and left it dangling. There was this one guy I hovered in front of for the longest time: he stood next to an empty wheelchair, his legs bent completely backward at his knees. I was trying to figure out how he was able to walk like that, when it dawned on me—it was a frigging miracle he was even standing! Gold flooded my little orb with . . . I think it was something like compassion.

I whispered, Oh, man, what happened to this guy? I certainly didn't want to appear an asshole if someone were to overhear my question. (Why this was a concern all of a sudden, I have no idea.)

The Voice whispered back, ***Some people are born with mangled bodies and if you're living in the poverty of a third-world country you're not even able to touch the idea of corrective surgery—it's inconceivable. Seu Miguel, however, is doing his work, asking for no money whatsoever because he, too, was born in extreme poverty. Since he was fourteen, he has worked hard labor at that brick factory, across the street. He would come home and stay up most of the night healing people.***

What's money? I had to ask, like a big dolt that I am, then I had to wait awhile until The Voice downloaded. It was so much information—I could have gone to work as a friggin accountant.

I hope you're not planning for me to be a CPA in my next human lifetime? I had to ask.

I swear I could hear him smiling. I think he did that to get my blowfish for being disrespectful and such a sheeebit in front of these Holy people, OR for something that I was going to do even before I'd done it.

SABRINA
MONTREAL, CANADA
JUNE 2000

CHAPTER 19

Sabrina's eyes darted around the room. Her brow knitted as she squinted to get a better focus. She had no idea where she was.

She heard her mother's voice off to her right. She's awake! Oh, God! Oh, God in heaven!

Sabrina tried to turn her head. Nothing.

Her mother's face came into view, all contorted—her eyes wrinkled from years of worry. Two deep crevasses, like parentheses, lined both sides of her sad lips. Veins of silver ran through her waves of red hair. Her mother had suddenly grown older. *Why?*

Sabrina puzzled further: *How strange. Where am I? We must be at Grandmère's by now,* but she saw no lace doilies, no soft pink comforter. The room was too white. Not a place she'd ever been before.

She tried to move her lips to speak, to ask. She could not. Nothing moved. She tried her hand, a finger to point. Nothing. *What has happened? Where am I?*

She watched strange people dressed in green smocks, pushing funny-looking machines around the room.

Flooded with feelings of I'm-going-to-throw-up-now-I'd-better-go- back-to-sleep rumbling around in the pit of her stomach, she pinched her eyes closed—luckily, her drugged sleep came quickly.

ZEEEP, THE ORB
PARAMANGUAIA, BRAZIL

CHAPTER 20

I knew The Voice had been gentle on me in the beginning because all of a sudden the tempo changed—I think The Voice got tired of my attitude and decided to take me for a spin through some kind of dimension without even telling me, 'cause one minute he's introducing me to Seu Miguel and stuffing me with numbers then spiking me with some beefed up Love potion and WHAMMO I'm off in another direction all together that felt like I was churning around in some giant turbine off the rudder of an enormous cruise ship, or-or . . . or . . . no, I'm caught in a pinball machine, that must be it! I swear—BOING—a feeling just whizzed by—BINGO-BOING—a sharp pain—PINGO—BINGO-BOING—What is that growing on my face? A short black hair? I look like a freaking cat—(Wow, now that thought certainly made no sense)—BING—What is happening to my back now? . . . (no answer, then I'm watching these blaring lights in some room and scared as hezzop)—PING-PING-PING-PING-PING-PING.

What a trip I was taking—it was like a joke that had no punch line—but I didn't have any choice but to go along with everything . . . I was still wondering if the Voice had slipped me a mickey when The Voice finally pulled me from that dikdik hezzopish machine. Man, I was stimulation-exhausted.

What . . . the hello . . . was that? I panted.

That's what it's like for a human to think.

That's Fitttt zzzzzzzzdts.

Stop that . . . please. I know a curse word when you mean a curse word.

Figured it out did ya?

I was on to you from the beginning, son

Oh.

And*?*

Well it's frustrating, all this BOINGIN' and PINGIN' around. You're telling me that a human's mind is *<u>that</u>* *out of control?"*

Yes, son*.*

All the time?

It is—if a human doesn't choose to make any choices.

No wonder humans have such a hard time on this planet.

It's not easy. It can get very complicated. If, however, they are able to slow down their thoughts . . . be selective—

How the heck does anybody, human or mammal, consciously slow down their thoughts, man?

I'm not surprised that a question like that would come from you—Zeeep the Manic Zipper Boy*. The Voice chuckled to himself.*

I resented that chuckle, however. No, I'm serious, I wanna know, I said.

Hold on, I'm going to show you.

Then . . .

WHAM, Oh oh, dikdik here we go again! I'm back in the BOING, BOING gettin' whacked around and this time Mr Bigs tells me that I'm in Seu Miguel's thoughts now. WHACK—Police, today?—PING—Armando needs to return that phone call today—BANG—this lawn needs cutting, gardener will say too hot, too much to do—BANG, BING, right, left, right, left, right, left, WHAM—I just got kissed by my wife, she smells so sweet—BING—need new shoes . . . go all the way to Brasilia? Long drive. When will I ever . . . ?—BOING . . .

So how do you like Seu Miguel's mind? *The Voice's voice is all static-y and getting further and further away.*

Speak up. I can't hear you.

I SAID, IT'S GOING A MILE-A-MINUTE YAMMER NOW. RIGHT?

NO SHEEBIT, I yelled.

JUST HOLD ON, I WANT YOU TO WATCH SOMETHING SEU MIGUEL does . . .

The Voice moved me from Seu Miguel's brain into Seu Miguel's eyes. Looking out of them, I was able to see what he sees: beautiful green grounds passing under tops of his white polished leather shoes, peeping their heads out from under the hem of his white shirt one at a time before disappearing. The scene moves over the grass: scattered gnarled foliage, dirt path by a fence of rock piled on rock, so smooth, pink, purple, scarlet, blue, ahhh. Yellow flower coming closer, closer, bigger, more detail, brilliant iridescent yellow filled with a dimension of rainbows, scattered with diamonds—I swear, this soft fragrance fills my orb, ahhhhhhh so nice. Seu Miguel's eyes close to black—I wait while he's taking the flower's perfume in—POP—suddenly I'm pulled into the green from the rolling hills, the beautiful whites and pinks from those luscious, amazing Brazilian clouds I'd fallen in love with on our trip in. I was so sensitized I even smelled a pending storm brewing and then I felt a whimsical thought float by . . . I love this feeling of the rain on its way . . . Hey, I realized that wasn't my thought, that musta been Seu Miguel's. Then when Seu Miguel took in a bunch of deep breaths, sure enough I was filled with this refreshing, cool-misty feeling . . . soothing, smoothing . . . ahhhhhhh . . . .

How do you feel now?

Floating on still—I say very slowly (which has never happened to me before in my entire life.) So-o-o-o this is how the human's do it . . . it works, my mind is nice and slooooow. I feel so-o-o-o great.

You look great.

Well, I must, 'cause I feel fabulous.

FISSSSHHHIT, POP. I'm <u>outside</u> of Seu Miguel.

Take a look.

I opened my eyes and my orb around me is all luminous and there's a friggin' light show going on. Outrageous!

Human Lesson 101: Meditation can change your frequency.

Well, that was brilliant—thanks.

Want to know more?

Wanna nap is what I wannn . . .

Coming out of the ride inside of Seu Miguel, my floating was very wobbly, I tried to drift beside Seu Miguel as he strolled across the courtyard, being greeted by tons of people dressed in . . . white. Nothing but white. Well, being a little fashion conscious since I had all these colors splashing around in my orb, I was thinking to myself, Hey, did everybody wake up this morning and ask, what are you wearing today? I think I'll wear white. Well, then since you're wearing white, I'll wear white. Then the next person says, Me too, I'll be wearing white. And then the next and the next. And vwha-lah, everyone arrived this morning wearing white—Whata group, these humans.

Sooos, why's everyone in white? I ask The Voice.

Because the Entities get mixed up when people wear colors—sometimes colors can throw them off, they all have different frequency patterns and it can interfere . . .

Interfere with what?

With his surgery.

Surgery! You mean like cutting?

Sort of—

Hold on! Who said anything about surgery? I thought he was just a psychic surgeon, ya know—wham-bang and wha-lah it's just magic that just happened—that kinda healin stuff, not blood and guts kinda stuff! Hezzop, Eeeooh had given me all the gorey details about this surgery stuff humans do. They did it to her in the zoo. I saw the gash all down her side! She thought it really sucked. Barbarian practice she said. Said she could have healed herself if they'd given her more time—

Zeeep. Stop. You'll see this surgery is very different, son. Come with me—*and try to calm yourself—you're shaking like a leaf.*

Leaf . . . like on a tree? Or like—leaf me alone I-wanna-get-outta-here.

Zeeep, buckle down. It's not what you think . . . c'mon . . .

. . . Now!

Okay, sheeesh.

We zipped over to the stage where Seu Miguel had headed, and I had a quick look at his tools for surgery resting on a small table. Ekkk! See?! They're using knives around here. I told you! My stomach was turning and I was getting lightheaded as I heard The Voice continue with his explanation, . . . ***they're as dull as the knives people use to spread butter on their toast for breakfast.***

Holy sheeebit! Now I <u>really</u> gotta get out of here before it's too late. What had The Voice gotten me into—some communal cannibalistic ritual? I was panicking here. The Voice had turned to the dark side, of this I was sure.

The Voice was watching me turn all shades of muddy colors, **What is wrong with you, Zeeep?** *He asked.*

I can't get behind this, Big Fella. I hope you understand. This is where I get off. When people are going to eat themselves for breakfast, this is as far as I go. I ain't stickin' around to watch this!

Well, I heard the loudest laugh I'd ever heard and the first time coming from The Voice. No, no, no, He was into his guffaw now . . . **No, Seu Miguel really doesn't need a knife at all to work.** ***As he works, I want you to observe closely so you can see the tip of the instrument he uses, it's nothing but a white-blue laser beam that makes the incision.***

I-yi-yi, I'm not dumb, I know incision is a nice word for SLICING SOMEONE UP! But The Voice just keeps on plowing right through my anxiety.

And because the Entities energy can move so fast, the wound will be healed almost immediately. He only needs to use one or two stitches to hold the wound long enough to heal, which is almost instantaneous.

Okay, so I knew what a laser beam was. Not. So I faked it with saying, Uh oh, okay. Well, that explains that. But I was revving my engine for a fast get away.

Let me try to explain . . . In truth, everything has a vibration, correct?

Yeah, yeah, yeah . . . In truth, I was slowly making my way to the nearest doorway.

Everything has an energy frequency. For instance, all colors have a certain frequency. Red has a very active, physical movement, whereas pink—being half of the red and half of the white—has a softer interchange, one that f lows but has an amazing power very much like that of say its cousin . . . orange. And pink is the vibration of Love.

Yeah, well then . . . what's white and who's its relative?

White is a huge, expansive, All-Knowing movement because it takes all the colors of light to make white. You went through the white light when you left your dolphin body and became the orb you are today . . . remember? It is in that transforming frequency—encompassing the All-ness where the Entities are able to easily do their work.

Just then Seu Miguel walked in. Okay, my interest was piqued. I stayed. Everyone had been waiting for him since early that morning. I looked around, there were hundreds of people perched on long benches everywhere, like birds on a wire—turning in unison, smiling, watching. I watched very closely as he strode amongst the people—but I was looking hard for a breakfast setup (still feeling very shaky) but I didn't see one. And good thing the sitting area was all open-air with lotsa shade, 'cause man, I was already pretty diksnik hot from all my revving.

My mind settled down when I got caught up in my inspection—a few people shouted out and some started sobbing with gratitude and reaching out to try and touch Seu Miguel as he passed. I also noticed off to the side of the room some people were quietly sitting with their eyes closed and this deep color of purple flowing off of them in a misty-like cloud. The Voice told me that was the color of respect and that these people were there to meditate while he worked, helping him collect and build the energy so the Entities could do the surgery.

Wait! I needed clarification. I thought Seu Miguel is doing the surgery.

Only Seu Miguel's body is being animated to help direct the laser-type energies, but in reality it is the entity doctors from the Otherworld, (where you just came from) who actually do the surgery.

Cool, I replied, lowering my jets as I watched Seu Miguel take the stage and ask for his first . . . victims.

I kinda had a clue after my experience inside Seu Miguel that celebrities like him were just human beings like all these other people. But then I saw something very peculiar happen when Seu Miguel sat down in his chair and closed his eyes. He asked everyone on those benches to say all that Portuguese prayer stuff again, and then he got real quiet, then FAP! the whole stage lit up with these huge columns of white light, then one of the light columns moved over and stood by Seu Miguel. Seu Miguel's body shook a little bit then WHAM the light completely took him over and an orb of blue-green light popped outta Seu Miguel and floated around and then took off to the right side of him. And pretty soon Seu Miguel's body stopped shaking.

The Voice was right there to explain, ***Seu Miguel is now in Entity and his soul's orb-body has just now disengaged from his physical body and will remain floating in space off to the upper right side of the room where it will stay for the duration while the Doctor Entities work.***

What is Seu Miguel doing during this . . . this disengagement? I asked.

He will be sleeping—which is to his benefit because of the tremendous hours of work and travel he does. According to the staff he really doesn't get a healthy amount of sleep and his wife is always so worried because she doesn't know what he's doing while he's out of body.

Well, what is he doing during that time?

He's usually in the Temple of Healing getting a good massage or something. For instance, sometimes he might come to work at Moradia de Dom José de Barros *(Mod-o-shee-a dee Dome shJo-zay day Ba-hoose)* ***with a terrible cold. And when he leaves his body for the Entities, there is no cold found in his body, but when he comes back he brings his cold with him.***

Why doesn't he leave it at the Temple?

Sometimes humans create colds and the like, because they think they need it.

So if he didn't think he had a need for that cold, he could leave it there and return without a cold?

Oh, yeah. It happens all the time. A little perk that goes with the job. But, he still is human and his unconscious programming at times keeps him from believing in the True Power he has access to.

I was so fascinated that without thinking, I flew over to Seu Miguel's orb and when I got close enough I could actually see his face inside. Talk about a mind-fizzzzdt! Can I talk to him, I wondered? Is he aware of what was happening while he's doing all this healing of people?

I could hear The Voice off to my right answering me in that: **Yes, I can read your mind and Yes, Seu Miguel's totally aware of everything but only on an unconscious level. Once he returns to his body, he won't recall anything—the staff will have to show him the video footage so he'll know what went on.**

Now, I gotta say, when Seu Miguel sat down he had blue eyes, but when he opened his eyes—when in Entity—they were brown and his facial features and body movements didn't look the way Seu Miguel had looked before. He looked and acted . . . like . . . like there was somebody else in his body—using it—I swear. Then I saw one of the white columns leave the stage and jump over and land on someone in the audience and all of a sudden that person just keeled right over SMACK onto the floor. Lucky there were all those people around to help, that's what I say.

Anyway, I heard The Voice start making this SNAP-SNAP-SNAPPING and I looked over and hezzop there was one of those white columns coming after me! Sheebit! I turned around to run like a porpoise on" speed" when suddenly I felt a rush of energy pulsing through my orb and everything in the room looked completely different. This scene was playing itself out like a fuzzy movie: the people were still in white on the benches, fanning the heat, listening to Seu Miguel talking Portuguese, little TV's flickering on the wall were running historical video footage of Seu Miguel in surgery—but the weird part is—I found myself taking short little orb-breaths because of the intensity of a lightshow of the Otherworld playing itself over that movie. The scene I saw forming before me had thousands and thousands and <u>thousands</u> of . . . of Angels (I'd remembered seeing them during my dolphin-to-orb transition) and they were all packed somehow into that little courtyard space and there they were wing, to wing, to wing. O133h, it makes me dizzy to think about it, but the room no longer had a roof, it couldn't possibly have one because there were too many of them, they extended way, way, way out into the heavens as far as I could distinguish—I realized I could see way beyond the physical world, I could see into the next world as well—the Earth <u>and</u> the Otherside, both at the same time!

Waitaminutewaitaminute—I was still doing the staccato breathing—whatisgoin'on?

I have just opened up your third eye, son.

Three eyes! Mygawd. How many eyes do I need? And just where the hezzop did you put this third eye? Is he thinking of going for the fly eye after this? Millions of eyes? Gawd, I'm a little in overwhelm here, bud, and I'm not breathin' too good, I told him.

With this eye—your mind's eye—you are now able to see everything that is actually going on—the physical world, as well other dimensions—and more dimensions will be revealed when needed.

More dimensions than this? Oh, thanks. First let me get used to . . . this . . .

My voice died out . . . because I was in the process . . . of . . . being . . . mesmerized. Wowiekazowwwie! This is some crazy eye, man, I heard myself say as I was scoping out a whole new terrain, white-light energy spewed throughout the room appearing like lightning flashes. ZZZZIP—ZZZZIP—ZZZAPP and they intermittently hit people meditating in the audience and I'd see the aura around their body light up so bright I could no longer see their physical form and when it would fade a bit, I'd see people shaking violently or grabbing at their hearts, tears flowing, looking like they knew something tremendous had just happened. Some had even passed-out flat on the ground and the people were scrambling around trying to help them—and even these helpers knew they were witnessing major miracles happening—over there, then over there, and oh look, did you see that? Fascinating.

I was so into the moment, I moved my third eye to the stage where Seu Miguel was standing. A huge, eight or nine-foot tall entity dressed like a king suddenly appeared out of nowhere and floated swiftly across the stage, aimed at Seu Miguel and landed on his body. Now this was the very first ghostly thing I'd ever seen in my whole entire life and my heart was beating a few hundred miles a minute. Although I was very light-headed, I managed to keep on watching as I saw an orb leave Seu Miguel's body.

Then The Voice went on telling me about the entity who had just surrounded Seu Miguel's body. ***He is the ruler known in the Bible and history books as King Solomon. He comes, as do other renowned doctors—or enlightened souls—to animate Seu Miguel's body, lending the knowledge of healing they had mastered in past lives or from the other realms. This afternoon the entity of King Solomon will be animating Seu Miguel's body, moving it around, speaking through it.***

Seu Miguel's hand pointed into the crowd and asked a bent-over Brazilian man dressed in tattered clothing—it looked like he hadn't had a nickel in his pocket for ages—to come forth. As he hobbled through the crowd from the very back of the waiting area, whew! the stench wafting from that guy was something else. People were grabbing their noses and getting out of his way fast. Sheebit!

I would have grabbed my nose, but I had no idea where I'd find the diksnik thing.

I felt kinda sorry for this guy though, he was probably in his thirties but looked like he was maybe sixty, all bent-over and had to hobble on two sticks he probably had found at the side of the road. But thankgawd there was a volunteer who had the decency and fortitude to help him up the stairs 'cause he wouldn'ta made it on his own, that's for sure.

As the odd-looking man hobbled across the stage floor, Seu Miguel met him half way with open arms, and touching his eyes softly he closed his eyes and all of a sudden this man went into a trance and immediately stood upright all on his own, like he had a completely different body. The guy no longer hobbled horribly as he stepped forward still using his canes, but he walked on his own over to the wall where the other people were standing in trance, and there he turned around and easily stood up against the wall.

Seu Miguel went to him and took the canes from his hands and tossed them into the stage beside him with a clatter, and the man looked fearful but he didn't fall down. Amazing. Every single eye in the house was on this man. No one took a breath, I swear, it was so quiet.

Seu Miguel told him to leave the wall and go sit down in a chair some helpers brought and put in the middle of the stage. The old man broke out in tears.

I can't! I can't, he said. Ten years it's been. I haven't been able to sit. Too much pain.

Seu Miguel led him over to the chair and ever so gently sat him down—no resistance whatsoever—and the man bawled 'cause I don't think he could believe what had just happened.

Seu Miguel reached down and pulled up the man's pant legs and oh my gawd, it was disgusting. I nearly retched right there. His leg had open wounds so bad you could see the bone: a bloody mess of scabs and oozing puss and big gigantic holes of skin were missing. Yiiik. And I heard a breath that everyone took at the very same time—like this—<u>uuuh!</u>—all at the same time. I could even hear what they were thinkin': no wonder he stunk so much: ohmygod what's Seu Miguel ever going do with that mess? is what they were thinkin'—and me, too, right along with 'em.

It's weird too, 'cause of what Seu Miguel <u>did</u> do. He stopped his healing work, pointed to the people that were shootin' everything with these video cameras. He told them to come closer—get up real close and record the miracle that was about to happen. Then ... he called up a bunch of doctors from the audience (he pointed exactly to where they were, too.) He asked them to inspect the wounds, got 'em to go right up close and even touch his leg if they wanted to. Not too many did.

Wonder why, heh? I'll tell you why. The doctors told the audience that this man had a flesh-eating bacterium attacking his system. Backup there! Meat-eating? Man is defiantly meat! There was a whole sanctuary of meat out there..

God, I could feel the panic that ran through the group, camera people and all, they were all about to flee I swear, until Seu Miguel yelled out, DON'T WORRY, EVERYONE! YOU WILL NOT BE AFFECTED! The Entities have assured me that they have had an energy grid around this man's body this whole morning session so that IT IS ABSOLUTELY SAFE, do you understand? ABSOLUTELY SAFE to be near him.

WHOOOSH—I could feel relief rush through the audience like a huge wave busting across a beach in the middle of a storm. Even though I'm not made of meat any longer, I too was relieved.

Seu Miguel held up a bottle of water and explained to the audience it was Holy Water, then took a swig and swished it around in his mouth and spat it right there onto the stage. He lifted the man's leg and poured water all over it—rubbing it in like a salve. I was shocked, and a little queasy, when he actually put his mouth on the revolting leg wounds and started to suck on that fitzbingbong spot! It looked like he was sucking out the globs of . . . well I guess it was the disease and spitting it into a metal bowl a nurse was holding. I could both see and feel a lot of nervousness, mixed with really intense fascination, that moved over that crowd. But fortunately I could see with my newly installed third eye: that the water was full of intense light energy, it was swirling down and around and even through his leg. Then these other light Entities started to pull off what looked like a second body of some sort that was around the outside of his physical body. It was silvery-like, elastic looking, the shape of his skin and muscles—but without any bones—all droopy like. It was weird watching this going on, it looked like a big, rubber foam blow-up doll flopping all around while the Entities were stretching and pulling it.

Then the light show began. ***What you see them doing now: the Entities are flooding every cell with a powerhouse of antiseptic-light, thoroughly saturating this man's tissues,*** *The Voice was explaining, but to me, it looked like the light show I'd seen on the water when the sun lit up the surface, glittering like, you know, little rainbow pinpoints, colors flashing just like . . . turning a diamond around, ping, ping, catching the glint of the sun.* ***The disease has obviously spread throughout his body,*** *The Voice went on, and the light show not only looked like it was around the man's body, but I could see that it was through it as well.*

I checked out with my regular eyes what Seu Miguel was doing—pouring more water and rubbing it in—then my third eye: The Entity Spirits around Seu

Miguel were talking to the soul in the man's body, asking it if they had permission to remove this disease completely. The man burst into blubbering sobs of gratitude as he nodded his head. The Voice explained, ***If there was any karma this man's soul had needed to experience further, his soul would have said no, and the work would have been stopped and cancelled, right there.***

The Entity Spirits then started pulling the elastic skin and muscle light-body right over the man's physical body (looked like putting on a tight glove) and dikdik if the man's skin didn't turn a bright pink. Just like that, bright pink. All over.

The healing is complete, Seu Miguel's in-Entity had said. Please stand, sir, and walk around. I couldn't believe it—just get up and walk all around that stage, no problem. Well the guy couldn't believe it either. He even was shaking his head, no. Heck yes, I'm with you Bub. But then he took his first step . . . little wobbly . . . then the second, then the third—the man's blubbering, wiping tears with his shirt sleeve, and he's goin' around telling everyone, No pain! 25 years, it's been. Then like a little kid, he starts marching around the stage. He was so captivating that he had everyone in front of the stage laughing as he actually started dancing and everyone started dancing with him too. I have to think it was more from the relief they felt; but if you think about it, he actually had infected others—with his good fortune! I think this was a perfect example of Point Zero in action the Voice had taught me about.

Meanwhile, Seu Miguel was on to the next task—The Entities don't do much laughing and dancin' and stuff, nope they're right on the job—next—next—pointing out into the audience and pickin' out the next victim, while some of the men on the staff were leadin' this guy down the stairs and he's just laughing and singing all the way. And guess what? That putrid smell? Gone. Yep. And thank gawd for that 'cause they took him through a door marked Infirmary.

The Voice explained, ***This is where everyone who has been physically operated on is taken to be watched by nurses for the next 24 hours. This man's body and soul has been through a major trauma and will be put into a deep recuperating sleep, so that the Entity Spirit nurses and doctors can keep working.***

I couldn't help it, I had to see what it was like in that room, so guess what? Yep, ZIP—I was close behind. But before zipping through that door, I looked back at the stage—using my third eye it looked like a giant circus was going out there. I got this feeling of excitement watching all that . . . etheric hubbub: lights swishin' and flashin'. I made a mental note: when I become a human, maybe I'll go check out what livin' in a circus would be like. What a rush.

Since I'd almost missed my timing, I squeezed, then—POP—right through the door of the Infirmary I went.

Inside, it was dark, real peaceful like, beds scattered around, some with sleeping people. I noticed the patients had been there for a longer period of time, because they all had different auras radiating lotsa colors—not like the blue-white that the old man still had.

Nurses were buzzing around looking like these little bees—attending the little frail petals of the convalescing, bringing them nectar: a special healing water that was glowing white-blue, brewed by the Entity Spirits to speed up and make sure the healing took hold. And they were feeding them a special soup, too. Whoa, full of that light, too. I could see the liquid go down and light up every cell and molecule. It was so fun watching all of this, when . . .

A scream rudely pulled me from my light-fantasy. WHAM. It felt like I'd just been slugged. The intense and ugly energy was coming from the stage area. I zipped back through the walls, and saw a woman, kicking wildly, screaming obscenities like a mad woman, while Seu Miguel's helpers where trying to hold her so that he could help her. It seemed she wanted nothing of it. I knew Seu Miguel had a lot of work ahead and I was wondering how in the world he was ever going to handle this one.

LILLIAN AND SABRINA
MONTREAL, CANADA
MAY, 2002

CHAPTER 21

It had been nearly a year since Sabrina had awakened from her coma. Before Sabrina woke up this morning from her normal night's sleep, she had been having a dream of getting to school in a hurry, she was very late but there she was, over at her best friend's house. They were playing dress-up in Janie's mother's clothes closet. Oh, how she loved looking at herself in a long, black velvet evening dress that was gathered around her waist with a rhinestone belt that glittered so much it was making her dizzy and the emerald, green, pattern-leather stilettos that were miles too big made everything seem so grown up. But when Janie applied the red lipstick on her mouth, Sabrina saw in the mirror how much she looked like her own mother—then this image faded softly—and she could see a true image on that shadow image: the face of her mother was looking down at her with a big smile, Good morning sweetie . . . want some breakfast?

Knowing now that reality was in *Grandmère's* bedroom with the morning light streaming in across the foot of her hospital bed, and having just freshly come from feelings of being free and loose and full of a kid's life, and now, knowing she was back in the staleness of her incarcerated body, she wanted to be able to tell her smiling mother, Please . . . please just let me finish my dream and fall back into playing dress-up with Janie. But her body was waking up and her thoughts about Janie had turned to the realization that her best friend in life had hardly come to see her after she'd awakened from her coma.

Lillian lifted the spoon to her daughter's lips and Sabrina touched the spoon with her tongue then took the mixture in. She had no idea what it was she was eating, maybe it was oatmeal this time, maybe grits, she couldn't tell, she had no feeling in her mouth and there was no taste. After the third bite she wanted to tell her mother, Enough! *Look at me, thought Sabrina, I need to find a way to tell her when it's enough but I can't because she isn't looking at my eyes.* Sabrina took the gruel but her next bite was too much. She tried to spit it out, but her mother kept putting it back in. When her mother finally put the spoon down, Sabrina was relieved and found her thoughts racing back to thinking about Janie.

Sabrina knew it was hard on Janie to have to be the one who talked all the time. She had seen the sadness in her eyes. She had heard it in her voice. A lot of what she talked about, Sabrina hadn't quite understood. Janie was talking about the years she had lived and matured—but these were the years Sabrina had slept through. Then her thoughts found a darker ground—self-pity screamed: *Why me? What did I do to deserve this? I can't stand this anymore—I just want to . . . to . . . die!* The pain of those thoughts let go walled tears.

Her mother ran over and covered her with hugs and kisses asking, What's wrong baby? What's wrong? But looking into her daughter's eyes Lillian realized whatever it was, she may never come to find out.

I'm so sorry, she'd said . . . I'm so sorry, Sabrina, rocking her for a long time back into calmness. Are you okay, now?

Her mother laid Sabrina back onto her pillows and wiped the residual tears from her eyes with the pad of her thumbs and patted the perspiration from her forehead with the side of her hand.

Sabrina blinked. She was exhausted and let go of a long shaky breath, noticing the smell of Grandmère was in the air. The sweet fragrance of *Lily of the Valley* lightened her gloom. It conjured the memory of the cheerful little blue perfume bottles sitting there, reflected on Grandmère's mirrored-glass vanity table. She was glad her mother had decided to move back to Grandmère's house after she came out of the coma. Grandmère was glad, too. She was old and Sabrina knew she cherished all the moments she had left with her and her mother. But now Sabrina didn't have Janie, or school, or anything that would pull her back into the past anymore—and maybe it was easier that way, she thought.

The one day Janie had come to see her, Sabrina had wanted to scribble: *How old am I*?—remembering that when she and Janie were best friends, they were eight years old. But now Janie looked so completely different—her hair was suddenly longer, clear to her waist. She had braces on her teeth and her voice was lower, different—not the Janie she was used to. With all the therapy from morning to night, then the moving, she hadn't been able to ask that one question to anyone, the question that had snuck through her mind quite often, mostly just before she'd fall to sleep at night, exhausted from the day . . . *How old am I?*

Her mother's answer broke into her thoughts of Janie, it was like she was in her head listening to that question because she said without hesitating: You'll be twelve in a few days, you know. We'll have a birthday cake and cookies and Grandmère and I have a wonderful present for you sweetheart. Then she reached over and took Sabrina's hand and started rubbing it, like she did so often when she wanted to do something nice for her. Sabrina watched her mother as she massaged her hands and wished she could feel the calming warmth of it. She missed that so much.

You were in a coma for three years, honey, she said, looking up from what she was doing. Lillian got up from her seat and moved to the bed, lying down next to her. With her head on the pillow, she cupped Sabrina's cheek and turned her face to her. Looking deep into her eyes, she said, Honey, there's something I need to talk to you about. *Was this the right time to ask? How would she say it?* she thought. Her fingers rested lightly against her mouth as she took a moment to carefully choose the words she needed. She cleared her throat and took a very deep breath.

It's been nearly a year since you've come out of your coma. Do you . . . do you . . . remember anything at all about the accident?

Sabrina's eyes searched for anything . . . anything . . . but no, nothing was in her memory. She made a considerable effort to blink once.

Sabrina had been in physical therapy for six months learning how to communicate. The only part of her body that was animated was her face. All the rest of her body was well—disconnected. She had learned to blink two times for yes, one time for no, and she was learning how to write with a pen in her mouth.

Lillian sat up, surveying her daughter lying in her bed like a big doll amongst pink and lace. She was propped up against king-sized pillows, two were under her arms to hold them up, and two were tucked under her knees. Next to her bed was her wheelchair filled stem-to-stern with gadgets—only the best for her daughter. She silently thanked her brother Abe for being there for them and making it all happen. Dear Abe—he surely must miss them not living with him in New York—she was sure—but again, they had been a burden of sorts . . . maybe . . . maybe because it might have made him feel . . . so vulnerable.

Lillian's thoughts of Abe were dismissed with a flutter of her eyelids. She wished to proceed with this talk and watching her words closely, she said, You were only eight years old, it was your birthday. We were on our way to Grandmère's house, remember?

Sabrina's blank stare was enough of an answer.

There was a storm that had blown in, Sabrina. We could hardly see to drive. If we had known, we wouldn't have . . . Well, I was singing just to stay calm. Then out of the fog this . . . this wall of a truck came right at us. I don't know where it came from but a ten-ton truck had jack-knifed on the black ice. They said that it might have come from the opposite side of the road, but no one knew for sure. It hit the side of the car where you were sleeping . . .

Sabrina's eyes suddenly filled with fear.

Her mother paused briefly, realizing her daughter was having a breakthrough and rubbed her arm and waited for her to fully connect with it.

Sabrina's memory came to her, at first thin and vague: the soft snow hitting the frosted window . . . but then the memories rushed in: vivid and harsh like a dam that bursts wide open—a horrible loud noise, the squealing sound of metal scraping metal, glass breaking and crunching all around her.

Sabrina . . . ? her mother broke in, seeing her daughters eye's looking around wildly—her memory perhaps too intense to continue.

I'm so sorry, honey. I . . . I just thought it's best that we talk about this. Sweetheart . . . do you want me to tell you more?

Sabrina eyes filled with tears that spilled when she blinked twice for yes.

Are you okay?

Sabrina blinked twice again.

I just want to make sure all your questions are answered as to why you are ..... what happened to . . .

Sabrina blinked her eyes three times: an indication she wanted to write something. Her mother put a pen into her mouth and a note pad up to her lips.

Awkwardly she began to write, Daddy?

Her mother's eyes clouded over as though she had just walked into a dark room in her mind. She answered hesitantly, Honey, he died . . . and Sabrina watched her mother's mouth move, but her words were fading off somewhere.

It was so quick I'm sure he didn't feel a thing . . . but he loved you very, very much, sweetheart.

She saw that her mother eyes focused on the tree house just out her bedroom window, wrapped in contorted branches of an old oak tree. Her father had built it for her and Patti Anne when they lived with Grandmère long ago. There had always been peals of laughter in that tree as she had played there with the kids in the neighborhood, and it was such a relief to Sabrina that she was feeling lighter and filmy and nonattached and not able to hear her mother's voice tell her of her dream of hope, and her vow: You will walk and talk again if I have anything to do with it. By the time Lillian looked back at her daughter's eyes, they seemed deadened and so very sad. Then they closed. And Sabrina fell into a deep, deep sleep.

Lillian looked at her daughter for the longest time - unable to move, unable to breathe, feeling nothing because it would hurt too much. Finally taking a bottomless breath, she realized that Sabrina looked again as she did all those years in the coma - cold and vacant.

Please Lord, not that, she pleaded, but a mother always knows somewhere in her heart what truly is so.

ZEEEP
A TRIP THROUGH SEU MIGUEL

CHAPTER 22

Whooooo! The staff was trying to carry the flailing screaming woman up to the stage to have Seu Miguel work on her and six large men were having one hezzop of a time.

Seu Miguel (still in entity) finally jumped down off the stage and went to where she was. He was trying to reach out, trying to lay his hand on the top of her head. The Voice said, ***It is important that he open her third eye before he can work.*** *But the woman was flailing, fists and arms flying equal with the strength of all the men that were trying to hold her as she hissed at Seu Miguel, even scratched at his eyes.*

Seu Miguel started saying the Lord's Prayer in a real loud voice and the audience joined in, loud and strong. She was violently thrashing around and six men were getting thrown here and there and they needed to hold her so that she wouldn't hurt herself and a video camera was smashed and people in the audience were trying to get away because they were getting punched too and everyone was holding their hands over their ears 'cause of her shrill screams and language that was the crudest and foulest I've ever heard.

I felt sorry for The Voice, man, if my language set him off, what was she doing? Concerned, I tried to fly above the crowd in search of The Voice, yelling out: Are you all right? Are you okay, Voice?

The Voice came to me through the din and didn't seem to be affected. ***I've seen it a thousand times, son. Dark spirits possess this woman—they're***

extremely afraid of the light—observe around her, what do you see? Use your third eye.

I hesitated to look—man, I'd had some nightmares when I was a little dolphin, and the sheebit I saw—but curiosity got the better of me. I changed my focus to my third eye—there, connected to her body were these dark gargoyle-looking beings: Grey, humped, and a really vile colored brown-chartreuse slime was oozing from their yucky, dried, scaly skin. The thick mucus looking like slim-ribbons hanging from their gristly lips and their hissing and growling sounded just like what was coming from that lady. Their eyes flashed blood-red, burning, I could actually feel their anger and hate, it seemed like it was coming up from a bottomless pit. But also, I saw white light being built right in the room and it was encircling the ghouls, making them even madder. The room was being packed with legions of Angels, it was like they had been heralded from every space in the heavens and more were on the way. But also, I saw more and more dark Entities coming through the walls . . . it felt like a war was about to rage.

Shee-bit! just fell out of my mouth and my orb was shaking like it might explode. The Voice suggested, ***Shift back to your regular way of seeing and do it now!*** *Good thing I did or it would have warped my fine-tuned orb body with all that intense fright I was projecting on it. But just before I did, I could see that the light was winning—it had nearly engulfed the dark beings. And I saw Seu Miguel actually had the woman calmed down a bit: he was holding her face in his hands making eye-to eye contact and he was talking to the woman in Portuguese while she was shaking madly, crying, pleading with Seu Miguel.*

What is she saying? I don' t understand a word she's saying. I'd only downloaded enough Portuguese for travel.

She says that these dark-infested beings intend to kill her before they'd ever give her over to the Light. But what they don't know, Zeeep, is that the Entities' Light can be the ultimate victor if this woman's soul has the courage to choose it for herself.

So why isn't she believing Seu Miguel? I mean, she came here somehow, so there must be a belief of some kind, on some level, that he'll be able to help her.

Her ego is way out of balance and attracting and holding the negative energy to her and as long as she cleaves to that, she hasn't a chance of receiving the Light <u>or</u> her healing.

Ego, what the hell is that? I can't find it in my downloaded information.

Concentrate, keep downloading, you'll bring it up, it's there under E-G-O.

As The Voice spelled the word it all came dancing across my mind: e-go (noun) 1. Self esteem 2. Inflated opinion of self 3. part of mind containing consciousness 4. Self 5. an ego out of balance is—an exaggerated sense of one's importance and a feeling of superiority over others—End download submission 8,200,585,481.

The biggest trap the human mind can fall into (a total and absolute illusion) is that one being can be superior over another.

You're superior over me, big fella.

Only because you have created that illusion. In fact, I am not. But let's get to the reason this woman is in so much trouble, shall we?

I digressed?

You digressed.

And the Voice went on to explain, ***You see, even though this woman lives in the fear she will never be released by the fiends—they, in reality, are an illusion.***

But they're real. Just look at all that hideous slime and nastiness.

Yes, they may exist but only because they have been created by her own fear—the fear of being controlled by bedeviled souls.

So if she had no fear of these buggers, they wouldn't exist?

Quite true. But we will learn more about how to do that later.

Well, hurry up this lady is in big trouble.

But the very thing that she has attracted and manifested—has been executed all by herself. It usually stems from a stored unconscious memory from a past life.

Wow, but can the human mind remember that far back?

Absolutely, but usually not consciously. They ultimately need some help to bring it from the unconscious. And that's what Seu Miguel's Entities are trying to do.

The human mind is pretty diksnik powerful.

Think about it—what has ever been created that wasn't thought of first?

Er . . . . Well . . . Man, give me some time on that one . . .

Even though this woman was told by her darkness that she will never be released by them—that they own her soul—the truth is, as long as she has a soul she always has the power of choice, no matter what, and that is what Seu Miguel is telling her now, over and over—that it is her choice to choose the light.

I looked around the room, all the Light-beings are just standing there waiting—for what? I had no idea. There was a lady in deep doo-doo and no one was doing anything but talking to her.

I yelled, Why can't they just jump on those guys and take 'em out, heck there's thousands of Angels and look, they're ten times bigger and they could just shoot that white light right through them and blow 'em to a billion bits. I mean, you said they were just her messy creation . . . just an illusion. What's going on? They're acting like a bunch of mushy jellyfish. Whadda buncha whoooooses! If it were me I'd—

Zeeep, they can't. One of the Laws of the Universe: the soul holds domain over its choices. They cannot receive the Light unless first they give the Light permission to take charge.

What? That's just crazy.

Crazy or not, that's the Law. If a parent did the walking for his toddler do you think the child would ever learn to walk on his own?

But it's so simple, why can't she just see it?

Another Law of the Universe: If a soul gives his/her power over to fear, they are looking away from the Light and if they are not looking toward the Light, how are they ever going to see it?

Tell her to turn around then! Sheeeesh!

Fear is the hook that stays. But if she chooses to put her blind faith in the Light—and it has to be on the unconscious as well as the conscious level—she can automatically have her soul restored instantaneously. That's called Grace.

So all this light stuff is called Grace?

Yes, that is what it's called.

Man, you know your stuff.

That's because, I AM of the Light. And you are of the Light. We are all One with the Light—

But we just keep forgetting, right?

That is correct, my son.

* * *

I hung around watching for three days. Seu Miguel's Entities had a vigil of holding the light around the woman and around-the-clock voluntary meditators came and went and Seu Miguel was allowed his body only for eating and sleeping and the body of the woman was put into a coma so she could be shown that she had choices.

The Voice pushed me over to the Otherworld. It was all very familiar to me because that was the place Eeeoo and I visited during our transition. It was nice to be back there again, beauty beyond words. I didn't quite understand why the woman was taken there by the Entities, but there they were gently taking her into the beautiful Temple of Orientation, up those steps and entering through that hallway full of columns. A buncha questions were piling up in my mind as we flew down the familiar majestic hallway.

I don't get it, Voice, she hasn't died or anything so why are they bringing her here?

Oh my boy, you don't have to die to come here. This is Home. People who live on Earth come here two or three times a week when they sleep or meditate—they just usually don't remember.

No kidding. You mean I could meet Eeeoo here anytime in my dreams?

Anytime. But you won't remember.

What good is that?

That's your call, son, *The Voice said, leading me into this huge room all lit with beautiful purples and blues. Aaaah, remembering how I loved this place, I found I was fighting being a little woozy with all the love vibe wafting around, until we found Seu Miguel's Entities helping the disturbed woman over at a table with a round screen-like surface.*

They are counseling her, taking her step by step through her life and showing her all the decisions she's made so far. Mind you, there is no judgment here—it is only to give her a more holistic view of the blueprint she chose before coming to Earth. Let's go closer, I don't think they'll mind.

Why wouldn't they mind? I wouldn't want some stupid strangers buttin' in on my private life . . .

Here, no one is a stranger. We are all One, so it really doesn't matter. What happens to one person can be information to help someone else. Besides, the Entities all know you are in training.

Oh.

As we moved in close to the screen, my heart jumped into my throat when I saw a little girl become visible like a hologram—as if I was in her life, watching her movie with her. This little girl looked all ratty, in some Brazilian city: shaking, cold, and starving to death, walking down filthy streets. When two men approached her, I had to stop myself from yelling, Beat it! Getoutta there fast!

But The Voice interrupted with an ***Ah-hem. Sorry, we cannot interfere in this. We are here just to watch and learn—got it?***

Check and recheck, I said real sarcastic-like, 'cause I only wanted to help.

You can't change what already is, if isn't yours to change.

I was relieved when I saw how kindly the men were being to her. They led her up the street to where they lived. They gave her a big plate of food and put her to sleep in a nice warm bedroom. I was pretty happy until I saw the movie jump forward, from one incident to the next, showing what those assholes were doing to her for the next ten years. The movie was intolerable for me to see from that point on. They had made her their sex slave and given her drugs and while she was out of her body taking a nice trip somewhere in the astral dimension to get away from all the pain in her life, that was when the nasty, etheric reptilian souls helped themselves to her as well.

I was pretty pissed off when The Voice suggested I watch again—I was so sick of watching these ghoulish tormented souls being mean to people. But The Voice told me that it was part of my training, he wanted me to see how they worked—how they wrapped themselves around her like big nasty snakes, hooking themselves in, and sucking from her essence until her . . . until her mind gave out and made her crazy. Well, I was getting nauseated to the max and if I'd had a stomach, I could have hurled a big load—aimed right at those creeps.

Strangely enough, the movie fast-forwarded again and revealed that it was her pimps who had arranged for her to go to receive Seu Miguel's help. I guess there is redemption after all.

As time went on, the Entities kept showing the woman the movie over and over, telling her what the real truth was about her life and the decisions she was making throughout. While at the same time, the Entities were talking to the dark souls attached to her. The light beings were listening to the demon-souls spew hate and vile anger and make threats of fearful things they would do to them—horrible things, inconceivable stuff. But the Entities just stood together in a circle around them and poured loving energy and thoughts on them and asked them to just look to the Light.

It's so simple, they were saying. There you'll find your original souls—they'll be right there, for you to claim—in the Light. Just turn and look for the Light.

One of the demons instead grew another neck, then a head popped out, and his voice, vile and sickening was screeching, I DON'T NEED YOUR LECTURES, I ALREADY KNOW THE TRUTH. I KNOW IT ALL. I DON'T NEED YOUR FUCKING HELP, and they were making it miserable—tightening themselves around her so she couldn't breathe. The Angels moved all around the woman, comforting her, but they didn't intervene.

I can't stand this! I told The Voice, the angels have the power, why are they just standing there? This is disgusting.

Do not fear, my son. They are helping her.

Diksnik! He was acting so coooool-ish and it was driving me soooo crazy-ish—I started hyperventilating.

The Light workers continued talking, Don't you see? You think you need to suck this woman's essence to live, isn't that right?

THAT'S RIGHT!

But you have your very own connection to the Source—to the Light. You don't need hers. Your direct connection is much more powerful than hers, anyway. The Source will feed you the Highest and Best energy there is—continually. You'll never have to worry about going without, ever again.

And while they talked and coerced, the Light filled all around the woman and the demons could not keep their grip and were POPPING off of her and, like moths to the flame, they were being pulled right into the Light and transformed immediately.

What just happened?

Well son, when the woman made the choice to look to the True Source, the illusion disappeared. They really had no souls because they weren't created by the Source, they were created by her.

But how can that be? She was the victim here.

Yes, but she thought she wasn't worthy of being with the Light because she believed it was her fault for how her life turned out.

How could she ever think that? She was just a poor little innocent kid.

Darkness and fear can make a child believe that they're not worthy. It's a very powerful force on Earth. There were hundreds and hundreds of negative thoughts and judgments that were being thrown at her every day by people who didn't understand she was just a little innocent girl—to them she was a whore, a woman of poor judgment to be punished—so she bought into it and did it to herself instead.

I was so relieved. Surrounded by Light the woman was totally free of those assholes even if she had created them. Her color had returned, her beauty is coming back, but if you looked around her you saw other demons she had not created, discarnate beings that kept hissing and biting the air trying to find a way to get back into her.

The Entities put the woman in a short coma so she could be protected from taking on anything more. There was still work to do on her because she still felt uncomfortable thinking of herself as being worthy—feeling unworthy was kind of a habit with her now.

The battle had raged for three days, Earth time.

When The Voice and I got back to the physical dimension, The Moradia de Dom José de Barros was packed to the rafters with people who had come to meditate and pray for this woman. Finally the woman was awakened in the Infirmary bed.

God forgive me! She said. She sat up, tears were streaming down her face and she looked to Seu Miguel who was in Entity by her bed and said, God forgive me! And I think she was pretty scared or something 'cause Seu Miguel held her hand and he was so cool, he said to her, You are forgiven dear one, if you forgive yourself first and forgive all who have used you and hurt you.

And then she said something really outstanding, she said, Mother Mary came to me and told me this same thing.

When was that? Seu Miguel asked her and he had the biggest smile 'cause I think he already knew the answer.

In my dream just now, she told him. Mother Mary had told her to look at her . . . and all I could see was this glorious light and then Mother Mary told me, All was forgiven.

And she looked at Seu Miguel like she couldn't believe everything and she asked him, Is that true, Seu Miguel? And his answer was brilliant—sounded just like what the The Voice would say. He said, It is, if you accept that it is so. And if you choose to let go of holding on to your past way of thinking. Look to the truth of things, my child. You are magnificent. You are worthy.

I choose to let go of it! I do. I let go of it all, she said. I accept that I am worthy of having the life I want. Then after a silence of drinking it all in, she said . . . I feel so free. I feel so light.

And I could see it, man! How can I explain it? Light was streaming into the gathering like a gigantic dam breaking over everyone. Angels were everywhere. It was like the darkness of her soul had been thrown into a washing machine and those attachments that had been stuck on to her had fallen off and she'd come out all bright and squeaky clean and I could see that those dark figures were crouched like they were goin' to pounce again but suddenly they started shrieking away from the intensity of the light like they were all being scalded to death, and their moaning and crying sounded like a shipwreck happening—the ocean was bubbling all up and around them and then pulling them down down down into the deep dark depths . . . where they came from.

That was a very dramatic description, son. That was quite well done.

Little too dramatic?

Coming from Zeeep the zipperboy? . . . No.

But the good news on top of this happy ending was that one of her attachments had had a soul and had turned around and had looked into the Light and was totally absorbed into it, and his laughter from the heavens was deafening.

And another cool thing that I noticed when it was all over—the woman that walked in so messed up, walked out an entirely new and different woman—heck she had color in her skin, she looked real peaceful and . . . she was acting normal. And when she walked out, she was hugging and thanking everyone in sight. Lotsa kisses, 'cause that's what Brazilians do . . . and you know what I think? I think everyone in the whole Moradia felt so high with . . . such . . . super duper . . . joy. And The Voice said something I'd heard around the Moradia: It's the humble that will inherit the Earth. Well, I think when I was swishing around over all those people humbled just Lovin' each other so much, just then that's when they inherited the Earth. I really think that's the truth of it.

Meanwhile, the main man, Miguel Sousa da Silva, well, his orb, floated over and entered his exhausted body and he went home to sleep—I think for a long long loooong time. The Moradia was closed for a whole week.

And I hovered in suspension—I had a lot of good stuff to think about.

* * *

I was stunned for the longest time. What had I just witnessed, man? What a trip that was! It was like The Voice had unzipped this magical curtain, pushed me through a hologram-movie, and downloaded an extraordinary experience into my memory banks. For the first time I was without any frigging words, I couldn't find my sarcastic ego to go play with, and I didn't care. Something had shifted in me, big time.

I look a little orb-drive through the garden sorting my thoughts. What a beautiful red flower . . . I had spent some extraordinary time—whooooo lookee at that . . . check out the big yellow one there mmmmmmmmmmm mm mmm smells so good—with my first human being—what an extremely interesting creature. What an adventure being able to crawl into a human's thoughts, while that person walked and talked and felt fear and experienced pain and fright and confusion and . . . I got to feel for the first time what it was like to be in a body that had shut down, none of the dots connecting, unable to move a muscle, while The Voice was butterfly free, collecting rambling thoughts and making them into something coherent—Ahhhh the tree there, how interesting the way it's all bent back and forth, looks like a sculpture—and I noticed something about myself, too; I was no longer being hounded with my panicked questions that I'd pulled out of some void that had no matching answers . . . and it felt . . . well . . . great. Yes it did. I took a deep breath of cool air, even though it was a hot day . . . I think it's called having an epiphany. Maybe I was a new—something—like that woman was a new woman.

Remember that feeling and take note of this moment, my son. This is what it's all about. The softening—so your soul can flow like a river through life. Congratulations, you've just moved closer to becoming a dog.

It didn't quite register, this thing about a dog. But really I didn't care. I was feeling too good.

I zipped out of the garden and flew up-up-up, as high as I could go then dropped like a rock. Ahhh . . . I'll admit I was feeling more relaxed—closer to being me, sensing my true power—but at the same time I was sensing that I was headed for a good ol' fashioned set-up. And once again, I knew I was about to be duped by the good-ol' Voice.

Come again? Whazat you say? Wasn't I in the middle of dropping? Oh yeah.

As I was dropping-dropping, I instinctively stopped and hovered at exactly two inches above the ground and then just happened to glance to the left of where I was floating. I turned slowly slowly, not believing my eyes . . . 'cause there before me I saw . . . I saw . . . a dog. Hadn't the Voice just said something about being ready to become a dog?

And suddenly I am looking at a scroungy, mangy, carcass of some poor dog lying half-dead by the side of the road looking as though it had been hit by a car and left to die.

This will do, *said The Voice.*

What?

Yes, this is the dog's body you will be using from here on.

This dead mutt?

It's not exactly a mutt and it isn't quite dead—yet.

You gotta be friggin' kidding me, man. I would have punched The Voice if it were at all possible!

I talked to the dog's soul inside and asked him if he was still using the body? He told me that he was planning to leave straight away, that if we wanted it we could have it.

No way.

Way.

What happened to my power of choice, man?

You're a dog now, not the same as a human.

You're friggin' nuts! This guy is ugly! He's all beat up, his hair's falling off, his ears flop, he can hardly breathe . . . Just then, the little orb inside the pooch left the body and floated off—ZIPP WHISH—then disappeared.

Excuse me, this may be a bit uncomfortable at first . . . *The Voice grunted as he pushed me inside.*

Ouch! Damn! It hurts like hell in here. Getmeouttahere, RIGHTNOW! This isn't fair. I HATE YOOOOOU!!!

Don't worry, have faith. I have help on the way. Trust me. This is all working for a very good reason—it couldn't be more perfect.

LILLIAN AND ABE
CANADA, 2002

CHAPTER 23

Just yesterday, after Grandmère's funeral, Lillian had been with some women friends at the local coffee house and something very strange had happened. A stranger, a woman just an ordinary woman, had passed their table, turned around, and come back. She was medium height, not beautiful in anyway, but she had a vibrant air about her.

Excuse me, she had said, you don't know me but I have a message for you. She was looking straight at Lillian.

Lillian's hand moved to her heart, For me? she'd asked. She couldn't deny the chill of recognition.

You have a daughter who's been in an accident, is this right?

The ladies looked around at each other, raising their brows.

Yes, Lillian said, . . . I'm sorry, do I know you?

Please, I know you don't know me . . . this is something I do . . . I'm a psychic. May I please give you a message about your little girl? I'm getting it so strong.

I-I-I . . . yes. Lillian could feel the heat flooding her cheeks.

The woman smiled. There is a healer in Brazil, a great healer that uses help from the Otherside. He will help your child.

What is his name and where will I find him? Lillian was embarrassed because there she was, before her all her friends, grabbing at any hope even from a stranger.

I don't know, but I get Brazil, and someone you know will tell you . . .

And if that wasn't enough, she went on, And someone has just passed in your life . . . Grandmère? Is that someone you know?

Lillian felt her veins go cold as ice. Y-y-yes, she stammered.

She's here and she's wanting you to know, My passing had nothing to do with what you did or didn't do. Please don't feel guilty. She loves you very much and is with you and your daughter through this hard time. She is fine and happy where she is now and is busy finding help for your daughter. The woman looked out at what seemed nothing, then looked at Lillian and said, That's it, hope it helps.

Lillian whispered a soft thank you.

Good luck. With that, the stranger smiled, turned and walked out of the café door.

Whoa, said the woman just to the left of Lillian. Ohmygosh, to her right.

Lillian stood, then fled to the bathroom, where behind the stall door, she held herself and rocked.

* * *

That memory had stayed on her shoulder and whispered its message throughout all last night . . . and there it was again today, poking and prodding her to go tell Abe about her message.

Her brother had driven up from New York and stayed to help her with all the details for the funeral. He had arrived his arrogant self but somehow had softened over the week. This transformation could be to her benefit when she told him about this afternoon . . . maybe. But it was weird, because like this psychic woman who had been so driven to give her the message—Lillian now felt pulled to ask anyone and everyone she knew if they had information about a Brazilian healer.

Oh, Abe wouldn't go for this, not for a minute. She hesitated, but her thoughts went on . . . wait a minute. It didn't matter. It couldn't matter. What mattered was that something extraordinary had happened. She had always felt deep in her being that Sabrina was born with a special mission and she was positive that the stranger—and Grandmère—had come especially to remind her not to give up.

The week before Grandmère had died, she had been embroiled in an argument with Abe. I'll sell my house, that will pay for it, Grandmère had said.

Abe stood up so he looked very big over her and had sternly said, marking his every word with authority, money is not the problem here, please. There are no more avenues left for Sabrina. Look, you must realize I have been dealing with this subject for my patients for ten years now. Hell, that's what my book is all about, Grandmère. When they find that they can't go on with their lives in the same way, my patients become so much more accepting of their fate; they see that they can carry on with a full life. They realize they only have to do it in a different way. All I'm saying is—that is what you and Lillian are going to have to do. Things are the way they are and we can go on from there.

Abe finished. He stood stiff with his chin forward, looking down at her.

Grandmère had been so angry that she had struggled to lift herself from her seat, grabbed her cane and left the room. Maybe it wasn't *wha*t Abe had said so much as *how* he had said it. And now she was gone and that was that.

She knew that Abe meant well, but it was her responsibility to step up and do what was needed. Abe had made up his mind, but maybe it wasn't the right time to put everything in a box like he wanted to do. Maybe this was a time to open her mind and think outside of that box. And, for the first time in her life, she was entertaining the idea that she could do it with or without Abe if she set her mind to it.

Lillian entered the room seeing her brother pouring over the paper work they had had to deal with since the burial. Calm and collected, she sat down in the chair opposite her brother, looking him square in the face.

Can we talk?

Uh, oh. I hate when a woman says that, it means—

Abe, I love you. I thank you for all you do.

Well, you're welcome—

But I have to say, Sabrina . . . something has happened with her, Abe. When she first came out of her coma she was ready and willing to carry on with her life, she was a trooper. She worked with the physical therapists and with all the wonderful machines you were able to get for us. And I can't thank you enough for that brother, and . . . I thank you for really being there for Ben when he . . . well . . . just, thank you. But Sabrina? I'm afraid you can't help anymore because I think you're going the wrong way with her.

Lillian saw her brother's eyes glaze over.

She got up and started to pace, *how she should say it* . . . For some reason, Abe, she has lost her will to live. After I told her about her father . . . she stopped . . . she stopped eating, she stopped . . . Lillian cleared her throat, then continued . . . after the operation: and you and I know it was successful. She, by all rights should have been talking again—even you said so. But her will was gone, Abe, so much so she chose a safe place to go—my worst fear—back into a coma. Her will has . . . and that's why . . . there is nothing more that you can give her.

Feeling effective, Lillian took on a stronger approach: And quite frankly, there is nothing more that we can take from you. I'm sorry.

He sat back, wondering how he could make her understand that she really had no other choice.

Abe's arrogance blocked his ability to listen, as it so often did. He knew what was best and that was all there was to it. Let's look at this, he started. You've sold your house, you have no insurance, and don't be silly, there is plenty I can do for you. And I *want* to do it for you.

On your terms, Lillian said.

Yes, on my terms. You'll have to trust me. Standing, he started to pace.

Lillie watched him move around the room, picking up things and putting them down.

I can't do that. I want to take my inheritance and—

What inheritance, it's tied up in probate—

Can you just be quiet and listen to what I have to say, can you do that?

He nodded, stood and continued pacing while she went through the whole story of the psychic and what she said about the Brazilian healer.

Normally, Abe would have gotten indignant, would have ranted and raved on and on about how irresponsible, how airy-fairy she was about everything. But hearing her request, his legs buckled and he found he had to sit down before he fell. Recalling Bob's glowing descriptions of the Brazilian shaman, months ago—waiting in the emergency room—flooded back to him and what about the story of the witchy woman knowing about Grandmère's death? He was becoming lightheaded...

He went for the scotch decanter on the leaded glass bar and filled a shot-glass, then downed it.

Lillian was surprised at his response; she'd never seen him like this.

He'd looked at his empty glass for a long time—rubbing it like a genie's bottle that would give him the answer to what he was asking—before he said, I'm sorry, sis. You two are the only family I have left. You're my only family. I missed out on . . . He cleared his throat, I guess you're right, I don't know what it's like to want to have hope for someone . . . I never had the chance . . . watching Mom and Dad being crushed . . . to death . . . his face crumpled into a little frightened child's face.

Lillie went to him, grabbed both her brother's hands and held them, looking into the pain in his eyes. He had been maybe five or six—so young. She hadn't been there; she was only a baby, always sick. They'd left her with her Godmother while they had gone on the camping trip.

We were having so much fun, Lillian. I'd caught my first fish. It was in a plastic cooler on ice right beside me. I was pounding on it like a drum, I was so proud. My dad was smiling, telling me what a great fishermen I'd become, we could go out together now. Dad and son . . . then . . .

Abe face had reddened and contorted to hold back the pain and tears. And as Lillian watched her brother, she couldn't stop the memory of the images in her own mind of the truck that came out of the fog and suddenly whipped her and her husband and Sabrina around and around and around, nothing making sense, going so fast . . . that horrible feeling of helplessness.

She tightened her grip on her brother's hands, feeling powerful compassion for his childhood horror, but found no words.

Tears finally slithered down and over the crags in Abe's face. How could this have happened twice in one family?

The two, together, could only shake their heads.

Okay, sis. We'll go to Brazil . . . we'll go to Brazil, Abe said.

ZEEEP: IN THE DOG
PARAMANGUAIA, BRAZIL
MAY, 2002

CHAPTER 24

Little bubbles of light bouncing around. POP in. POP PING out. Growing red. Blue—bluer—intense blue—Wow. Getting bigger and bigger. SNAP. I heard voices but couldn't understand what the fitzbingbong they're saying. I was so dikdik peezonked at The Voice stuffing me in this mongrel's carcass... a dog... I was a frikin' ding-dong dog! I could have spit. Hah, spit. I could hardly swallow much less hack-a-lougie, man.

Eventually my body started to feel lighter and lighter, finally fading away the horrific pain. What a relief that was. I looked through the sky to a place from where I was—I could see the interior of that wretched little body: broken bones on my left front and back paw, a deep gash, not to mention all the fur that was missing all over.

Upon thinking: "licking will make it feel better," I freaked! Why do I have to lick myself, that's disgusting?! Why would I even consider it? I heard The Voice trying to explain, something about... ***what dogs do****, but I shut him off. I'm not ever listening to that A-hole again.*

I was soooo exhausted, I couldn't move a single muscle in that crummy doggie body. Just lay there and listened to a pumping—WHOOSH WHOOSH—goin' through my veins for the longest time. I felt like I'd been without water for a billion years—who knew, maybe this rat sheebit body had been. Food... I couldn't bring up a recall of what that was . . . had it been so long that I—a diksnik dog—could no longer remember . . . food . . . ? I couldn't even find a . . . desire for food. How pathetic. Ouch, the diksnik hot sun's burning the skin on this body all the way through to the bones. I don't care what The Voice says . . . I'm just gonna let this dog's body die. That's right. I am. That'll show him.

Then I started having these really weird thoughts I'd never thought before and I had my suspicions The Voice was downloading without my permission at that time:

. . . I would like to live . . . I want to live more than anything . . .

. . . I want to love a human. To be loved by a human. It's very important.

. . . It's a dog's job. That's why I'm lying here. I'm doing my job.

WHAAAAA? Now I am thinkin' dog thoughts? I'm screwed. I'm soooo screwed! Then more friggin' thoughts:

. . . Maybe, sometimes it takes something bad to happen before something good can happen . . . and the rest of the words I didn't hear 'cause the sound faded out as I slid deep into a welcome sleep: away from the pain, away from sadness . . .

And there in this dream coming on, I could hear Eeeoo calling for me. I could see her in a far off place playing on a green hillside and the sky so blue. She was a little girl . . . a cute little human girl with blonde bouncy hair. Only, how'd I know? I couldn't see her face—or really see what she looked like—I only knew I wanted to be with her, where she was. I didn't care that she was human. I didn't care that I was no longer a dolphin, or an orb. I didn't even care any longer that I was a diksnik dog . . . I DIDN'T CARE. All I cared about was that I wanted to be with Eeeoo or whoever she was now. I wanted to be with her so bad my hair hurt. I just wanted to be running with her among little bubbles of light, bouncing around. Popping in Popping out. Growing red. Changing to blue.

MARIANA VITÓRIA AND RAFAEL
PARAMANGUAIA, BRAZIL
JUNE, 2002

CHAPTER 25

The hot sun was falling onto the mud walls of a building that the little girl and boy were walking past in the village of Paramanguaia. School had let out some time ago, and the children were on their way home. Mariana Vitória Mosques had been late to pick up her brother, and of course, like all siblings when they're mad about something, they're not being so nice to each other.

Oh, no! Mariana Vitória stopped short and without thinking, pushed her five-year-old brother out of the way of something she'd seen in her peripheral vision. As an older sister, she knew it was her job to protect him.

Annoyed, Rafael pushed back, Don't! he said with a growl.

No-no-no. I see something. Stay here. You hear me?

Rafael didn't answer—what do you say to someone who bosses you around all the time and because she's the older you have to take it. He didn't dare move though. He watched his sister as she crept cautiously over to the ditch along the side of the dirt road.

Mariana Vitória held her breath and couldn't believe what she was seeing—there, nearly hidden in the grass, was a little doggy's body just lying there all lifeless. Mariana Vitória always hated seeing animals being hurt—let alone dead. She pinched her eyes closed fast and yelled, Come over here, Rafael. You go look. I can't, she said as she was pacing in a circle, shaking her hands like silly girls do when they're all grossed out.

Do I gotta do everything for you, stupid? Rafael walked over to where she was looking. He stepped over the bank and tiptoed over to the dog, dropped to his knees and started gently petting his clumpy fur. Aaaah, are you okay? he said in a little tiny voice.

Look out! He might bite.

Are you okay, little puppy? Wanting to put his face closer but he couldn't because Mariana Vitória just might be right.

Eeew . . . I can't look, Rafael. Just tell me, just tell me, is he still breathing? Eeew.

The dog still hadn't moved.

How can you tell? he asked without looking away in case he might miss a twitch that would tell him there was hope.

Mariana Vitória had come closer and was staring down at the dog, still afraid to look too closely, Is his stomach going up and down?

I don't think so.

Oh, no, oh no . . . she was nearly in tears. Touch his nose, but be very careful he doesn't bite. Feel if he's breathing? Eeeew, her hands were still shaking in that silly way.

Holding his breath, Rafael started to put his finger on the dried rough skin of the doggy's nose, he'd flinched a few times, and tried again. He thought he felt little puffs of air but he wasn't sure. He looked at the deep red sores on its head and where its fur was nearly gone but he was thinking the whole time, *he's so cute, he's just exactly the kind of dog I've always wanted . . .* He sat back on his knees and let out a sigh and was surprised when he felt warm tears sliding down his cheek and a hurt in his throat that was so bad he couldn't talk. He couldn't tell Mariana Vitória that he thought maybe the doggy <u>was</u> dead. *The <u>exact</u> kind of dog I'd love . . . Wait! Did a foot move?* Yes, it moved again. Rafael caught his breath and pushed his words past the lump and said with great excitement, Mariana Vitória, I think he's still alive!

Are you positive? She squatted beside him.

Rafael leaned forward and tried to slip his hands under the doggie's back and stomach, trying to pick him up, but Mariana Vitória grabbed his arm so he jumped and pulled away.

Don't touch him! You could hurt him more. Dad said never pick up someone who's been hurt, they could have something broken and you could break them more.

Rafael stood up and quickly clasped his hands behind his back—he certainly didn't want to hurt the little doggie—not ever.

Mariana Vitória couldn't believe that her little brat brother who never did what he was told was listening to her now. What surprised her more was the feeling that he could be kind of sweet. Seeing her little brother's wet face and brown eyes looking up at her through shards of his black hair—he actually looked innocent and angelic.

Softening, she said, We've got to be really careful, Rafael.

Mariana Vitória looked out into the field where Mr. Sanchez's carthorses grazed. There seemed to be plenty of junk in the pile where the rooster and his brood hung out. Look, we're going to need a stretcher of some sort. Then she started to run into the field yelling, C'mon Rafael, I see something we can use.

* * *

As the two children walked home, passing by houses and store shutters pulled down for the night, the girl noticed the strangeness of their shadowed images f loating across the low-light on the brick walls as they carried the limp doggy on the dirty board they'd found in the rubbish.

Passing an open hut, Mariana Vitória secretly hoped Julio was at home—it was getting too late and they really needed help—Rafael had been tripping a lot and every time, she cringed and now her stomach hurt.

Stop, Rafael. Let's put him down for a minute.

Rafael felt relieved at the suggestion and gratefully moved with her to the bench in front of the door where they set the crude stretcher down very gently. The doggy hadn't moved a bit. This worried Mariana Vitória, but she wasn't going to let Rafael know.

Peeking inside, all that Mariana Vitória and Rafael could see was *Senhora* Dominguez lighting her open fire in the pit that rested next to the front window. The villagers' houses usually had no chimney but plenty of open holes under the roof for the smoke to escape.

Is Julio here? Rafael yelled in.

Julio's *Mãe* was busy preparing dinner and stoking up the fire for the evening's heat and didn't hear his question. She never heard a word they said, even when they talked straight to her face. Julio was always taking advantage of her poor hearing. Resigning, they weakly said, *Adeus* . . . and went back outside to pick up their precious package and slowly walk on.

It was the end of fall, the nights seemed to rush in faster and colder, and soon June would be gone and Brazil's fields would be turning to the winter's dry yellow. The sun was gone and the children's parents would be looking at the clock and getting into the truck to come and find them.

Finally, the kids turned onto the street where they lived and were thankful that they hadn't yet seen their family truck pulling out—maybe they hadn't returned yet from their trip into Tupani, Mato Grosso do Norte. Mariana Vitória shivered a little as she looked down at the scrawny unconscious dog in the dark—she shivered not from fear of facing their parents or from the cold breeze that was whipping her skirt and tousling her waist-length auburn hair—but from a strange excitement she felt. There was a new bond between her and her brother, and she knew how much he'd wanted a dog. She was going to save the life of this sweet little creature no matter what it took—and the idea was giving her all the courage she was going to need.

ZEEEP, IN THE VOID
PARAMANGUAIA, BRAZIL 2002

CHAPTER 26

In the Void, I could hear The Voice speaking to me.

Hey, wake up Zeeep. What a great idea you had.

Whaa? Where am I? Who am I? Sheesh, I couldn't get my bearings to save my life.

Let's go.

Go where? Do what?

We're going to work.

Wait-wait-wait. What are you talking about? I can't go anywhere. I got this fitzbingbong discombobulated dog carcass you shoved me into and it's not going anywhere right now.

Well, while we're waiting for Mariana Vitória and Rafael to save your life, we can get some really good work done.

I don't feel like working, I'm too peezonked at you right now to go anywhere, especially with you.

Even if you could be with Eeeoo for a while?

Man, I perked up like sex on wheels. Eeeoo? Where is she? I asked.

She is on a healing mission, acting as a walk-in.

What the hezzop is a walk-in?

A walk-in is when there has been an exchange agreement between two souls, one will leave and the other will take over that body and life.

Yep. Sounds very familiar. Not.

In this case, Eeooo has been granted a mission. There is a little girl in a coma right now, she is very confused because she has experienced a shock that keeps her in a place of darkness. Her spirit is so traumatized from a car accident that she has to be taken to a place where she can be wrapped in a cocoon of Love until she can function again. In the interim, Eeooo has taken on this little girl's body and persona temporarily to see if she can assist her in finding some kind of balance and peace.

So let me get this right . . . Eeooo is a little girl now?

Yes, son.

Wow, I just dreamt this! Woweeeeee. Does this little girl have blond hair?

Yes, quite a cute little thing.

That's her! That's her! What can I do?

You're going to be teaching her some things you have been learning.

I'll be teaching Eeooo . . . ?

So does this mean you're up for the task?

As ready as a cockroach in a hot frying pan with a gun getting ready to shoot a squirrel.

A cockroach in a hot frying pan . . .

Never mind, I'm so excited I'm getting my thoughts all gibberywiggled.

So does that mean . . . yes?

Yes-yes-yes, a thousand times yessssss.

A little over-kill, son.

C'mon, tell me what you want me to do, yessssss. I wanna be with Eeeoo again, yesssssss!!!!!! My aura was getting bigger and bigger I was so excited.

You must know, however, that there is a hitch.

Oh look folks! Watch as the heavy ball drops and crushes all of Zeeep's dreams, I said. Vizzzzzzzummmpt. My aura had shrunk.

Not at all . . . It's only that she just won't remember you—

Eeeoo won't remember the love of all her lives, how can that be?

Right now she only has the intelligence and memory of that little girl. Her name is Sabrina. Little Sabrina doesn't know you—it'll be like meeting a stranger. Can you handle this?

Uh . . . sure . . . I mean, what are my options? Wait out my fate in a wrecked and busted-up canine cadaver—yeah my favorite thing to do. Get real.

I knew you'd come through. I'm proud of you son.

Okay, so I'm gonna help Eeeoo with a mission, yessss. Okay, let's get to work.

Oh, and there's another thing—

You said only ONE hitch—no fair.

I'm not going to be able to go with you—

What?

You'll be on your own for a while.

Why, where are you going to be?

I'll have to make sure your dog body makes it through, otherwise we're going to have to . . . Well, let's just say, you need that body.

Yeah, like a zebra needs spots.

Don't.

I won't.

Good. ***I just hope you were paying attention to your lessons.***

Okay, let me get this straight. So Eeooo is really Sabrina now and has no memory of me and I'm supposed to do what?

You first must get her to trust you, then get her interested in wanting to be happy and strong again, then when it's the right moment we'll go into the dark together where Sabrina's soul is choosing to stay and we can coax her out.

You think I'm ready for this?

Absolutely.

Wait! One question. Am I a dolphin or a dog or an orb or what?

A dog.

Wait, I don't know how to be a dog yet—

Wing it, son.

And The Voice left the Void.

SABRINA
MONTREAL, CANADA, 2002

CHAPTER 27

Lillian was right, Sabrina had not wanted to be a prisoner in her own body—and in fact she wasn't most of the time. How was Lillian to know that Sabrina was walking around the room, looking at her, talking to her, answering her questions? How could Lillian know the unexplained breeze in the closed room was actually a kiss from Sabrina?

Sabrina had found other worlds to visit where she didn't need words to speak or a body to take her places. Even though it looked as though she was incarcerated and asleep in a broken body, she could still have choices, and her choice was a dream-state where she could create everything she didn't have on the earth. She had even found a companion, a small white and caramel colored dog. He called himself Chico or Pico or something, she couldn't understand him sometimes because he talked too fast but he was a dog so maybe she was just making everything up but she could have sworn he'd told her that, There is no time or space where they were and what was in the present was really in the future, and not to worry, because there really is no time or place anyway.

She thought he was a very funny dog with funny ideas that didn't make much sense, but then who ever heard of a dog that could talk? This was a magical place, however, and she wouldn't change a thing. Besides, he was making her laugh and that was such a welcome relief.

She loved running through bright colored fields of grass, playing with the little orbs of light that taught her how to twirl in circles without getting dizzy. The twirling took her up and up into levels of different-ness.

One level was like walking into a painting of numbers—these numbers held together structures: beautiful buildings that could have never stayed together on her earthly planet. Then she could twirl up to the next level and see the very same building in a whole different way. She could put her hand on a wall and hear an amazing symphony playing, then touch a different space and two symphonies would play together, and then become a whole different piece of music. She particularly loved this level, she could have stayed there forever, but her little dog friend would want to take her somewhere else, or she'd hear someone speaking off somewhere, and that would vibrate her light body very hard.

We have to turn you now, sweetheart, someone would say back in her bedroom on the physical level, and suddenly she would find herself being pulled back—like she was in a giant vacuum built only for Heavy Duty Suck—returning her to her physical body, and pain would come thrashing through her awareness like a maverick horse pounding through an ocean wave.

The anguish of her physical body being turned over was always intense. She'd become nauseous and the black fright feelings would enter her bloodstream like little needles and intensify the pain all the more. She'd learned that if she could put her mind somewhere back up on a level she'd just visited, then she could get some relief. This worked well for her as long as the doctor's didn't inject a drug into her system.

When they did, then she knew she was in for a ride with no controls. Her light body was thrown around like a bowling ball in a sewer system: slammed up against a wall, dropped down a shaft that never ended, or jiggled so hard she'd swear she'd just been plugged into an electrical socket. She had learned to just go with it, relax as best she could, disengage, and know it was temporary—to fight would only make it worse. But sometimes it swept her to memories in the past— memories of her father.

She was always looking for him, and he was always calling her . . . *Sabrina, I'm here Sabrina* . . . and she'd end up at a big door that SLAMMED shut right before she could go through, and then there was the sound of many doors slamming SLAMSLAMSLAM and she would be so upset she would go to the place where she could twilight sleep: a place where there were no thoughts and there was nothing except her gentle dog friend licking her face sweetly, lying as close as he could to her, loving her.

When the drug finally wore off, she would find her spirit in that flat space, where her light body could affect nothing. She was imprisoned in a cavity of total exhaustion, and her soul felt unattached. The dog told her that she had been in a place called the lower Astral, a place that spiraled counter-clockwise—down, down, down—a mucky grey place where she needed to wait with prayers when she saw the haunting shadows creeping about, making sucking noises—looking for a piece of created energy they could attach themselves to. These were the dark forms that didn't believe there was a Source of energy that was theirs alone. They only knew that they could pull energy from other creations of light.

That was their hell, until they came to know better and could give in and turn to the Light that waited for them—and with the help of Angels, be swept right into a big steaming pool filled with white light—the Source of All Unconditional Loving. She loved watching this. She loved feeling the waves of ecstasy that rolled over her when this happened.

She really didn't understand what the little dog was telling her, but he made her feel safe somehow, maybe because he was always there at her side when she needed him.

If there were anything Sabrina could tell her mother, it would be, Please tell the doctors to stop giving me the drugs, I'd rather have the pain. Please find a more gentle way. With all the knowledge here on this Earth, surely there must be an alternative. But somehow she knew that was an impossible request, because her mother and the doctors were so limited in their beliefs. She wished they could meet the dog and let him teach them the magnificent things in the dimensions where he lived.

In that intense light, she had many conversations with her dog friend—sometimes with words, sometimes with pictures that turned into words. It was all so different there and she was learning so much. During most visits, they went together to a place called the Temple of Healing where they rebuilt her body over and over. She loved that game: learning where the heart was and how it pumped, how blood was made and how it moved through the web of veins. When they came across what looked like a dead-zone (void of energy) or a diseased zone (an erratic or static energy) in her body, they'd push blood filled with light—with their imagination—into those areas. When they did this, the weird feelings and gurgling sounds they made reminded her of when she and her sister use to make water balloons and squish them in their hands.

She always wanted to learn more from her dog friend. At the end of their play sessions, she and her furry friend would look at the perfect body they had created and laugh and laugh and laugh. She didn't know why they were laughing so much, but it made her feel so good.

She wanted to tell her mother what she was doing so Lillian could stop worrying. Sabrina created beautiful picture messages in her mind, then gave the pictures to an angel in the Otherside. That was a game she loved, too.

Yesterday she'd created this scene: A woman would go into a coffee shop, walk past her mother, stop, turn around, go to her and say, *Everything is going to be alright. Someday your daughter will be whole again, do not fear. There are plans being made.* Then Sabrina summoned an angel to take the message to her mother on Earth.

Of all of the games they had played, that was her favorite creation game.

MARIANA VITÓRIA AND RAFAEL
PARAMANGUAIA, BRAZIL
JUNE, 2002

CHAPTER 28

When the children had first arrived at their home, Pousada Raiar do Sol *(Po-sa-da Hi-yar-jch do Sole),* with the injured dog, their parents had been positive—as positive as circumstances allowed. Their father, Martim, *(Mar-cheem)* stood watching their mother, Flavia, while she buzzed around the kitchen giving instructions to the kids and attending the little hurt doggie, speaking to him in a soft whisper: asking, where do you come from little doggie, I bet you have a family somewhere that misses you terribly, and let me see . . . do you have any broken bones? As she gently laid him down in a cardboard box with many towels folded at the bottom, she covered him with a cotton baby blanket the children had found at the back of the clothes closet, and she tucked him in like he was one of her own kids and put the box by the stove to keep him warm.

Mariana Vitória and Rafael sat beside the box, looking in and joined in the soft talking while Martim—being the more practical—walked back and forth looking at what was going on from all angles and finally cleared his throat to speak.

Kids, he said, I'm afraid this little one may not make it through the night so don't get your hopes up. And don't get too close to it—he may have rabies or something. Be very careful, he could bite. Then he added, do you hear me?

Just in case they were off somewhere in their minds. They both said Yes, in unison because their minds indeed were somewhere else.

Daddy! Rafael's lower lip started to grow, and his mouth dropped at the edges. We have to save him. Call a doctor, daddy.

Rafael. Son. Listen, there is no way we will be able to get him to Brazileia to see any vet until the morning and even then, the trip might be very hard on him. Martim didn't like that he had to be the bearer of harsh reality, but he was their dad and he had a responsibility.

Mariana Vitória ran her hand under her nose, sniffing back the tears. No, daddy. He's gonna be alright. I just know it, she said.

We'll all just say a little prayer and if he decides he has to go during the night, at least the angels will take him to the Otherside where he will get a whole new body and be happy and healthy again. Through the children's sniffing he asked, Do you kids understand what I'm saying?

Yes, daddy, they both said then made up little prayers, each one of them, telling the angels to take care of him and make him well.

We'll get up extra early and take him to the vet tomorrow, now get some sleep. Martim and Flavia kissed the kids goodnight and even though they wanted to stay in the kitchen and sleep next to the little doggie, they were sent to their rooms. Remember, their mother told them, the faster you sleep, the faster morning will come and the faster they would be able to take him to the vet.

* * *

The night lay quiet all around Rafael and Mariana Vitória but the full moon was so bright through the windows it was almost like daylight. When a dark storm cloud passed by, the room darkened and fear poked at their attempt to sleep. They knew a little doggie's life was at stake—they would have to be heroes, even though they hadn't an inkling about how to accomplish that.

Rafael whispered through the stillness, Mariana Vitória?

What?

What about Seu Miguel dos Milagres?

Are you kidding? He's much too important. He'd <u>never</u> help us.

But what else can we do?

Dunno.

Me neither. And I been thinking all night long, so much my brain's got real tired.

Okay then, if we go to Seu Miguel's, we gotta go right now.

Now? Rafael pulled the covers over his head.

Yeah, right now. Get dressed.

Still under the covers he said, This minute? Can't we think some more?

Mariana Vitória made her voice shaky while she wiggled her moonlit fingers in front of her wide eyes and made a creepy noise—wh-o-o-o-o-o-o. You're not scared of the *Fulnios*, are you Rafael? Ohhhh Rafael . . . Indian ghosts! only come out! after dark! you kno-oo-oo-www—

Stop that! His voice was high and whiney and still under the covers. Let's not go by the *Fulnios*, we'll take another street. Can we . . . please?

We can't, we have to go by the *Fulnios*, she kept teasing.

Rafael started to cry, No! We have to go around the *Fulnios*— Don't cry. We'll have to go through Alfonzo's gang territory then. Why?

'Cause, that's the only other way. I don't like Alfonzo.

Me neither.

Well . . . maybe we should wait for morning . . .

He got no answer, but the silence was deafening. Rafael gulped and then sat straight up, tossing his blankets to the f loor and said in a loud whisper I'm not afraid. You afraid?

We can't let the doggie die 'cause we're a bunch of scaredy . . .

Then let's go!

* * *

Night things were super different than day things. Going out at night in Paramanguaia was not something anyone did, especially children. The only ones out were the night people, the ones that were addicted to fear: the gangs that marauded the streets on their motorcycles, that got in fights, stole anything not inside, set off firecrackers and shot bullets into the air, blared loud music daring anyone to get mad.

Then there were the ghosts and spirits the children had read so much about. The ghosts of the Brazilian-African Indians—the *Fulnios*—they had a way of getting into your head and possessing you, everyone knew that. Tonight the children must be extremely courageous. They climbed into their clothes. Mariana Vitória grabbed Rafael's baby blanket away from him—the one he snuggled with every night so he could go to sleep.

Hey! Rafael was shocked to see his sister acting so nasty.

Hey, yourself. You're a big boy now. You don't need this anymore—the doggie does.

Rafael stood up straight, ready to fight for the only security he could be sure of. His bottom lip jutted out over his chin—but even though he didn't like it, he knew his stupid sister—just this one time—was right. Tonight he had to be a big boy.

They opened their bedroom door and sneaked very, very quietly down the hallway, passing door after door in the Pousada that housed the sleeping sick people that came to see Seu Miguel.

In the kitchen, the children picked up the box with the doggie inside, after covering him with Rafael's blanket and headed for the courtyard that led outside.

They had to undo the front door bolt very slowly without a sound. Mariana Vitória felt sweat pop out over her lip and her heart was beating so hard she thought its pa-dum pa-dum would awaken someone. But Rafael was acting so grown up she unexpectedly felt a kinship with him—a trust she had never before allowed.

The night air had a dampness that somehow revealed the largeness around them—without the hum of the day, without the comfort of walls, without an adult and it all felt . . . too large, too vast, too unknown. Being outside made both of the kids' hands and knees shake.

The moon slipped from underneath the cloud, clear and bright, showing them the way through the water-rutted dirt road that led to Main Street. There, dim street lamps made it a little easier to see when the moon was shrouded in the ghostly vapors of passing clouds.

Mariana Vitória and Rafael checked the doggie regularly—feeling relief when they heard his small whimpers—it meant he was still alive.

What shall we name him? Rafael asked, keeping his mind as still as he could. Naming him would be comforting.

Shhhh, said Mariana Vitória, leading the way.

Still finding comfort in the name game, he ran though his mind all his favorite names . . . none of them seemed right but it kept his mind off the "what ifs" threatening to freeze his courage.

Looking in all directions Mariana Vitória realized she had never seen the town at night before except from the car when the family was driving home. It was strange to see Main Street in the bright moonlight—storefronts and windows all boarded up with heavy wrought-iron bars and gates. Shivers went up her spine—was it because of the gangs? Her chills rapidly got worse when she heard the drone of motorcycles in the distance, turning onto Main Street.

Rafael! Hide! Now!

They scrambled into a shadow beside the side wall of a storefront and hid, listening breathlessly to the putt-putt of the approaching motorcycles as they slowed: flashing beams of light crisscrossing and dancing over the storefronts just across the street. The motorbikes were coming closer and closer.

It dawned on Mariana Vitória, Oh Mother Mary and Santa Rita, please let this be dad's security guards, not gang members. Her father had hired security for their Pousada Raiar do Sol, to protect the naive visiting Americans and Europeans who nonchalantly strolled the streets, impervious to the night dangers.

Sweat dripped down Mariana Vitória's forehead as she realized—if their dad's guards found them, she and her brother would still be in enormous trouble. The children remained in the shadows, holding their breath, hoping the doggie wouldn't whimper. They started breathing again when they knew, yes, it was their dad's police guards—and only two. But two too many if they were found.

Who's hiding there! The children jumped at the demanding voices coming at them from behind the flashlights. Mariana Vitória and Rafael almost wet their pants they were so scared. Mariana Vitória abruptly pulled her brother further back into the shadows but in doing so the little doggie gave out a squeal.

You'd better come out now or we'll start shooting, and the helmeted silhouetted shadows popped the leather holsters flaps and removed their guns.

Rafael whispered, Be sure to take the doggie to Seu Miguel. Be very quiet, stay back.

This statement sounded very strange to Mariana Vitória until she saw him suddenly stand up to be seen by the police guards.

It's me, he bravely said. Then in a louder voice, It's only me, don't shoot, then he stepped out heroically in front of the motorcycles.

Not believing the courageous actions of her brother, Mariana Vitória could hardly swallow. One of the men stepped out from behind the flashlights and could clearly be seen. Rafael? What the hell are you doing out here kid?

I . . . I'm running away from home. I'm running away . . . 'cause . . .

No you're not. Not now. The guards had heard from Martim about this little one always getting himself in trouble. Jump on. We're taking you home. C'mon.

As Mariana Vitória tried to adjust her hold on the doggie, her foot slipped on the gravel.

Wait, what was that? Is there someone with you? The other guard said, looking further into the shadows.

No! said Rafael as he broke away and started running down the street getting the guards attention away from his sister and the doggie.

Hey, you little brat! They both ran after Rafael until one grabbed him up by the waist and started walking back toward the bikes with him, his legs kicking the air and yelling at the top of his lungs. Mariana Vitória was just about to give herself up to help her brother when she noticed a bunch of teenagers running out into the street.

Hey! What are you doing to that kid? Put him down! They were brandishing knives and flashing them in the moonlight.

Move on. This has nothing to do with you.

Rafael was squirming so much now that he managed to wriggle out of the guards grip and run off into the shadows and hide while the gang had it out with the guards: yelling, cursing and threatening to tear them apart. Meanwhile, sleeping neighbors came to their doors bellowing to keep it down, some people need to sleep, some responsible people get up at five and go to work! Get outta here! NOW!

Rafael appeared at Mariana Vitória's side, Let's get going, he said. Mariana Vitória grabbed him and hugged him hard. You're crazy. What were you thinking?

Rafael brushed it off, How's the doggie?

I think he's getting worse; he hasn't made a sound or moved at all in a while.

They waited until the patrols had moved down the street out of sight, before they started running carefully from one shadow to the other. They knew the little dog was suffering with all the jostling, but what could they do? At least he had moved a little.

As Mariana Vitória and Rafael crossed the field where they had found the doggie that afternoon, to their amazement they saw little orbs of light the size of baseballs—floating just above the grasses here and there—disappearing and reappearing. Their parents had told them about the special energy packets that helped Seu Miguel heal people, and this must be what they looked like. Orbs were little bubbles of energy, it had something to do with the ten feet of crystal bedrock that lay deep below The Moradia de Dom José de Barros and their town. At school, Mariana Vitória had learned that a tiny crystal could power a clock—so what could 10 miles of thick crystal power? Was that why there were so many miracles happening every day? she wondered. The children stopped and gasped in fascination, for the closer they got to The Moradia de Dom José de Barros they could see more and more orbs—hundreds then thousands!

When they reached Seu Miguel's house—located on the grounds back of The Moradia de Dom José de Barros—there were no lights on inside. Bravely, they banged on the front door. There was no answer. When they heard no whimpers coming from their little doggie, they realized time was getting short and they banged as loud as they could!

It was a few minutes before Armando, Seu Miguel's assistant, swung the door open—unsmiling—his nightclothes all rumpled and his hair standing straight up in all directions. The children had to hold back a giggle—they had only seen Armando meticulously dressed with every hair in place.

What are you two doing out so late? His voice was gruff.

P-p-please, Armando. We have to see Seu Miguel! It is very, very important. Little Rafael's eyes were big and wide and his chest all puffed up with purpose as they lifted the box for Armando to see.

Armando either wasn't interested or was very tired, because he stifled a hefty yawn. I'm sorry, children, I certainly can't wake him—you should know that. He has a thousand people to heal tomorrow and it's *imperative* he gets his rest.

The children stopped in shock. They looked through their tears at the small, shaking doggie in the box as they placed it on the porch—would they have to watch it . . . just die?

You children shouldn't be out this late. Let me call your dad.

No! Please.

Hearts racing, they turned to go, then turned back. Their parents must never find out. What if Armando calls them anyway? Now, what will they do?

They had to think of something and it had to be quick. Mariana Vitória and Rafael picked up the box, but they still couldn't move.

Seu Miguel suddenly appeared at the door in his robe and slippers saying, In my dream, I was told that I had someone to heal tonight—who is ill?

Rafael and Mariana Vitória took the box over to Seu Miguel and set it down.

A little doggie we found!

A flicker of hope lit their faces as Seu Miguel kneeled and peered in tenderly. The kids kneeled beside the box and Rafael's big dark eyes sparkled as he looked up at Seu Miguel and said, I know that you healed Armando when he was crushed at the brick factory. I know you healed my grandmother of cancer in her back. I know you saved my mother's life so that she could have me—but can you save animals, too?

Seu Miguel winked and smiled and got to his feet. Well, shall we find out?

* * *

Headlights swished across The Moradia de Dom José de Barros's walls as a car pulled into Seu Miguel's driveway. Recognizing the car, Mariana Vitória and Rafael gulped hard. They knew they were in big trouble. It was their father.

Martim got out, slamming the car door, looking very angry but relieved to see his children. I had a feeling that this would be where I'd find you two. Rafael, what the heck possessed—

Please, we have work to do. Seu Miguel beckoned everyone inside. As they entered Armando lit the candles in the wall sconces as Seu Miguel gently lifted the doggie out of the box and carried him over to his big sitting chair. Everyone gathered around to watch. Seu Miguel closed his eyes and he shuddered—his body was being taken over by the enlightened Entity Doctor, St. Francis of Assisi who was there to animate his body to instigate the job. Seu Miguel's borrowed hands moved over the shaking creature while everyone bowed their heads. Armando led them in a prayer to the Source of Allness to bring all the Beings of Light forward, with the intention of healing this little dog. A flash of brilliant white light immediately filled the room. It was hard for anyone to look at the white tube of light formed around Seu Miguel and the doggie for any length of time. Squinting, the children were able to hear the flutter of angel wings and to see ghostly figures and orbs of intense colors moving around in the room.

Mariana Vitória jumped suddenly. She felt someone's warm hands pushing her over to where Seu Miguel was. Then that something took her hands and placed them on Seu Miguel's hands. She felt a strange electrical tingle run up through her body and out her hands. She could feel them becoming very, very hot.

The doggy started shaking, small *yip-yip-yipping* escaped his lips, the children thought it was sounding like he may be trying to speak.

Whazzis? Ohmygawd, where am I?

Eeeooo? Eeooo? Where did you go? We were having so much fun . .

Oh, oh. That was when it dawned on me I was no longer in that wonderful dream with Eeooo any longer but I was back in that dingdong, scroungy, half-dead doggy body The Voice had stuck me into and whooooo-ooooo ouch ouch ouch! Could someone please turn down the diksnik volume? It's so loud in here . . .

Nope? . . . Ah, c'mon! Mr. Voice? You there?

Nope?

Wow, I'm super—sensitive to sound in this little crappy body and I'm lookin' out of these doggie eyes, thinkin' I guess doggies come with built in third-eyes, too, 'cause all I could see were these wild bright colors everywhere flying all which ways: spewing outta this big bright blob of light that was moving up, up, up, then jump over—what looked like—people made of white light and . . . they were doing weird things like they were pumping into me this . . . this . . . this energy out of their hands. Whoo-weeee. It was feeling good. And amazingly I was feeling better and better and the funniest thing . . . all the pain was draining out of that body bag I was in . . . and . . . it was so cool 'cause I was feeling this amazing Love vibe—more than I've ever felt before—it was so overwhelming I was drifting off somewhere to a la-la-land of bliss . . . what a rush! I was feeling so grateful from being released from pain 'cause dogs must be able to cry with joy, 'cause, man, that what the hezzop I'm-a doin' right now.

Rafael's wide-eyes blinked in disbelief as he watched the doggie's foot, all swollen and red, change to a light pink. Look, he is moving his bad leg! he said.

After a moment, Seu Miguel opened his eyes as the light in the room started to dim and returned to the candle-lit glow that was present before. Everyone watched as Seu Miguel's shiny dark-brown eyes blinked wildly as they slowly changed back to their usual bright blue.

Smiling, Seu Miguel gently said, The healing is finished, my friends.

Mariana Vitória and Rafael smiled up at Seu Miguel in deep gratitude.

Martim, unable to speak, put his big hands on his children's shoulders, pulling them to him. A feeling of loving warmth swept over the children letting them know that they wouldn't have to worry about being in trouble after all.

The children gasped in joy as the doggie struggled to his feet, and took a few wobbly steps.

Okay! These pegs work after all. A-a-a-and . . . maybe not.

The doggie sat back down on his haunches and started to pant looking straight at Seu Miguel.

Heh, heh, heh . . . hey, I gotta tell you, man, I'm very impressed and . . . well, thanks. A lot . . . no I really mean it, heh, heh, heh.

It looked as though the little doggy was actually smiling up at Seu Miguel. But when his nub-of-a-tail, which had been so still before, started wagging, the children couldn't hold back their shouts of glee!

Is he okay to play with now? they asked.

Oh no-no-no-no. Tell 'em no, there big fella! No-no-no-no— I'm just a little tender still.

Seu Miguel answered, his voice soft and thoughtful, Let the doggy sleep for a few days. That will be sufficient rest before you two can play with him. Then he added, You know this little one is going to need a name, don't you?

Martim had told Rafael many times that they could not have pets. He was concerned that some of the travelers at the Pousada might not look kindly on having an animal around.

Rafael looked up at his father, Can we keep him, please daddy?

Martim did not answer.

Seu Miguel smiled and said, This dog is very special, Martim—

Oh, yeah, you got that right.

He will work with the Entities helping our visitors to heal—

Okay, didn't know that . . .

He is an extraordinary dog—

O-kay—

I can see that he can do for others what I just did for him.

Martim looked puzzled. You mean, this dog can heal people?

I don't find them too often, but I know one when I see one, said Seu Miguel.

Me? No way. Wait a minute . . . just ask The Voice—You gotta know The Voice—he's the first to tell you I gotta a whole lot more to learn . . . I mean, what all you light people did—that was phenomenal, no that was truly amazing! I was really impressed . . .

Seu Miguel looked straight in the little dog's eyes and stroked his head, smiling at him.

You really think some day . . . ?

Seu Miguel smiled and winked.

Whoa!

Then Seu Miguel looked at Martim and said, So that's what you tell your boarders at the pousada. Okay? And don't be surprised if he becomes well known at all the other pousadas as well.

Mariana Vitória boldly stepped forward hugging her father's arm, Then we will call him Xico (Shee-coo) the Medium, right Dad?

Zeeep! Zeeep is my name, you . . . you . . . little person. Call me Zeeep!

Martim smiled, running his fingers through his hair and taking a deep breath, I guess I'm outnumbered here . . . Okay. Xico the Medium, it is . . . but only if it's okay with Rafael.

Rafael. Ol' Buddy. Tell them my name is Zeeep not . . . not—

Rafael grinned from ear-to-ear, Xico the Medium . . . my own dog, he said. And Mariana Vitória's, too.

Ohhhhh nooooooooooooooooooo not Shheeeee-coooo—sounds so . . . so . . foreign.

Rafael's prayer had finally come true. And Zeeep still would have to get used to it.

Xico . . . sheeeesh!

ZEEEP AND THE VOICE IN THE VOID

. . . So what do you think?

What? About being a stupid dog?

I know what you think about that.

Where the hezzop were you?

I was right there. Seu Miguel and I go back a long way.

I never heard or saw you . . .

You have to ask, or say my name. You should know that by now.

I fergit . . .

I like that Seu Miguel guy a lot, though. And getting my body all patched up was pretty cool. I'm really going to be hangin' with the dude, doing healing stuff?

Well, yes. If you pay attention to your lessons and don't . . . forgit.

Oh, sheeesh. And speakin' of sheeesh, My name is Zeeep. Can' t you do anything about that?

Xico is a good Brazilian name. It's a famous name among Brazil's Spiritists.

Famous, huh?

Very Famous. Xico Xavier was a brilliant medium, and best friends with Seu Miguel.

Big deal. Zeeep's a famous name back in the pond and I want it back.

How did you do with little Sabrina in her dream?

Oh, man, it was weird, weird . . . . just weird.

. . . ?

Well, it felt like I was with Eeeoo alright, you know, all the same good feelin's were there but it was strange we couldn't do all the things we use to do, you know? Like what we had in common back in the pond.

Yes, little girls don't do dolphin things.

And she only felt like she was half—like the other half was somewhere else.

I told you that the other half was Sabrina's soul and she was being healed at the Temple of Healing at the same time.

I know, I know I know, it's just . . . I've never had to share Eeeoo before. And I've never felt her being so sad. She was happy being with me and all but I gotta tell ya . . . when I had to go 'cause you stuffed me back in that ding-dong doggie body—I mean you just whipped me out just like that—and I think we both had separation anxiety 'cause it hurt like hezzop 'cause I miss her so much and I know she misses me . . . I don't think I can go through that again.

And, son, it's all part of what you need to do to help Sabrina. You want to help that sweet child, don't you?

Yeah. Guess I'm gonna have to learn to . . . trust you . . . huh?

That's a good start.

I still think you're a smart ass.

Better than no ass at all.

Hey! You made a joke.

You're a good teacher.

—PART TWO—

THE HEALING

LILLIAN, ABE AND SABRINA
BARRA DO BURGES, MATO GROSSO, BRAZIL
2002

CHAPTER 29

Touch down. Barra do Burges, Mato Grosso, Brazil *(Baha do Bushz-ee, My-you Gross-oh, Bra-zeel)*

Looking out the window, Lillian could hardly make out the soft green rolling hillsides of Barra do Burges, through the condensation caused by the intense heat and humidity. She stretched, weary from the twenty-one hour journey.

The pilot's voice came over the speaker, Good morning, Dr. Latham. We will be sitting on the runway for a few minutes—there is a lot of traffic this morning. We apologize for the delay. Please remain in your seats with your seat belts fastened. Thank you.

Lillie smiled over at Abe. He was sleeping so deeply she hadn't the heart to wake him. Even looking over at her comatose child, wrapped in soft blankets amidst the machines, she smiled. Though her body ached from the hard seat she'd been confined to for the last 14 hours, her mind was filled with excitement. Yes, her head, her shoulders, and even her butt ached. But why was this . . . this sadness there?

Why . . . ?

She remembered. Maybe it was because . . . of the heavy thoughts she'd been having on the flight. They had appeared right after the flight attendant had offered her a cocktail. Oh, how she had wanted a glass of wine but she had refused, knowing—now—that a thirst for something stronger might soon follow. The memories . . . she had been feeling so guilty about Grandmère during the trip and was missing her so much. So guilty. Grandmère was the woman that had given her everything she'd ever wanted, been there for her in every way . . . and that night . . . the night when Grandmère had needed her.

* * *

She'd been downstairs trying to pay bills with the money they didn't have. Miserable, she was throwing blame at everyone and everything she could think of.

She hadn't heard Grandmère fall. She hadn't heard her calls. Lillian had been so mad at her that night—she had been so nasty to her. She had told Grandmère they had no choice—they were going to have to sell her house—Sabrina came first. Lillian remembered that she had yelled, "Grandmère, you're old! Your life is almost over. We'll find you a nice home with other old people—people you can relate to." She hadn't stopped there, "I am just so damn tired, tired of taking care of . . . of invalids 24-7. I need a life. I have no life!" Oh why had she been so cruel?

Lillian had been drinking that night. All that month, she had been on a hate rampage, mostly at herself. Drinking was the only way she could find to feel better. Just a little bit of relief, that was all she needed . . . then soon, she needed more, then a little more.

That night she wasn't even aware of how much she'd had to drink—even that escape wasn't working. She'd phoned Abe and lambasted him, too. I'm doing this all by myself and you're in some penthouse in New York, diddlin' chicks. It's not even my Mother, Abe. Why should I have to take care of my husband's mother? He just ups and dies and leaves me with all this shit . . . blah, blah, blah, she'd gone on and on . . .

Abe had been amazingly calm, she'd remembered. He had suggested that she contact her sister-in-law and get her to come out and help her, but Lillian wouldn't have it. They'd never gotten along—especially after Ben's death. No, she knew she'd only end up having to take care of her, too. She had begged Abe to come up with a solution but he had cooled, then hung up.

Lillian had slammed down the phone, kept slamming it four or five times then burst into a yelling and crying fit that went on and on. By the time Lillian had collected herself long enough to remember to check on

Grandmère, she'd found her lying on the floor in a large pool of blood, gurgling, Lillie . . . Lillie.

She was already so far away that Lillian could hear her talking to the angels. Lillian had begged, stroking her hair, Grandmère please, please forgive me. I am so sorry. I've been so selfish. I'll do better, you'll see. Don't die . . . I love you so much. You have given Sabrina and me so much love and I was so . . . she couldn't go on.

Grandmère's breathing stopped.

The silence was so large without her breaths, Lillian was afraid to take her own next breath. She lay her face next to Grandmère and sobbed, Please go to where Sabrina has gone if you can and be there with her, she needs you. Ask her to come back . . . to me . . . . please.

By the time the ambulance had arrived, Lillie had sobered up some and the horror of what she'd done was dawning.

* * *

Her mind came rushing back into the hiss of the plane's overhead air vent and the hum of its fuselage.

She looked over at her daughter sleeping quietly on the gurney; strapped in her blankets, IV swaying gently as they taxied. She'd never stirred at all during her coma, even though Lillian had massaged her body daily. She suddenly felt so exhausted. Exhaustion always took her into a dark place—her foul thoughts running amuck.

Danser avec le diable, Grandmère would have said. Dance with the Devil. The dance can take you away if you let it. Stop it now. Watch your thoughts then change them. Be responsible, *ma plus chère*. Stop being so lazy.

Be responsible, stop being lazy? That scared Lillian. What in the world did that mean? I am being responsible. It was <u>me</u> that talked Abe into bringing them to Brazil. Was that lazy? Lillian could distinctly hear Grandmère's voice say, *Non cherie*, <u>your thoughts</u>. Be responsible for your thoughts.

She looked over at Sabrina and found her resentment had gracefully changed to love. She could feel Grandmère's presence and knew somehow she <u>was</u> helping Sabrina, like the psychic woman had said. And she could feel that she was helping her as well.

She had felt good refusing alcohol from the flight attendant. Grandmère's death was a harsh lesson but she realized that she was learning something else that was helping her cope—Love. She didn't know how but she was getting the lesson: exhaustion makes people stupid, drinking makes people cruel, drinking and exhaustion make people stupid and cruel.

She relaxed, knowing that she really wasn't alone, there was something bigger than her that felt like Love. She took some deep breaths like Grandmère had shown her, visualized creating a white light bubble around her entire body and let the breath out slowly. Letting go of resentment, letting go, just letting go, she said to herself.

She found her thoughts changing. Grandmère had been right. She was realizing she really was grateful. Grateful that Abe had consented to come with them. It couldn't have worked better, actually. It was truly a blessing that he was able to pay for the entire trip, that he had access to this jet, that he was an MD and that Sabrina's situation was his field of expertise. The only problem: he had told her at the very last moment he really needed to attend an important conference in Rio for one of the two weeks they had planned to stay. His best friend, Bob was meeting him there.

She'd never really liked Bob. He was a womanizer just like her brother and the two of them together gawking at nymphets drove her crazy. She looked over at her brother in the seat across from her—his head was back, his jaw so relaxed as he slept—he started snoring. Lillian found herself wanting to poke him but she didn't want to deal with his temper—he hated to be awakened. Actually, since this trip began, Abe was proving to be an imperial pain. So far he had only seemed like another child to take care of. His whining had been nearly unbearable, thinking he had stooped so low to have to carry their luggage—a spoiled little rich brat.

She'd caught herself again. Stop!

She said a silent prayer—she hadn't done that in ages. She was finding words of gratitude that her brother was with them. She knew if any emergencies were to happen he would be there for them—even though she had prepped for hours with the nurse, she hadn't even come close to mastering her nursing duties. It was as though their journey there had been blessed—what were the chances that Abe would learn of John of God only weeks before the psychic woman in the restaurant had so boldly offered the same information?

She was grateful for that, too.

After all they had been through: Benjamin's death, Sabrina's coma, Grandmère's death, all their sibling fights, the tears and horrors of their childhood—and now she was watching her brother fast asleep, snoring.

What about that one night she'd fallen asleep in the hospital bed with Sabrina? In the middle of the night she had woken up—she could have sworn that Sabrina had been awake and had said "It's okay, Mommy," but when she looked closely she had seen no indication that Sabrina had moved. Still, in her heart she knew that Sabrina had wanted her to know . . . Everything would be okay.

The plane taxied to its place and the attendant opened the door, letting in a shaft of brilliant sunlight. Lillian rubbed her throbbing temples and reached over to awaken her brother, coughing mid-snore. She looked at him and loved him dearly and laughed fondly at his awkward awakening. He stood with a *humpf* and was into the role of the wise doctor in a matter of seconds. Lillian watched him arranging for the exit and rose to her feet, helping lift Sabrina into the wheelchair and adjust her limp body.

ErrrrkErrrrkErrrrk! The shrill alarm jerked Lillie from her thoughts and sent her heart to a fast patter—something was going wrong with Sabrina's equipment. Abe was pulling and reseating tubes, adjusting from the button panel and making entries into the laptop computer before shutting off the alarm.

Panic gripped Lillian. Oh, God, she thought, what if this happened while Abe was away in Rio? She needed him with her, that was evident. She must talk to him about changing his plans. Taking deep breaths helped her to center as she grabbed her luggage from under her seat and collected Sabrina's belongings, but her stomach was still churning all the way into the terminal—even after they had loaded Sabrina and her equipment into the medical van.

The trip through the city was amazing to Lillian . . . talk about space age . . . looking out the window at the astonishing architecture passing by—it was straight out of *The Jetsons,* a TV show that she and her brother had watched in the Sixties. She looked over at Abe sleeping, and wished he was awake to share the memory.

She watched the city fade away into the green rolling hillsides, great billowing clouds building up and up in the sky. Looking to the road ahead, she watched the small, dirty, Brazilian-made cars and the beat-up trucks that belched black billowing smoke—it was a war of dominion over the single lane that was winding its way through the hills toward Paramanguaia where Medium Miguel of Miracles was.

XICO
PARAMANGUAIA, BRAZIL
JUNE, 2002

CHAPTER 30

Fitzzzzzzzst it was hot in here. Heh-a-heh-a-heh where the hezzop am I? Oh dikdsnik my head hurts. Oh yeah, sheebit . . . I was still in that doggie body. And now I had legs on which I must . . . stand.

Umph! I was up. I had tried them out once before . . . a-a-a-and not too successfully as I remember. It's hard when you've never had legs before . . . Well, maybe many, many lifetimes ago. Then I had to figure out . . . . how do these things work again? I wiggled them back-and-forth, okay okay, that kinda worked. And then I looked around backward and there it was . . . what was this thing that stuck out of my butt? Now, what was it used for? What in the hezzop was that for? Oh yeah, I can wiggle that back and forth—oh yippy. Big friggin' whoop.

So far, I wasn't impressed with the equipment I had to work with. And this icky smelly fur. Whew! Oh God, it was so exasperating. I had a whole different package and no instructions.

Hoime kjpk htlkdt kjlkt pdlflke mvnl was comin' from somewhere in the near distance.

Wha waz that?

Voices. Not The *Voice—wherever he was now—I had no idea. Maybe it was human voices. Weird sounding voices though—little puny voices. Squeaky little voices. Maybe little people.*

So there I was . . . wondering, just where the hell I was. Why can't I remember anything? Is this dog's brain I'm using so stupid that I can't remember diddilysquat? Is that it?

Well, let's see if I can figure this out . . . okay, okay, one minute I was lying on a road, flies buzzing everywhere, buzzzzing buzzing buzzing, vile creatures . . . and little nasty ants picking at me, then . . . then The Voice showed up and wanted to send me to go on a mission. Yeah. I can't remember too much about . . . something about . . . my . . . helping Eeeoo who is now a little girl . . . and the little girl is Eeeoo who doesn't remember me . . . and then I'm hearing little people talking outside the box I'm in. Yeah, I was in a box. I could see it was a box. So hot. Oh dear, this is so complicated . . . and now I see faces looking over the edge of that box, faces with BIG voices and BIG eyes. And everything was so LOUD. Pllllllease turn it down. Oh, oh, the box is moving, I'm moving, everything is moving . . . FLOPPLOPPLOPGR ERRRRRISH—

MOVE AWAY FROM THE SIDE OF THE BOX, I was yelling over all the noise . . .

HI, XICO . . . ARE YOU FEELING BETTER? Someone was talking to someone named Sheee-coo.

Then it all came back to me . . . Mariana Vitória and Rafael. And they named me that . . . that name. Why? Zeeep was a good name—a diksnik good name. Well, The Voice had said they were going to save my life and I guess they had. Couldn't remember how. Oh I'd been sooooo out of it . . . whew it was so hot in there heh-a-heh-a-heh.

I . . . remember . . . vaguely there was this big man . . . or somethin'—oh what is wrong with this BRAIN? Think-think-think brain. Oh . . . yeah, and there were these people made out of . . . light, yeah light and there were hundreds and hundreds of them and lots of streaks of lights flashing everywhere and I remember this big man with the name of Seu Miguel something . . . and my body felt really funny like electricity was running all through it and it felt bad and good at the same time. I'd go into this deep, deep sleep and then they'd wake me up and ask me a bunch of questions . . . like . . . like .. . diksnik I can't remember . . . and then The Voice was there, talking to 'em, tellin''em—all about me being a dolphin and all and then he told them about Eeeoo and the mission we were on, and that I was learning to heal people. That I would be helping Seu Miguel heal people . . . Wow . . . That's huge! Next there would . . .

Xico, Mariana Vitória's voice pulled me out of my recollections and her hand was coming over the top side of the box and she—ow-ow-ow oh shebit—and she was lifting me up-up-up and then I saw that I was in this big room and she was putting me down on these . . . legs . . . I was supposed to walk on, ow-ow-ow. Well,

I guess they worked pretty good as they were getting me across the floor . . . doin' purdy good . . . faster now . . . fall down . . . get up . . .

Oh, oh, I'd bumped right into Rafael, sorry pal. I'm having a time here.

Xico, he said. Come here, Xico.

Why are they calling me that awful name? Zeeep! Zeeep! Zeeep! Is my name, I was really getting madder and madder and I was trying to tell them and all that was coming out of my mouth was this . . . Yip,yip,yip—such a disgusting sound—then Whooo-ooo-ooo yip yip—<u>Oh what have I gotten myself into?</u>

VOICE? VOICE? WHERE ARE YOU VOICE? I was yipping. And I had never been so relieved to hear that Omnipresent One say, ***Yes Xico. What can I do for you?***

Heh-a-heh-a-heh—it's so hot—heh-a-heh-a-heh—I'm breathing so funny—

You're panting.

Panting! Wha for?

That's how you cool your body off.

Oh great. I have to spazzz to cool my body off?

Anything else you wanna know?

The volume—how do you turn it down?

You don't. That's a perk. Dogs have excellent hearing. Comes in handy for all sorts of things.

Like what?

I'll let you work with it and see what you can come up with. What else can I do for you?

What can you do for me? Figure it out. You're not stupid.

Well, son. Your body is healed thanks to all these wonderful humans who worked so hard to save your life.

Oh yeah, . . . thanks. Now what?

We'll I think you can do better than that. They have worked very hard, you owe them deep appreciation and not a smarty attitude.

Well, maybe I'll have a better attitude tomorrow when I'm not so . . dishcombooblebeebelated.

See that you do.

Fitzzzzzzbezzzzst.

Mariana Vitória and Rafael are your new masters. And so are their parents.

Masters? I don't gots no fitzzzztst masters—no how, no way. I'm a free agent.

You do now—you're a dog. And dogs have a pack mentality.

What? Whazat? I'm soooo afraid to ask.

Humans are the Alphas—the leaders of the pack—and you obey everything they say because you are part of their pack.

Oh yeah? Not likely.

Oh, son. They are in charge because they are supposed to take care of you. Don't you understand? You're not in the wild anymore; it's a whole new game being a domestic dog.

So, these people take care of me right? So, this means . . . What does this mean?

Well, they give you shelter, they feed you, they take care of you. They love you.

Wait wait wait, back up a little there. They feed me, yes?

Yes.

You mean I can't hunt my own food?

Not a good idea, no. But, you'll see, Flavia is a great cook.

They cook my food?

You'll love it.

I'll get spoiled to death, is what.

Possibly.

And fat. And repulsive.

Not likely.

Don't I get a say in any of this?

Well, you can show them how happy you are that they went to all that trouble . . .

How?

By wagging your tail.

You mean that thing that's stickin' outta my butt? Is that <u>all</u> it's good for?

Just about. It'll let them know what you're thinking and how you are feeling.

Let me get this straight . . . I have my brain sticking out of my butt now?

At that point, The Voice let out one of his GREAT GUFFAWS and wouldn't stop laughing.

Hey hey hey. STOP IT! STOP! I yelled. Remember the volume? Remember all that sensitive hearing equipment? Remember . . . ?

Oh, I'm sorry. It's just*—he was trying to whisper but it was only making him laugh louder.*

Sooooo big fella, you're laughing at a dolphin who's just trying to figure out this whole doggy mess—<u>is that nice?</u>

I'm sorry, son. I'll try to be more considerate.

You better because this is very confusing to me because I have to run a dolphin intellect in a brain half the size I'm used to and it's frustrating . . . so you gotta help me here—

Sorry, how can I help? *And I could still hear a chuckle coming on.*

Stop with the chuckle and tell me so I can get this straight. Just—where—am—I? And what's with the hot box?

You are in the kitchen, next to this stove, the warmest place in the pousada. You've been very sick and the kids were taking care of you. And look, they painted a picture of you on the outside of the box in honor of you.

That's not me, that's a dog.

Heh-hem.

Leave me alone. I'm tired. I've got to stay up and learn a whole new language . . . yip yip, yip yipp yip—This will take me all night.

Oh dear, this is going to be much harder than I thought, *whispered The Voice.*

Just go away. Go Away. I was sick of dealing with The Voice so I turned my attention to Mariana Vitória and Rafael who were acting mighty weird just then. They were down on all fours acting like . . . they were dogs. They are making the same Yip Yip noises that I was making. And shaking their behinds. Cuuuute, I'm thinkin'. I'll just humor them. Okay! I can play this game.

So I started running around like crazy and they liked it . . . a lot . . . made them laugh. And when they started laughing real hard and yipping back at me, my little tail started whipping back and forth, going a mile a minute—whish whish whish but it was a nub so it was more like ffff-fff-fff. And I learned when I would hold my mouth a certain way, lift my lip and show my teeth, they'd laugh so hard and say, Oh, look! He's smiling, isn't that cute? So I'd try to remember what I did, and did it now and then and they'd laugh some more and gave me some food to eat . . . Yes, I have to admit, it was really good . . . yes, <u>I like cooked food</u> . . . But the part I liked the best was when Mariana Vitória would rub my ears, ohhhhhhh-ahhhh, yesssss, ah, a little to the right, yessss, then Rafael would rub my ears at the same time, ohmygawd, heaven—a stereo ear rub—the best! Yes I was settling into this new lifestyle after all. And they were really gentle with me, with all my wounds and stuff, which I really appreciated . . . Sometimes Rafael would kiss me and hug me, so I kissed him back—right on the lips—and for some reason he didn't like that so much . . . oh man, this doggy human thing is really hard to get used to.

But the cool thing, as it turned out, this new package was really goood at picking up smells. Dolphins never could smell things all that well. But dogs—we're great at this.

I was so into the smells, I became get obsessed with 'em—yep, a smell addiction was what I developed. One smell would lead to another and another and another one and pretty soon it would lead me outside where I could smell complete histories in one-mighty-whiff. Sniffffff Ahhhhhhh. And if another dog peed somewhere, I could go over to where he peed and I could get to know everything about him: what kind of hair he had, what kind of dog he was, where he lived, was this his territory, was he Alpha dog, what he thought about stuff, like females, like sex . . . stuff like that. And once I had it all down then I'd leave my calling card—just tryin' to be social, 'cause who knows, maybe we'd meet up sometime and have a go at it, you know—find out who would be the one to rule this territory. Back at the pond, I'd get into a rumble or two, now and then—it's a guy thing. I figured I'd carry my prowess into my dog-dom too. Yesssss.

Now if it was a girl dog, it was a different thing. I figured I could find out what kind of sex she liked and where she lived and then I could go over and do her any time I liked—but I probably wouldn't . . . well, because . . . I still loved Eeeoo. But again, Eeeoo did know how much I loved sex, and yes, maybe she'd understand under these circumstances—me being a dog now and all.

I, on the other hand, felt pretty safe from worry about Eeeoo doing the deed . . . I mean she was just a little girl in a coma . . . what were the chances? Oh. I am bad. So bad. I just can't help it . . . sex makes me behave . . . badly . . . have bad bad thoughts. Yes, it does.

Good thing The Voice wasn't around just now, huh?

* * *

A month later, I was all settled into my new body. I was totally used to it. It was feeling pretty good. I was running a lot.

Every morning I'd be down at the fields where the other dogs met and we'd have races through the hills—absolutely exhilarating it was—reminded me of my dolphin days of racing! And not to dog my bark but I did win every single race—just like back at the pond. Yeah, I liked being with the village dogs, all of them characters, taught me a whole lot—a lot about the way of the dog. And Mariana Vitória and Rafael would throw this ball and I just couldn't help it, every time I'd have to chase after it, I know it sounds crazy how I loved chasing that stupid ball, how I craved it . . . and how I loved to twirl in about a million circles, around and around and around—what a rush! And sniffing everything in sight—the best—and I think what was happening as time went on, my dolphin brain was morphing into the dog brain and they were becoming compatible or something like that.

Anyway, I've got a story that will knock the socks off anyone's feet. One night, after a whole day of hangin' out with the boys, I was home, just walking around the Pousada, sniffin' like I like to do and walking among the feet of the humans under the dinner table where I could get some fantastic eats, like I like to do, and I was just minding my business until I looked up at this man, sitting there just plain as day, and he had this huge lizard on his back. Yeh, I said lizard. Huge Lizard. As BIG as him. And it would hizzzzzzzz when it saw that I was looking at it. I don't think that guy knew the lizard was on his back, and I don't think any of the humans could see it, cause they would have freaked. I freaked. I started barking at it, trying to get it off that guy's back. I mean, this Lizard looked really mean—big orange eyes with a stripe in the middle of its pupils, and it had scales all over it and slime running down its mouth when it hizzzzed and spitttttt at me. It tried to scare me when it knew I was the only one that could see it. It was making itself bigger and bigger and bigger! Till it was enormous! Could almost touch the ceiling! Then it shrunk back to its original size. Now it was just . . . nasty.

And I thought it might be my job to get rid of that guy so I was barking away at it, showing my teeth like I knew business, I had my hackles stickin' straight up, rufffff rufff grrrrrrrrr I was growling, deep and meeeean . . . and guess what? Mariana Vitória and Rafael came out and started yelling at me. They told me to shut up and go lay down! Bad dog they called me! And when I wouldn't stop,'cause I thought it was pretty important I keep doin' my job—I mean that reptile- thing could have bitten someone—and they smacked me right on my butt. How humiliatin'. It really smarted.

So I did what they told me, I shut up and went and lay down in my bed in the kitchen. And that guy got up, and went to his room and so did the lizard. And not one of those humans could see the lizard on that guy's back.

How gross was that?

FLAVIA, MARIANA VITÓRIA, RAFAEL
PARAMANGUAIA, BRAZIL
JUNE, 2002

CHAPTER 31

The kitchen smelled earthy and fresh. Piles of vegetables pulled only moments ago from the garden lay waiting to be sorted, washed and chopped. Local women tended to the ritual of preparing the healthy diet requested by Seu Miguel's entities. Just this afternoon, Seu Miguel had sat in trance while his staff jotted down the dietary information being imparted: his patients were to have no pork, no pepper, no alcohol. The vibrations of these substances would interfere with the work that the staff did as the visitors slept.

Flavia Mosques was the hub of the kitchen. She always knew what needed to be done and in what order. Her kitchen ran like a fine clock—tick-tick-tick—simmer chicken and small red potatoes in fine oils and herbs—tick-tick-tick—preheat oven, braid rising bread dough—tick-tick-tick—prepare lettuces and vegetables—tick-tick-tick—preheat pans for vegetable sauté—tick-tick-tick—roll out pie dough—tick-tick-tick.

Mariana Vitória carried Xico into the kitchen, looking for her mother. Mom? I got to talk to you. It's *really* important.

Okay . . . Flavia surveyed her kitchen, checking that everything was in motion, tick-tick-tick. She wiped her hands on her apron, while looking at the clock. Just give me a minute, she said.

Mariana Vitória knew her mother had to have everything ready at 6:00PM when the patients all gathered in the dining area.

I'll be in the courtyard, Mom, Mariana Vitória said, walking in that direction.

Be there in a moment, sweetie.

Mariana Vitória thought the courtyard was a magic land. On the lawn, tables and chairs were set in graceful groupings. Martim and his right hand man, Tadeu, had built a ten-foot high mountain/water fountain at the end of the yard, under the tank that sat at the top of the roof. Once a day the water flowed down the mountain, watering the plants and flowers that Flavia had planted.

Mariana Vitória put Xico on the ground and let him run and play in the grass.

Tick-tick-tick, she felt her mother's arrival at her side.

You need to talk to me? Flavia sat down beside her on the faux rocks. Xico ran up and dropped a ball at their feet coaxing a throw with a fierce tail wagging. He knew he was in trouble—Mariana Vitória was being so reserved and he wasn't used to this energy coming from her. He tried to fluff it up a bit by spinning at least 10 times, then again in the opposite way.

Mom, Xico was barking at that poor man who just arrived.

And?

He wouldn't leave him alone all day. Seu Miguel said Xico would be helping people heal, not making them feel worse.

Xico stopped his busy panting and found a position belly-close to the ground, maybe that would make them see that he was really no threat, no threat at all.

Maybe Xico knows something that we don't, Mariana Vitória.

I do—heh-heh-heh-heh—gimme a break here, that crazy lizard has no business being on that man's back and did you hear how he hisssssed at me? Huh? I had to tell him to get off. You think I'm rude? Well, I think that lizard is pathetic and I . . . Oh, well.

Xico was feeling pretty low until he heard a familiar voice shout, Xico! Xico, c'mere boy! He was up like a shot and running toward his buddy, Rafael.

Hi-Hi-Hi! How ya doin', how ya doin? You know I'm doin' my job, doncha—ya gotta tell 'em bud. Tell 'em. Heh-heh-heh-heh

Mariana Vitória sighed, irritated by the interruption. What's wrong with that man?

He has cancer, sweetheart.

But why would Xico bark at him?

I can only guess that somehow he's doing his job.

How?

Not sure. If Xico specializes in healing . . . well, this is what I understand about healers . . . I know, that Seu Miguel himself—as a man—doesn't do the healing. He allows the energy of the entities to flow through his body to help the person who needs healing. Maybe Xico does the same . . .

Oh, oh! Rafael ol'buddy. Don't . . . . no no no no . . . HEY!!!!

Mom? Do you think the entities might be . . . ghosts?

Rafael appeared holding Xico upside down.

No-no-no I can't breathe Bud. Owwwww my legs.

Mariana Vitória grabbed Xico away from Rafael and righted him. Hey brat, it hurts Xico when you hold him that way, hold him the way I showed you.

Mariana Vitória—my hero.

What ghost? asked Rafael.

Never mind and go away! Mariana Vitória was not inviting him into this grownup conversation. Rafael crawled onto his mother's lap. Mom, did she tell you about that TV show we saw about ghosts? he asked.

No, dear.

Xico squirmed, *was that lizard . . . a ghost?* He'd been there, he too had seen that TV show. He really didn't like watching TV though, it had a spiky energy that made his brain go too slow.

Mariana Vitória's lips tightened into a hard line. She said, Mom, I can't talk to you about this if Rafael's here.

I think we can do just fine, Mariana Vitória. Flavia smoothed her son's hair, You want to know what I think a ghost is and what an entity is, right?

Right.

Right, Rafael mimicked.

Yeh, yeh. Me, too.

My understanding is that ghosts are spirits that have left the physical body but they don't realize that they're dead. They're confused because they are no longer in the physical world but they are stuck in a void between the physical world and the Otherside.

What's the Otherside?

It's where you go when you go to sleep, baby. When you're alive, you float around in this astral world all night and you're able to come back every morning because you have a silver cord that pulls you back. But when you die, your cord gets cut.

Rafael, eyes all round and big, asked, And when you die, then you fly around, and you can't come back . . . and then what happens?

Then, angels and helpers come and find you and take you with them to the brightest light there is—and to a very lovely world.

You really think that's true? asked Mariana Vitória.

Rafael looks very serious, his finger poking his cheek. Oh yes, this sounds very true—I remember this.

Mariana Vitória hit him again, What do you mean you remember this—Mom, how can he remember?

Well, he hasn't been here with us very long on Earth. It wasn't too long ago that that was where he came from.

Yeh, yeh . . . that's right. The Voice says there's a place called the Astral. One level on this Astral dimension has this really low, dull vibration and the other was much higher. Yes . . . yes, the higher one . . .that was where he'd seen the Doctors that were working with Seu Miguel the night he healed his leg. That was the dimension where he had actually seen the energy that was being used by the doctors for healing.

Can you actually see the energy Seu Miguel's entities use to heal people? Mariana Vitória asked her mother.

Absolutely. You've seen the photos on the walls of The Morida Seu Jose—the ones that have white streaks of light right beside him while he's doing a healing on a person, right?

Oh, so that was what that was, I always wondered.

You know? Flavia continued, When he worked on me . . . I remember I felt this amazing whoosh of energy as it pulsated through my whole body.

What's pulsated mean? Asked Rafael.

It's like . . . Flavia blew softly through her slightly opened lips, whew—whew—whew—she said, making it sound like a soft heartbeat. Like when you bend over upside down: that's what you feel . . .

Rafael flopped his body in half, touching his toes with his fingers. I feel it! Whew whew—whew—whew—

Mariana Vitória ignored his antics, Really? What *else* did it feel like?

Well . . . it's hard to explain to someone until they experience it . . . I remember feeling very warm, but then becoming really cold. I think the energies change as your body responds to the healing work that's going on.

Did it hurt?

Well, sometimes yes. But I think the hurt was just me thinking too hard about it. I know when I was giving birth to you, I could help the pain become so much less when I relaxed and accepted the pain. So when Seu Miguel's entities worked on me, I found if I just thanked the entities for what they were doing, the pain went away.

Went away. Just like that?

Just like that.

Really . . .

Mariana Vitória's face got all contorted. Xico wondered what she was thinking.

What are you thinking? Flavia asked her daughter.

Xico loved how some people could hear his thoughts sometimes. He vowed that he was going to learn how to read people's thoughts, too.

All of a sudden he heard that Big Voice as loud as if it were right next to him—

You, my son, already know how to read people's thoughts, just listen next time.

OK, Xico answered in his mind and wondered if The Voice had heard.

Yes, I heard, The Voice said.

Xico barked and wagged his tail, turning in circles and circles and circles. He did that when he had a backup of happy energy that he needed to get rid of quickly.

Mariana Vitória was laughing. Look! Xico's doing it again. Why does he do that?

Flavia was laughing.

Rafael was not: he was serious when he said, You should ask him someday. He might just tell you.

Xico stopped—that was profound, he thought, and took up the challenge. He concentrated. He tried real hard to send them a message:

Lizard . . . There was a huge lizard on that man. Huge . . . Lizard.

Xico was not sure anyone had heard. It was going to take practice.

XICO
PARAMANGUAIA, BRAZIL, JUNE 2002

CHAPTER 32

I must have been dreaming deeply in between my flipping and flopping around all night, barely sleeping. Every new position was uncomfortable and every itch demanded attention.

Eee'zz tiii-m-ee . . .

Uh? I was halfway into coherent reality and halfway out.

It's . . . time . . . to go to work*. The Voice said, making a connection this time.*

I knew something was up the minute I lay down for the night, thinking I'd be getting a good night's rest. Hah, the dreaded moment was upon me.

Okay, I blurted, What do I have to do?

You'll know.

How?

You already know.

What . . . ?

First, you've got to get your body up and running.

Laying on my back, looking up at the ceiling I could see the outline of a figure filled with amazingly bright light, so bright it hurt my eyes. Was this the first time I was actually seeing The Voice? It was a little unnerving but I found myself exceptionally calm.

I've already got my body up and running after every flea walking around on my back. Could we make a deal here?

Deal?

I rolled over and got to my feet, but the itching was getting the better part of my standing, so my butt hit the dirt and my back leg started thrashing behind my ear. I was miserable. Yeah, before I check in to work for you, could you please do something about these fleas?

You are a dog after all.

That's true, but you know what kind of dog I'd be without these blinking fleas?

Flealess?

Yeah . . . and happy . . . H-A-P-P-Y and COMFORTABLE. Wouldn't you rather work with a HAPPY, COMFORTABLE dog?

The blindingly bright figure moved across the room to the doorway as if beckoning me to follow, **I'll speak to Mariana Vitória about getting you a bath,** *saying it like the deal was already cemented.*

Can't you do better than that, being so Omnipotent and all?

What would you have me to do?

Talk to the fleas. Tell them: Medium Xico, Healer in Residence, is off limits. There and then, I'd made up my mind, if he wasn't going to do for me, then I wasn't the least bit interested in this so-called healing work.

Well, all I can do is ask, there still is the Universal Law of Choice—I can't override that law.

Insects can make choices?

I swore I'd seen a flea jump off my back and stick his tongue out at me.

In a very limited way, yes.

I was not about to fight this out—I realized I was licked. Never mind, I said, What do ya want me to do?

Think real hard . . . *The glow moved through the kitchen doorway. I followed. Then it hit me . . . Oh no! Not the guy with the lizard?*

I know it looks overwhelming for your first case, but I'll be here every step of the way. I just cannot do it without you.

Why not?

You have the physical body. I do not.

Gotcha.

The walls lit up as we moved down the hallway and lit the darkened dining room as we passed through and proceeded to the hallway where the rooms were.

As I was wondering what the Lizard was doing on the man's back, The Voice chimed in on my thoughts. ***Fear created it.***

That man's fear is able to create a whole lizard?

Believe me, it wasn't me. Where I come from there are no insects and there are no lizards. But humans get hold of some of the most perfect ideas and run with them in the craziest ways.

I believed him . . . remembering the man this afternoon walking toward me with not one lizard but a whole bunch of 'em hangin from him . . . . yukkkky.

What does this human-type guy need with all those lizards?

Who knows? He certainly doesn't <u>need</u> them. Just remember, any creation made by anything other than The Omnipresent is a fake. And the fakes have no real power without the fear they command. When you get those creatures to the Light, they'll pop right off of him and then you can do your job.

Uh, I was wondering, just what is my job?

It's simply this—

And CRACK! All spaces were suddenly filled with Light, everywhere around and through me was filled with Illumination . . . I could see every molecule, sense all that was to be sensed: eons that had come before, eons that were to come, everything was ALL in one single fraction of a moment.

Holy Wow!

Your job is to call on that Force, the Divine Source, with all your <u>might</u> and <u>intention</u> and all will pale in its presence and return to its perfect order. Believe, and it will be so.

The message was so loud and powerful that I looked around thinking that we had woken everybody up from their sleep, but then it dawned on me that, hezzop, we could have been exploding bombs on that divine level and all but a very few of the human-types would have been able to hear us.

I gotta sit down for a minute, boss.

You'll be just fine at this job, you come with the best credentials, you know—you're a dog now. D-o-g spelled backwards—

I know, I know.

Feel better?

No I didn't feel better—I'd seen that man go where Mariana Vitória and Rafael had been playing this afternoon and I didn't want one of them to jump off on the kids! I knew my job that night was important and that we needed to go do it—but I needed more information. I just can't figure out why humans collect all those creatures?

Son, it's not easy being human—they're prone to making a lot of mistakes. It's their job.

Job? I felt the breeze moving in from the open windows at the end of the hallway. It was turning out to be a very balmy night and the gentle wind helped calm my apprehension.

Their souls have chosen to come here to learn what it's like to create.

The Voice continued, **It's been said many times, ye are all Gods.**

But doesn't it scare you a little bit? I've been watching TV with Mariana Vitória and Rafael. I see the things they're creating , the things they've been creating for eons? War. Pollution. Hate. All that.

No. I am not about fear. Fear was man-made to control others.

So, all the vampires and the devils, they're man-made, too?

Bingo.

Well, I've heard also that the Big Man Upstairs is a little full of himself. He's angry, He's hateful and vengeful, He beats out his commands on brimstone and fire . . .

That God was man-made to control others. The noise you experienced? That CR ACK? That sound filled everything with intense Light. Do you know what it was made of?

No. Do it again, I dig it.

And he did, and I got the same amazing WOW feeling.

That was pure unadulterated Love—the most Powerful, the most Forgiving, the most Enlightening, the most Creative—and that's why it heals the sick. That's why it changes the world.

That's the real deal?

That's the part of yourself, the part of everyone and everything that exists, no matter how much fear is created. When that part of Everything is believed as the REAL DEAL—from the very center of the Heart—then the human soul can come Home to stay for good.

But why can't he stay Home now?

Because he must clear himself of all of his lower frequencies—of his creations—because if he cleaves to them, he isn't at a high enough frequency to be able to stay. He gets pulled down every time.

So you have that frequency?

I do.

Then why are you hangin' out with me?

Then I just happened to remember looking at the man sitting at the table that afternoon, and the lizards jumping on other people one by one as he spoke to them. Then he got up and he walked real slow-like, like he was in real pain.

I'll let you figure that out for yourself.

Well I just gotta say, not to be critical, but sometimes you come off having this super subtle voice—pin-drop quiet sometimes. And I have super hearing, believe me. And when I have to listen to all the other voices going on in my head, it ain't easy . . . Oh, oh. I just realized . . . I've been hangin' around humans too much—I've never had so many voices before.

Listen to those voices son. If they speak negatively or fearfully—that is not Me.

Who is it then?

Those are the voices of the Ego.

When is it you?

Any Voice that comes from Love . . . that's Me. This voice will be proactive for your Highest Good.

How will I know it's for my Highest Good?

You will feel it. And it will feel very Peaceful. And when you act on what I say and trust me implicitly, then my voice gets louder and stronger, my son.

The hallway I was being led down was a horror show, if I chose to look at all the human manifestations hanging around people's doors. It was like a virtual battleground of hideous creatures.

Door number One—a lot of bad smelling slime, a weird looking insect. Two—a few hybrid animals of some sort: hairy, thick and grotesque Three—not bad. Four—I don't even want to talk about it. Disgusting! No wonder they were sick, I was thinking, while I kept my intentions very clear: I was looking for room9. Even when the manifestations hissed or growled or shrieked—there was a lot of shrieking—I knew better than to take it personally, after all, I was virtually walking around in people's dreams and it had nothing to do with me.

Very good deduction,** The Voice commended, **you're catching on.

We came to a halt before the door with the number Nine on it.

This is it? I shuttered, my teeth started to chatter, ('cause that's what I do when I'm filled up with too much static energy.) Was I up to this?

Don't worry, in comparison to other creations, a little lizard can't be all that bad, right?

I started scratching at the door—get this thing over as soon as possible—I kept thinking. I stopped and listened, no response. I took in a deep breath and let it out slowly. I asked The Voice, Okay, just so I know. How did this man create a lizard?

Through thought forms—they're very powerful. If people could realize just how powerful their thinking is, they would want to change the destructive, negative ones immediately. This particular lizard thought form was created during a fearful moment when he was a child, three years old, living in a small village at the south tip of Brazil. He was with his older brother watching a particularly, gory, violent horror movie on TV, going against their Parents' permission. So there was that element of guilt already established. At the same time, their parents were in the next room having a horrible fight—yelling and throwing things. The parents separated that night and got a divorce soon after. The youngster felt it was his entire fault, because he knew he wasn't supposed to be watching that movie.

No sheebit? What does that have to do with lizards, man? Maybe I couldn't hear the answer over the scratching I was doing, 'cause I put my whole body into it. I stopped briefly, I could hear shuffling behind the door.

. . . ***I'm telling you this, the lizard is not the problem here*** *. . . was the only part I heard.*

Okay, good to know. I should be able to handle this lickity-split and be back home in time for a good ball tossin' game with Rafael, I thought.

The man finally opened the door and to my dismay—behind the thin, tousle-headed old guy standing before me in his pajamas—was a room filled with lizards: on the walls, on the floors, the ceilings, even on the bed he was sleeping in. Most of them were scurrying around as they all watched me through the dark, their red eyes blinking and glowing.

Lizards aren't the problem, man? Did you fart or something—and it blew up a big important part of your brain? Look at em!

Don't be concerned, it's all an illusion.

I gulped. Uh, this man is a bit on the compulsive-obsessive side. Why so many?

These are the negative thoughts that got created every time the original fear was triggered.

You mean the fear that he made his mother and dad get a divorce?

No, something else happened other than their divorce, son.

What was it?

It's hidden very deeply, so deeply it's hard to see.

But you can see it, can't you?

Every time he relieved that fear, it created a thought that took on the form of a lizard. It's built a moving barrier around the memory and now

it can't be seen. Only his subconscious knows what it is. And he's been carrying this burden around all his life and each form has taken on a life of its own.

Thankfully, the man was completely oblivious of the lizards. He smiled down at me, What's a little guy like you doing up so late? Do you wanna come in? Okay, little poochie, c'mon in. Minha casa é sua casa.

I answered with an obligatory tail wag but didn't move.

I need you to spend the night with this man, *The Voice said.*

Are you kidding? I can't go in there. Did you get a look at the friends he hangs out with?

You want to learn how to heal don't you?

Well . . .

Then go on in.

Okay! Just don't be so pushy.

I entered with great trepidation. The little old man shut the door. Tension was rising as well as the room's temperature. Heh-heh-heh, I panted. It felt like steam was scorching my lungs.

Hey? What goin' on. Whaddo I do now? I panted harder. I was freaking.

It's okay. The man has a fever. He's here to see Seu Miguel because he is very sick.

The man looked ashen and held his stomach, he sank to the bed and lay down and the lizards were crawling all over him.

Poor guy, no wonder he was so sick. Can't we get him a can of bug spray or something?

The Lizards looked at me and started hissing . . . a foul smell was permeating the room. What had I got myself into? By the time this night was over, I would surely be consumed.

Voice? Where are you, Voice?

The lizards were coming over to me, stacking themselves on top of each other.

Their nasty breath was in my face.

Yo, Voice? What do I do now?

Figure it out, what did I teach you? Think!

Yeah, think fast! I'm thinkin', cause I'm gonna be melted to a doggie pancake with all these toxic fumes being expelled . . . then by some miracle, I remembered my lessons: I was not alone. I had a power greater than me and you'd better believe I called on it. DIVINE FORCE! BE HERE NOW! I declared with my most forceful intention, three times.

To the poor man it just sounded like barking and he shhhhhed me. But as the room suddenly flashed with Light—my good pal had not let me down—all the lizards started popping and exploding into thin air and eventually every one of them had vanished.

Whoa! I was stunned. I couldn't move. Couldn't breathe. But the old man instantly took a breath of relief and tension eased in his face and body.

Don't worry they're gone for now. That is, until they get re-created by this human. So you've got to work fast.

Why me? Why was I the one that was so important? You got all the energy you need, man. I can go home. I wanna go home.

You're the one that has a physical body.

So? Big deal!

We need you to hold our light in the physical world. We can't do our job without you. Don't you get it?

Okay, I gotta job . . . I need to do this so I can be with Eeeoo . . . . okay, I remembered.

By the time I calmed down, my doggie-itis had kicked in, and I'm all over that room sniffin' the air, sniffin' the floor, sniffin' under the bed, looking for any creature that may still be lurkin'.

Wheeeweee! Those varmints left a real rank smell. Phooey, I snorted.

Oh, sorry, I'll just take care of that real quick, *The Voice said.*

Flowers, much better, thanks.

I looked at the poor man, but he seemed to be resting much more peacefully. That made me feel much better and gave me encouragement for the next task—whatever that was to be.

Can we give this guy a name, for goodness sake? Give him a little dignity?

The name his mother gave him is Howard, but he hates that name. It has run in the family for five generations. Why humans do that to their children, I'm not quite sure. If they realized that the collective vibration of all those previous generations was attached to a name, they'd reconsider.

Why? The man was now looking straight at me. I was getting very uncomfortable.

Not every Howard in his family was exemplary—some weren't evolved, some were just evil—and now he has to carry their baggage too.

Might make him stronger.

Good point.

Yep. I was feeling sorry for the dude. I jumped up on the bed beside him. He started petting me real nice.

But it could also be his undoing.

Feeling a bonding going on, I said, hey you could disconnect those vibes, Boss. You can do that.

Not without his permission. And first, he has to become aware of it.

Can't someone just tell him? I'll tell him . . . and I tried, but it just came out sounding like a little woof. A pathetic wooffff at that.

You could tell him one hundred and two times, and he still would not be able to hear.

I don't get it . . . if someone tells you something, you become aware -

Can you make anything out of a foreign language . . . like for instance . . . Swahili?

Like Swa—whaaaa?

Exactly. Because you have no way of interpreting what you hear.

I nudged up close to the guy. I was feeling really sorry for him. I really have a lot of work ahead of me. Then it dawned on me to ask, Hey, . . . did we get permission?

When Howard asked Seu Miguel and his entities to heal him, that was a form of permission. And guess who Seu Miguel dos Milagres and the gang turned to?

Your Source-ness?

Looking over, Howard was smiling at me and patting my head. C'mon boy, he said, as he lay down.

I don't have to sleep with the guy, do I? We can go now, can't we? The lizzies are all gone.

Yes, this is why we're here, son. So sleep as close to his diaphragm as you can get. When he moves, you move, got that?

Check. I shuddered but for the life of me I couldn't budge. What if Howard summoned some more of his reptilian creations while I was sleeping?

Let's go to work. Take your position.

Position. I crawled under the blanket and snuggled in a ball right by his gurgling stomach, but I could feel that there was a change in the room. I peeked out from under the blanket.

Suddenly, the room filled with hundreds of angels and two very tall beings made completely with light. It was such a spectacular sight I had to get my breath. I realized what with these Beings and hundreds of angels flapping around, that we couldn't possibly be in Howard's little Pousada room any longer. But we were.

Xico, I'd like you to meet King Solomon . . .

I crawled out from under the covers and extended my paw, staring with my mouth gaping open. The twenty-foot tall, velvet-robed figure before me looked like a King made of light; his crown was a splendor, gleaming of rubies, emeralds and diamonds. His beard was full, glistening white, flowing to his knees. Under bushy white brows his eyes peered out—a strong, steel blue.

The Voice broke my stare, waving his shining hand in front of my face, ***Earth to Xico.***

Wow, not THE King Solomon!?

One and the same, *said The Voice.*

Gadzooks, I've heard so much about you, your Majesty. I watched a whole TV program about you—it went on for a week. I loved it! How old are you now by the way?

When King Solomon laughed, there was no sound but the air around him undulated in the colors of a many rainbows, I had to blink to stop from tearing it was so magnificent.

Solomon is one of the mightiest holders of energy working for me.

Pleased to meet you, I yipped, turning in circles, 'cause I do that to say hi. My behavior was making Howard clap his hands and shhhhhhh me. The King only smiled.

The other Light Being stepped forward. He was half as tall.

And this is Doctor Enesto Espirito de Águia. He's one of the Entity doctors who uses Seu Miguel's body when he needs to do surgery. Right now he will be working on removing the cancer—cleaning it all out.

How'd the cancer get there?

Many reasons, but mostly because of the stress he put on his body by thinking negatively for so long. He listened to his ego and believed it was his God.

I can understand how he could do that,

Yes, and like I said, human thought is very, very powerful.

How's the Doctor gonna clean out the cancer?

Where he is, he is able to go to that area in the body and match the frequency of the healthy tissue. The body is very smart once it's reminded of the correct frequency. And from where the doctor is, <u>there is no time or space</u>, so the healing can appear to be instantaneous in the physical body.

Wow! So that's how it's done.

Basically, yes. But the human still has choice, and he can change it back if he chooses.

Why would he choose that?

It's complicated... many reasons... it may have to do with the contract he made before he came into this life and what he chooses to learn because of it.

Is that that Karma stuff I hear about around here—

Pay attention now, they want to meet you.

Next to the magnificent king, the doctor looked rather tame. Although he, too, was brilliant with light, his suit was cut like it was from the 1930s, his hair was a glorious mane of white waves but his full mustache made him look much too serious. The doctor looked down at me . . . not a fan of dogs I'm sure.

Pleased to meet you, I said to Dr. Santos. But you're not going to make me do surgery are you? I'm a lot squeamish at the sight of blood. I wouldn't be of any help to you at all . . . zilch . . . nope . . . nada.

Dr. Santos didn't smile; he just waved his hand like he was dismissing me.

Not the friendliest guy, I thought.

The Voice spoke for him, **They have ways other than cutting the flesh. They can do surgery in the Etheric and be just as effective.**

Is that where we are now, in the Etheric?

Both. Howard and you are in the Earth (or the material energy) and the help is coming from the Etheric (or ethers, as it's referred to sometimes.) You see in the reality of Allness, there's no time and space.

Oh, I think I get it now—it all so clear . . . Not!

That's okay, you'll see how it works as we go along.

I snuggled next to Howard, he gave me the best ear rub, looked into my eyes, and told me what a pretty dog I was. What's with the pretty? I'm handsome. I've got a . . .you-know-what.

All along I was looking for any lizards that might have been missed. But suddenly I was getting really sleepy and I could feel Howard was, too.

The Voice continued, **Howard might be feeling a little pain now and then, just depends on how fast his mind can get out of his way and allow everyone to do their work. We're putting you two to sleep right now, get him over to dreamland fast and keep him there, he'll trust a dog to do that. Howard loves dogs—that's to our advantage.**

I just have one question.

Yes?

Are you all going to be doing all that glowing so brightly thing the whole time? I can't sleep with the lights on, that's just how I am.

With that, everything went dark in the room.

Better?

Yep.

Now you might see some bright flashes every so often, that can't be helped. We'll be doing some internal incisions with what looks like a blue laser beam.

No problem.

If you run into any trouble, which you're so good at doing, just remember to call on us . . . because after all you are . . .

A dog . . . I know.

As I dropped off to sleep I had a very strange sensation. I felt I was sleeping next to a part of myself and was now being reunited. I felt like I was complete—I was watching myself watch myself. I entered into Howard's mind like it was my own. It felt very small, teeny-tiny, completely blocked off from the vastness I just left. I traveled around in this space for a while just trying to get used to it, trying not to let claustrophobia take over. It got so that I could hardly breathe—my chest was so tight I had to cough just to get my next breath. I coughed again and again until I realized I didn't need to make the same choices as Howard.

I decided to choose instead . . . relax relax, gotta relax, and next thing I knew, FOW! FOW! FOW! I was being shot like a ball in an Arcade game board into every nook and cranny, into every membrane, into every molecule, into the nucleus of a molecule, into the space between all matter—where once again I could breathe freely in the hugeness and vastness in which I had returned to.

Looking around, I realized I had returned to the place where I lived before I'd come to be a dog, the place where Howard and all souls on Earth all hailed from.

In a split second it was revealed to me what I was to do here . . . I took a deep breath in—let it out—creating a wave in this ocean of life, to keep breathing for Howard until he could remember what he had forgotten: to relax, to accept, to stop choosing to be so small, to be so restricted, to stop choosing to be what some other fractured soul had told him to be. To finally be the soul that he was as he breathed in, breathed out, found the rhythm in the dance of heaven that was his—he and his soul—alone. This wasn't about being a human or a dog; it was about being open to all infinite possibilities.

Then it came upon me, the urge to speak, not in doggy language, but the language he could hear, the language of the Heart. I knew it was the Voice speaking through me, because you wouldn't catch me talkin' so intelligent like. Not in my nature!

What is it that you need? What part of you lives in the dark? *I channeled.*

I heard a child's voice so far away and so weak I had to ask it to speak up. The small voice spoke but it was no louder. It said: My heart. It's so dark down here. I've lost it. I've lost my heart. I've gone to that place where I heard it beating—because that's where it's supposed to be—but I can't find it there.

Help me! Help me, please!

I looked over and I saw a very small five-year-old boy. He was so tiny he could fit in a sewing thimble. The garden around him was dead: tangled and full of thorns. I wasn't feeling all that comfortable there, but I knew it was only an illusion he was living in. An illusion he'd created. Believe me, any minute, I expected to see thousands of those nasty reptiles to come meandering out flicking their nasty split tongues while they screeched.

Let me ask you this: When did you give your heart away and to whom did you give it? *I surprised myself with the questions I was asking and the way I asked them, it was kinda cool being so intelligent.*

The boy started to weep with a man's voice.

Why do you weep, sir?

Taking a moment to calm himself, he said, I-I-I don't' remember.

But my friend, where we are now—this moment in the All of time—you do know everything.

I do?

Open your mind to that possibility and the answer will be yours.

I paused and waited while I saw the boy get to his feet and start running. I raced after, but it seemed we both were running in place. None of the dreary landscape was changing.

I-I-I-can't. I've tried.

Give it a shot.

Why should I, you're only a dog.

He nearly tripped, looking back at me.

I was getting a little winded but managed a mouthful, ***I am that . . . if that is what you choose . . . me to be.***

Luckily, I was able to side-step, just missing him when he suddenly stopped and dropped to his knees, gulping in air from his all-out sprint. I was relentless and pranced over, continuing with my questions.

What if I were a part of yourself, would that make you feel more trusting?

Are you kidding? I'd feel worse. I hate any and all of myself.

Ah, I said, waiting a few beats. Did you hear what you just said?

I heard. My life is a misery, every day I live in hell.

I was still trying to get used to this man's voice coming out of such an innocent-looking child's face.

What would you feel like if you lived in Heaven?

I don't know . . . it's been so long.

If you were able to remember what Heaven was like what would it be?

Leave me alone, go away, you bad doggy!

What if I were to tell you—right here, right now, where it's safe—that it was okay, you could remember anything and you'd be alright.

I'd say you tell fibs. My mommy gets mad at me when I fib.

Okay, you like the game of pretend, don't you?

I watched his child-face light up. Yeah, I'm good at pretend.

Yeah, kids are great at this . . . Let's pretend . . . you have a huge brain, as big as the Universe—

The whole wide Universe?

As big as the Universe . . . and beyond.

Wow! My head would really look weird. I-I'd have a real fat head! He slapped his head and laughed at his joke. Then he laughed harder and threw his head back, I could see his teeth as he rocked laughing and laughing.

I laughed, too. And when he was catching his breath, I said, **What if I told you that your human brain really does contain the Universe just the size it is?**

He was thinking now, smiling, thinking.

Howard, some of your scientists say you only use a tiny part of your brain . . . what about the other ninety-six percent?

The little boy started morphing into a young man, contemplating a much larger question. The garden started to take on faint color and the tangles began to unwind a bit.

I've wondered . . . I've always wanted to know . . . His voice was younger now, much more in keeping with the physical form he was displaying.

What do you think is the answer?

I don't know.

Exactly! That is the correct answer. You don't know. But what do you feel?

I feel like I really want to know.

What if I told you—everything you feel is what your mind already knows.

Then I do know everything.

Are you trying to please me with the answer you think I want? Or do you really believe what you are saying? *At this point, I noticed that I was sounding harsh but I couldn't stop, words were pouring out of my mouth and my voice had suddenly turned into a shrill woman's voice.* **SPEAK UP, YOUNG MAN!** *It was his mother. When she appeared, the young man shrank into the little boy again and started to sob.*

I-I-I don't know . . . what . . . why?

Who are you trying to please? *My voice was normal again, soft, and yet firm.*

The little boy continued, My mommy, my poppy, my teachers. Then his voice became a man's voice, My lover, my friends . . .

How about yourself, how about Howard?

I hate that NAME don't call me that! That was my uncle's name and my grandfather's name . . . when he . . . he molested me. I H-H-H-HATE ME!

How old were you?

His voice once again became a kids voice, shaky and unsure. Five. He hurt me. He's hurting me down there! He's got his hand on my mouth and he's hurting . . . ohhh it hurts so bad . . . NO!

Then the little guy just stared and was silent for the longest time.

Where did you go Howie? I asked after a while cause I was really scared something had happened to him. Again his voice came through, tiny and barely heard. Don't tell Mommy. Don't tell anybody or Grandpa will kill them with a hatchet. He'll cut off their heads and feed them to the dogs . . .

Whew! I had to take a breath cause all the sudden I was as afraid as the little boy . . . I'm a dog, I'd never eat anything that disgusting but never said anything like that. Instead, I drew in a deep breath and said very calmly with a voice that certainly wasn't a dog's . . . It was a voice of The Voice . . . ***Son, It was not your fault when your parents got killed in the flood.***

Grandpa told me! It was all my fault and I would go to Hell! Howard now appeared as a grown man blubbering in his tears and I was a little doggy watching him . . . what was going on?

He'd kill my mommy and my daddy if I told anyone. I didn't tell and they died anyway.

When did they die?

I watched Grandpa and Uncle Howard stab them TO DEATH!

I was really mixed up now . . . The Voice had said they died in a flood and the boy was saying his uncle stabbed them to death.

In a grown man's voice he goes on, Yes, and I'm in Hell and I know who you are . . . you're the devil tempting me.

Softly I asked, Now that you're a grown man, do you think that a five-year-old boy lost in a flood, sitting on the roof, watching as your parents and uncle drown—do you really think that it was your fault?

Aren't you listening, you little mutt? My Uncle stabbed my parents!

Is that really the truth? Think . . . you are on a roof of your house, water all around, your Grandpa is there beside you . . . what is he saying, Howard . . . ?

He's acting crazy! He's yelling at them! He's got an ax in his hand and he's bending over the water yelling for my uncle to grab on . . . my uncle grabs the ax and the ax slips from my grandpa's hand and hits my . . . mother and she goes under the water and my father goes under the water to try and get her and . . .

What? What is happening Howard?

They never come up . . . they never come up.

It's not your fault, little one.

It is . . . it is! I should have . . . I should have pushed my grandpa in, then they would have been safe . . .

He was trying to save your parents, does that make sense?

NO! NO, OF COURSE NOT, he said, red faced with rage, spitting every word. I noticed as he ranted, as he wailed, the garden had unwound itself, was re-growing straight and tall, blossoms becoming brilliant with color.

I sat before him and just wagged my tail. He looked around at his garden and started laughing, deep from his gut, as tears spilled from his eyes.

If you were in heaven and everything was perfect, would you still have to save your parents? *It was The Voice speaking this time and I was so relieved.*

No . . . only me . . .

All your life you've never loved yourself and you've never been able to love anyone else . . . What have you learned, my son?

It really wasn't my fault; there was nothing I could have done. I really have to learn to love myself first . . . before I can ever learn to love others. Yeah...yeah. Then he let out a sigh of relief. He knew that was the truth—the truth that would save himself from himself. Then the man looked at me, and smiled, I'm so tired, I have to sleep now. And he lay down in the soft green grass being blown by a soft breeze.

So I crawled over and snuggled in close to him.

XICO
PARAMANGUAIA, BRAZIL

CHAPTER 33

It was a new day. I was feeling super confident after the successful night with my first patient.

The old man was in the bathroom singing to himself when I went to the door and scratched and whimpered. He thanked me as he opened the door and I raced out. I had to pee something fierce! I gave the courtyard wall a good dousing.

Someone was at the front gate, I could hear it, I could smell it. I was so speedy I couldn't even feel the grass below me. I was on my job. Yessss, I had to announce, to sniff out each and every guest that came through the Pousada gates. I gave myself the job and I took it very seriously.

To my surprise a crowd of small people were arriving—friends of Mariana Vitória and Rafael—boy did they smell sweet: little candy people, my fav. I could dance around and smile, make 'em giggle—I decided that maybe I could take a day off from my duties. I saw all kinds of soft energy whirling around: whoosh, whooshing by. All the bones in my body were happy. I felt fantastic—I'd definitely take the day off.

I circled around exactly seven times and lay down so I could enjoy the whirling energy that bounced off every wall—and every wall had my own pee-smell. The Mosques's Posada was my domain.

I ruled.

I was in my own heaven, just layin' there whiffin' it all in, listening to all the laughter and yam yamyamyam, watching Mariana Vitória putting pointy hats on the little people, Flavia bringing trays and trays of little foods for them to eat, Martim lifting up Rafael like he was a king, flying him around and around in the air like a bird and then landing him there, right on Martim's shoulders way, way up high.

Man, that looked like so much fun, I really wanted to be up there, too. I even jumped up as high as I could get about 9 to 10 times trying to let them know yippinyippin, IwannaIwanna, but that day Rafael was everyone's favorite. Everybody was throwing special good feelings at Rafael and no amount of tricks I could perform made people pay attention to me—well, maybe for a few minutes to say shut up or calm down. What was this? Magic day for Rafael? How did he rate? I didn't get it. Whoooo after a while it was exhausting trying to compete with that little boy person.

Nobody cared about me. Suddenly I felt soooo depressed. After skulking back to my bed and curling up whisper-quiet for awhile, I decided I was gettin' hungry, Mariana Vitória hadn't remembered to feed me—of course. Maybe I'd try that small food. I don't know, it looked like everybody was enjoying it, so why not me? It turns out begging for people food is kinda fun. Sweet food can give you a nice high, yesssss. It can rev you up really high frrrrvvvvvvvoom yesss!!!! Pretty soon I was getting into the kids whirly whirly energy, the more they ate that little sweet food the more they loved to runnnnnnn and jump and yell and scream and heh-heh-heh and I loved the running and yelling and running-around-like-crazy-fast-and—faster-stuff. It felt like I was really back in my element. And I was lovin' chasin' and barkin' at the little bright red energy balls that spewed off their bodies—I'd try to pop 'em with my teeth—

But then I stopped 'cause . . .

'Cause with my very high caliber hearing, over all the yelling and laughing I could hear this creepy deep sounding rrrrrrrr goin' on just outside the Posada gate. When it buzzzzzed, <u>I knew</u> I had to stop all this playin' around and get back in my job mode.

New people were arriving.

Faster than the wind, I was at the front gate . . . heh-heh-heh something was up and I knew it. I got down really low right underneath the gate and sniffed hard— wifffffffft—whatever was on the Otherside of the gate smelled particularly nasty and I could feel that spiky energy.

Tadeu opened the gate. Look out! I did my warning circling exactly 10 times and barking, barking for him to be very, very careful, there were suspicious people out there. But Tadeu didn't stop one-second to ask me what was up, no, he just opened the gate right up. Since he was ignoring me, when I saw my chance I scooted out to see who it was.

There was quite a commotion going on so I protected Tadeu while we watched these two big doors pop open from the back of this huge people car—biggest one I've ever seen—two big shiny red bumps on the roof, windows all round and a bunch of words on the side. A-M-B-U-L-A-N-C-E it spelled. I spelled it but I wasn't much of a reader, The Voice never downloaded instructions. Said no dog ever read so not to worry about it.

Men jumped out of the car-thing, yelling at other men inside who were moving around things that were going bee-beep-beep and little lights were flashing and TV screens were flickering. That patch of hair on my shoulders was standing straight up—something was really wrong.

Then a strange smelling woman stepped out and a tall man with the same smell got out, then this long bed contraption came clang-banging out of the door and its feet popped out and started rolling on the street, then the men inside jumped out carrying some more stuff I'd never seen before.

Now, this man and woman were the kind of people I watch closely and sniff at often because these were the kind—with the nasty smell and spiky black and red colors around them—who can walk around and shoot dark grey-red little barbs of energy out into the air and hook right into someone and start sucking. It was amazing to see their victims grow paler and paler and get so exhausted that they had to excuse themselves to go lie down. Fascinating but frustrating.

Flavia, Martim, and staff were welcoming the smelly man and woman, helping with the luggage, and directing the men with the floating bed toward one of the pousada rooms.

I tried to YipYipYipYip! and warn everyone what the hezzop was going on with these two but—womp, ouch!—I got smacked on my butt and Bad dog, go lay down. Whaaa, don't' they get it? Every time I try to do my job . . .

But, I did not listen, nope, 'cause I had a mission and I would continue to do my job—it is my duty to guard and protect—and you don't know it, folks, but you all are in grave danger here. You don't have a smeller like I have a smeller so get real!

So I didn't go to my bed in the kitchen, not this time, nope. I carried on . . . bravely.

I followed way far behind the group as the spikey people were taken to one of the pousada's rooms. I sneaked into that room on quiet feet careful not to be seen and flattened down under a cot. From there I could catch glimpses of long brown ringlets on the little girl's head, and I could see that her lips were the color of the vanilla cake I'd eaten earlier. That little girl lay so quiet, wrapped in wires and stuff hanging out of her skinny body . . . but . . . then there was another girl standing next to the bed all brilliant with otherworldly color—the girl that was looking right at me and smiling.

I shivered. She seemed so familiar. Somewhere off in a space that wasn't Earth, memories of us playing in a breeze-blown garden off on the Otherside . . . was it? Was it? My heart started beatin' like a crazy . . . Yes, I knew this little girl well, but something was very different about her . . . she didn't smell the same.

LILLIAN AND ABE

Oh my God, Abe, there's a dog under Sabrina's bed. Get that thing out of here before it gives her some strange Brazilian disease. Get him out now!

The lady's anger looked like fire sparks flying everywhere. The man's hand moved into the darkness where Xico hid and chased him from one side of the bed to the other. Then came the broom whishing and prickling—but Xico was still faster.

Call Martim and Flavia, this is disgraceful. What kind of barbaric place is this anyway? Letting dogs in the rooms.

No phones here, Lillian.

Don't you smile at me like that, Abe, go and get them. Please.

I don't want to interrupt their party again. I'll leave the door open so we can scare him out.

XICO/ZEEEP
AND
EEEOO/SABRINA

Little did they know after all I've been through nothing scares me. *I'll stay right here if I choose to. This room's my territory, I've marked it carefully—all the walls and the furniture. What's wrong with people, they should know that they are just guests here.*

The woman stood close to the pale little girl as if to protect her from me. Abraham James, go and get them now! her voice made my hackles shoot up and my lip curl.

After the man left, the mean lady's eyes were hot pokers boring into me as she waited, broom in hand. Suddenly, I thought someone had reached out and slugged me, that's how hard it hit me. It was the very minute the bright shiny-colored little girl crawled under the bed with me, smiling and looking straight into my eyes. My heart started bang bangin' harder and I got all shaky 'cause this amazing vibration roared from her, a wind of familiar feelings, the . . . very same *. . . sonar frequency that Eeeoo pulsated at. . . Eeooo . . . Eeoooo?*

The Voice, who I had not heard from for a long time, unexpectedly broke through, ***Xico, my son—this is Eeeoo.***

I know I know!

You must find a way to stay with the little girl over there on the stretcher. That is Sabrina.

I know I know! But does Eeeooo remember me? Does she recognize me? C'mon c'mon I gotta know.

My tail stub started whipping the floor, I panted so rapidly and my body burned, were my wildest dreams coming true? The bright girl before me, rubbing my head so tenderly was Eeeoo, the love of my life. And the foul smelling woman with the broom, throwing scorching eye-darts at me . . . was Sabrina's mother? And Eeooo was Sabrina and . . .

Oh man.

The Voice went on, **As you know it will be your mission to help this body named Sabrina to heal, or Eeeoo will have to leave and go and start her human life again as someone else.**

What? My hopes were dashed, this job was way over my head. I thought Eeooo and I were to be working together. I can't do this alone. I'm not a healer yet. Seu Miguel's the healer.

Eeeoo is here so you can help her heal Sabrina's body. This is your destiny together, son.

The iridescent girl smiled. I wanted to cry I was so confused. This is not good news. The pressure, I said.

You can do it.

How did you get Sabrina's mother to come all the way to Brazil—this is fantastic.

I didn't. Eeeoo did.

How?

You see, she did research at the Temple of Knowledge on the Otherside before she took the job. She scanned your total life's plan—

My life? How'd she do that?

It was all there in a hologram projector. She found out you'd be working with Seu Miguel down here in Brazil. Eeeoo figured out a way she could get Sabrina's mother to bring her to Brazil by sending an angel with a message to the coffee shop.

Huh? I don't giddit. An angel served Sabrina's mother coffee? How'd anyone ever hire an angel to waitress—I mean the wings alone—

That's not how it went . . .

Oh, soooo Sabrina's mom drinks her coffee and finds this message at the bottom of the coffee cup: Hello, you don't know me, my name is Eeeoo, I live inside your daughter and could you please drag her to Brazil because there's a dog there I need to be with and he'll heal your little girl. Did I get that right?

The shiny bright girl started giggling and said, So it is you, Zeeep! I just knew it, the very same sense of humor!

Eeeoo? My dream really was coming true at last.

Her face glowed as she kissed my forehead and my cheek and my . . . snout. It sure wasn't the same as nuzzling with Eeeoo back in the pond, but as I licked the air, I was enveloped totally in the fiery moment.

Xico!

My bubble popped. Martim's red face was huge before me as his hands pulled me out from under the cot. The bright girl disappeared, POP! Eeeooo! I cried. My heart slammed in my chest, I was in big trouble—again! I would surely be sent to the back room for the duration of their stay, I knew it. I couldn't let this happen—to heal Sabrina was my destiny—Voice! would someone please fill him in fast?

But Martim was taking me out the door under his arm, sayin' So sorry, ma'm, this won't happen again, and there she was again, the bright Eeeoo girl was floating after me, yelling, No! No! And I could feel my heart tearing right in half! I squirmed so hard it felt like my ribs were collapsing. I had to get down, run away and hide, and I had to do it fast.

Then, the bright Eeeoo girl turned and whooshed back to the human Sabrina girl and got sucked into the girl's body.

No . . . no . . . don't—a weak voice was coming from Sabrina, her eyes flickered then opened, looking around, frightened.

The tall man started yelling, Sabrina! God in Heaven you're awake. It's a miracle. Oh God.

The mean woman rushed to Sabrina. She looked like she was afraid to touch her but really wanted to. She looked like she wanted to talk to her, but no words were coming out, just tears and laughter at the same time.

Still carrying me, Martim turned around and went to Sabrina. I looked up at him, he was smiling bigger than I'd ever seen before. Sabrina looked up at me, but in her eyes I could still see Eeeoo. I barked to thank her and Sabrina's sweet mouth said, Chi . . . co . . .

The mean woman gasped, Chico? Chico, who is Chico?

Martim held me up, This is Xico.

This dog?

This dog.

How in the hell would Sabrina know that, Lillian? the tall man asked.

God, it's so strange, Abe. I can't believe Chico was her first word in years. So strange! The woman's eyes were softening as she looked over at me.

Finally Martim formally introduced me, This is Xico. This is our resident healing dog, this is typical of the magic he can perform.

I owe you an apology, said the woman. I'm sorry. I'm usually not this . . . rude to people. I'm a little jet lagged. Abe and I have been snapping at each other the whole trip—we're sister and brother. It's a bad habit. I hope you understand. She threw her hands in the air, Of course Chico can stay.

I knew I was back on the job. I yipped exactly three times to make sure.

LILLIAN

Lillian awoke with a dull headache. She looked around—everything was unfamiliar. She had to concentrate hard . . . Where am I? She sat up, still drugged from lack of sleep, moving her feet to the cold tile—she was used to a thick lawn of soft carpet first thing in the morning. She cradled her head, Where . . . ? Brazil popped into her head. Yes that was it. Brazil. Dread was moving through her body. What was that all about? She wondered. Jet lag, still. Then she realized . . . what was at stake. What if they came all this way, spent all this money, and what if nothing got better?

She stood and stretched hard—yes, she realized, today represented a step off a cliff into the abyss. Sharp doubt filled her mind. Trying to shake the panic and dark thoughts she shuffled to the bathroom with half-opened eyes and asked her reflection in the mirror, what in the heck am I doing here? This is crazy.

What? Abe's voice came from his cot in the other room.

Abe, get ready for breakfast, this is Sabrina's big day, she called out while splashing her face with cold water. She started to brush her teeth, and then stopped short. Oh, God. What had she done? She wasn't supposed to drink the water in Brazil. What about the shower? Should she be careful there, too? This must be what they meant when they talked about culture shock. Everything seemed so unfamiliar. It made her grouchy. She'd have to work on that. But right now she was too exhausted to care.

She massaged her forehead with her fingers and wondered where she had packed the aspirin. Her stomach churned while she considered packing up and getting the hell-out-of-there. What had possessed her to come here? Were they really that desperate?

As she looked in the mirror, she realized that she was seeing the dark, ugly, doubting part of herself. And if she gave this part any more power, there would be no hope for Sabrina. Remember last night? A miracle had already happened. Sabrina had talked for the first time. Martim said last night that this was a place where miracles were a normal way of life and to expect that more miracles were on the way. She remembered she'd read somewhere if you were open to accepting and surrender, then you could allow the miracles to happen.

She forced a smile to her lips and watched the sour image in the mirror transform to someone much more pleasant. What good would ever come from thinking about fear?

She knew would need to prepare her mind for the days to come with prayer and hope—to give this place a chance and do it 150%.

SARGENTO RODRIGUES

A month ago, Sargento Fernando Osvaldo Rodrigues—elaborate braided cords and badges decorating his military jacket—had arrived in a black official SUV, determined to get rid of Seu Miguel once and for all. The streets in front of The Moradia de Dom José de Barros were already lined with police cars, parked defiantly wherever they wished.

Outside the gates, he met with his police corps and gave them their orders: once inside The Moradia de Dom José de Barros they must spread out, make their presence known—intimidation their tactic—when Seu Miguel was deprived of his audience, his practice will disappear. Rodrigues, himself, would go to the center of the hive and stir the bees there.

Rodrigues and his men strode menacingly into The Moradia de Dom José de Barros. Ignoring Armando's questions, Sargento Rodrigues pushed past him and made his way up front to stand before the stage where Seu Miguel, in entity, was doing physical surgery before hundreds of people. The officers stood out in the crowd like black thorns amongst white flowers.

Rodrigues stroked his gun holster as he looked through slitted eyes, X-raying Seu Miguel's every move on the stage. His assignment—to inspect the Spiritist healing center, The Moradia de Dom José de Barros, and devise a way to shut it down. He represented an influential group of jealous Brazilian medical doctors intent on stopping Seu Miguel from practicing. Hefty amounts of money had flowed from their briefcases, all cash—a handshake the only contract

As he observed Seu Miguel make incisions into the skin of a standing patient, the Dignitary watched carefully for any grimace that would reveal pain—he saw no indication. He jotted a note on his pad—*Using illegal drugs*—he wrote, but questioned *how are they still standing*? He looked for guide wires and marveled to himself—*excellent craftsmanship of illusion*—smirking as he wrote, dotting his i's with a loud pop against the paper.

His conspirators had advised him that the negative vibrations emanating from his scrutiny had the potential of being extremely invasive to Seu Miguel's surgery procedure. He knew fear. He knew how to manipulate it. He did it well.

He didn't realize that this tactic posed no threat to King Solomon or the other light beings working from the invisible world—they had ways of containing such energy so that it didn't leak out into the high frequency ethers. They encapsulated it in a bubble of intense light. The white light was a great cleanser and neutralizer—once recycled—it acted as a restorative. What held this energy in place in the physical plane was the abundance of prayer—the two sides working together made it strong.

No, it was Miguel Sousa da Silva, the man that was the possible weak link. When the entities worked, Seu Miguel's soul needed to stay completely away from his physical body and to refuse to engage in any thoughts of fear of any kind. Fear hooked him too close to his physical body. He had to be diligent in keeping his thoughts in incessant prayer—a Christ consciousness always kept him protected in a heavenly perfect state.

The corrupt dignitary didn't know this, of course, but he could sense the potential advantage he had over his opponent. Fear had run rampant for eons—fear served him and his ego—manipulating fear gave him exquisite pleasure . . . even if it were illusionary.

On many previous occasions, these same nonbelievers had employed Sargento Fernando Osvaldo Rodrigues. He'd made an arrest on some trumped-up charge and carted Seu Miguel off to jail right in the middle of many healing sessions, then incarcerated him until his assigned hearing day before the Court. It almost bored him it was so easy. There were many dubious government officials. It was, however, the ones that offered him large sums of money he was interested in, otherwise, he would have been happy to leave the poor man alone. He actually liked Seu Miguel.

When they were younger, the incarcerations had been much worse. Seu Miguel could be imprisoned sometimes for months. Many times he had suffered brutal beatings and witch-hunt interrogations. Thank God, Sargento Fernando Osvaldo Rodriques had only to bring him in. He wasn't sure he could have been so brutal. The last few times he had demanded his clients spare Seu Miguel the brutality, otherwise they could look elsewhere. Of course, he knew there was no place else they could look. He made the decision to plead for Seu Miguel after he witnessed how Seu Miguel had used the opportunity to heal those imprisoned alongside of him. The court had considered such good deeds as evidence for his defense. This had only sent the powers in the medical system into a deeper rage.

Sargento Fernando Osvaldo Rodrigues was in for a surprise when Seu Miguel, still in entity, finished working on his patient. Before moving on to the next patient, he had turned around and spoken directly to the dignitary.

Sir, may we do a healing for you, right now?

The officers in the crowd bristled. They posed for attack. The dignitary blushed, turning around to the crowd and bellowed in a jerky deep voice, Seu Miguel, you know by now that I don't believe in what you do and never will. Besides, I am perfectly healthy. He slapped the side of his pants with the baton he carried and grimaced up at the healer.

Yes, to a certain extent, you are. But what about your blind son?

My son? This was a low blow and he could feel the punch in the core of his stomach. He grabbed both ends of his baton, holding it across his body, and glared.

Seu Miguel went on, His eyes have been affected by a *disease* that took his eyesight at birth. Is this not so?

The Dignitary sucked in his breath, disease? He knew Seu Miguel, the man, knew of his son's blindness, but pointing out that he knew it was the result of a disease was startling.

You see Rodrigues, where we are, we can see everything. And from where we are, we can see how to make changes to give your son his eyesight back.

The man stammered, I-I-I don't know what method you use to ascertain this information but I'm not pleased that you feed on people's most intimate weaknesses. That, sir, is the WORK OF THE DEVIL, and what you are doing is JUST THAT! I'm here to expose you for what you are. Turning with a stamp, he pompously marched right through the audience with a stone-cold look that masked the hurt that had bludgeoned his heart every day of his life since his son was born. There was a possibility that, in front of all these people, Seu Miguel could expose a sexually transmitted disease he had given his wife. Then came a familiar horror of a thought, *it's my fault my son is blind.*

Hurting as he was, he became more than ever intent on getting Seu Miguel now.

On his way out he stopped and watched a small boy being wheeled in on a chair, soon to be worked on by Seu Miguel. The something that stopped him, somehow stopped his anger too—the boy was the same age as his son and a resembled him closely. He lifted his chin, set it hard and disguised his fascination as he returned to the hall to watch what Seu Miguel would do with this child.

After he released his troops, Sergeant Hernando Oswego Rodrigues had intended to drive straight back to Brasilia, but a broken drive-train in his SUV changed his plans.

Martim put his head under the hood to help him try to find the problem even though he would have liked to thrash him—good thing he hadn't been brought up that way. Instead, he called a mechanic friend and arranged for their meeting.

Sargento Fernando Osvaldo Rodrigues thought about having dinner at the local market, then decided to find a place to stay first. He had asked the mechanic which was the best and cleanest Pousada available. Martim's was the best.

As he entered Pousada Raiar do Sol (Martim's hostelry,) Flavia Mosques greeted him as she did most everyone—like an old friend. But when Martim returned from working with Seu Miguel, he recognized this unpleasant man who had made such a scene that very afternoon, the man he'd helped under his SUV's hood. He was about to approach him and ask him to leave until he found him off in a corner of the grassy courtyard stroking and baby-talking with Xico.

Martim had a gut feeling that there were invisible elements at work and that he'd better leave well enough alone. He watched the dignitary head off toward his room and Xico follow close behind wagging his tail. As Sargento Fernando Osvaldo Rodrigues put the key in the lock, Xico was leaning against his leg.

XICO
JUNE 2002
(THE MORNING AFTER SABRIA'S ARRIVAL)

Hey, some hero I am. I got put out last night to go take a dump and I didn't get invited back into Sabrina's room. I scratched, but I think they were sleeping too hard to wake up. But I'm not stupid. Got it all figured out. I've poised my little body right up against the door and the nano-second they open the door: Whoops, oh gosh, there's that little Xico dog, oh my, isn't that cutest thing? C'mon in, Xico. See how that works?

So here I am, a friggin' doorstop.

ABE

Abe stepped into his pants. He needed an excuse for air. And . . . he'd have to find another bathroom, his sister had locked the door.

I'll bring you some coffee, he yelled to Lillian and opened the door for his escape just before Lillian yelled behind him, Please come back soon, I need help dressing Sabrina before we go. Ignoring her, Abe mindlessly stumbled over the deep-sleeping Xico—propelling the little terrier to his feet and down the hallway—with dramatic yips of pain.

Dammit, Abe said with no remorse. He had decided that the miracle he'd seen last night was coincidence. He had no respect for this mutt—a so called miracle-worker. Hogwash.

As he headed down the hallway, he noticed high windows and flowers in pots hanging along the walls. Nice touch, he thought as he made his way to the dining room filled with people all dressed in white. They were standing in line helping themselves to a buffet of breads, breakfast cereals, fresh fruit, and pastries.

Abe glanced at scrambled eggs, sautéed zucchini, baked tomatoes, pan-potatoes. Nothing there interested him. So he strode straight to the coffee as he planned his cigarette on the patio, hoping he wouldn't run into any f lack from these healthy-minded freaks.

Outside, his first puff was heaven. It had been nearly 24 hours since he'd had his last hit. The plane ride and being around all of Sabrina's equipment had demanded a detour from his habit—the wait had been hell. He took another drag and coughed it out. Once he felt relief from the pain in his lungs he contemplated asking Seu Miguel to help release him from this addiction, but he didn't want to get his hopes up. No, this was Sabrina's time, not his—besides what in the world would he do once he returned to New York? It was an urban custom and he really didn't want to segregate himself from all his friends.

He watched a white-bearded man dressed in white, cross the yard coming straight toward him. Abe wanted to get up and leave rather than start a conversation. He knew they had nothing in common until he saw the man pull a cigarette from his breast pocket and dangle it in his lips while he searched for matches.

Gotta light, sir?

Sure. Abe flicked his 24K gold lighter holding it out.

Wasn't sure we could smoke around here, but I thought if I were part of a united team, I bloody hell could get away with it, he said with an English accent.

I figured Martim wouldn't say anything, said Abe, The Germans here would kill him rather than go without.

Bravo. The bearded man savored his inhale, holding it before releasing.

What are you in for?

Beg pardon?

Your reason for coming?

Oh. I'm dying. Not a blame thing he can do for me.

Nothing?

Quite.

Then why did you come?

Why? His eyes looked faraway.

Yeah, I mean if he can't help you . . .

Well, old man, I figured if he was getting help from the Otherside, then he should know how to help me to get over there in peace.

Otherside?

Right, it's my understanding that's where we all go when we croak.

We go someplace when we die? I thought this was it. We live, we die.

We don't really die.

You know that for a fact? Abe was seriously debating if he wanted to continue this conversation.

Quite a fact, chum.

How? Curiosity had grabbed him.

I've already died once.

Really?

Right so. Had a heart attack. They rushed me to the hospital and I could hear the blokes hitting on my chest and yelling to one another for this and that. I had tried to tell them I couldn't bloody breathe but not a word could they hear—I couldn't move one thing in my whole body. I remember thinking, By God, this is it. I'm bloody dead here.

You see that light, like they say?

Not sure about the light, but I saw a lot of strange patterns and symbols. Blokes made of bright white light of some sort. Then there were a lot of questions. Lots of voices. Telling me . . . go back, George. Had me a daughter. She bloody needed her father. She was hopped up on drugs of all kinds. Don't know how . . . Don't know how I suddenly knew . . . knew how I could help my little girl. I was shown the future. Given all the answers—right there in this huge room of some sort. Next thing . . . I was back in that body racked in pain.

So you think you got this information from . . . the Otherside?

Quite so.

And your kid?

She's now a nurse in the homeless shelters, helping others get off the stuff.

Nice story.

Bollocks . . . and I sleep bloody well, to boot.

XICO

After the rude awakening this morning, I was back with a vengeance—on a mission, I was. Putting one paw in front of another real soft, all sneaky cat-like, I dropped to my belly and started crawlin'. Friggin cold floor was scratchin' like crazy but I was on this maneuver: focused, unstoppable. Slowly I inched my eyes around the door so I could see where Sabrina was. I had to catch my breath the moment I saw her, she was sooooo pretty—like a little angel. Her Mom was sitting her up like a rag doll dressin' her in a white frilly dress. I looked high, low, side-to-side, didn't see the girl made of colored light so I guessed she'd gone back into Sabrina's body to stay.

Uh, oh. Footsteps, clickie-click down the hall. Got back on my cat feet and and slipped back into my hidin' place. Waited . . . knew there would be the right time to put my plan into effect: if I stayed out of sight I could stay real close to Sabrina, follow her to the Moradia. That was my plan . . . until . . .

The men, same ones as last night, pushin' a gurney, went right into Sabrina's room and then whisked her right outta there faster than grass through a goose, in this two-wheeled chair contraption I'd never seen before. It was choked full of all kinds of machinery hangin' and clanking. I had to follow super-duper careful . . . could get stuffed in a room somewhere if they'd a caught me (they do that when they think I'm a bad dog.) No. you gotta be smart around here or you can end up . . . well let's just say—you have to be really smart to <u>get out</u> of some of those situations you end up in.

Okay, I was up, runnin' headon. Dikdik they were fast these guys, What?! Oh, man. Didn't think they'd get that apparatus through the door quite so quick. The door smacked me right in my face—missed by a mere mega-fraction . . . fitzbit!

Plan B. This one I've used a lot. I ran to the front door and started to act as crazy as I could: yipyipyipyipyip I'd say, panting hard, turning exactly seven circles, before the reverse seven—it always gets attention. So I put Plan B put into effect, I was killing myself . . . but nada, nitch . . . nothin'. Rats! I had to get through that door, dikdik!

I looked around. Everyone had their attention on something else. Why is it? When you don't want to be seen, all of a sudden, everyone's got this super vision. But when you need attention, everyone becomes instantly blind.

Sos I kept it up, it had to work, there was no plan C. I was whippin' around in circles like crazy and mid-circle when I spot two hot-lookin' young women I knew, crossin' the yard toward the door. They always liked me. Always cooin' 'n' makin' these kissie noises every time they'd see me. (Quite embarrassing, however, when I'm trying to create an impression of dignity, which I try to do . . . being the resident healer, and all.)

See, I'd spent healing nights with these fine ladies when they first arrived—which led them, I'm sure, to believe we were tight. Not really. I thought they were silly. Heck, they really didn't take any of my, or Seu Miguel's work, seriously. Like after having their invisible surgery, they'd stayed up all day talkin' and playin' cards rather than sleepin' for 24 hours like Armando told them to. Invisible surgery is sometimes harder on people than the visible surgery because they can't see any incision, can't feel the kind of pain they'd feel if they were in one of those hospitals where most people go. But if they could see on the inside of their bodies like I could, they'd sure as hezzop know better. There is an incision. It's just on the inside where no one can't see it, man.

Armando always tells everyone the rules for surgery: sleep 24 hours and have someone bring you meals, no pork, no alcohol, no coffee, and no sex. One of the ladies didn't listen, had sex, and started hemorrhaging that night. That's when I was given the assignment to stay next to her, so the entities could re-do the surgery and stop the bleeding. It was my job—glad to do it.

So all of a sudden I had an idea! I could use my connection to these ladies to my advantage. They owed me a favor, big time. So I circled exactly 14 times (7 times counterclockwise, 7 clockwise) and barked 21 times exactly right at their feet, (so dikdik obvious) until—guess what?

It worked. They opened that door and let me out. Yesssss!

Freeeee again.

Once outside, I flew down the road to the Moradia. My feet goin' so fast I swear, couldn't feel 'em even touch the ground—don't think they actually did—going so fast—Uh oh, horse pulling cart—head for their feet, dodge right, left! Dikdik, she's freaked out. I'm running out in front of her, thinks I'm a big fast rat or something, she's rearing-up, sets the cart whole on its side. I can't look back, Eeeeeug. Crashin. Bangin.' Nasty sound. I left behind a bunch o' faint cursing in Portuguese and the poor horse screamin' back in the dust, made note I'd apologize the next time I saw her, but right now, Sabrina needed me. This time I would be there for her. I would remain true to my promise no matter what. Nope. I no longer was the slovenly brat dolphin that didn't care about anything. I was a dog, learning to be responsible. I had a purpose and a debt to pay. I had an important job and I would do it for Eeooo—er—Sabrina.

Finally, I came peeling around the corner—The Moradia de Dom José de Barros ahead—I see that my job was not going to be easy, having to make my way through hundreds and hundreds of people. I'm pantin' hard but I have to find Sabrina in this crowd. Weaving in and out of a forest of feet, lookin', sniffin', lookin', sniffin', can't find Sabrina's sweet scent. Boy, if people walked down at the level I walked, they'd be appalled at the stench. Lucky for them . . . they have been spared . . . and that's all I have to say about that.

I'm lookin' for wheels, wheels wheels wheels—nope, nope nope. Shebit. Keep lookin. Wheels? Big wheels. Hey . . . right here! Huge wheels. Two. Same kind of chair as Sabrina's. Got up on my hind legs, looked around, nobody there. Quickly assessing the situation, I decided I'd just wait for her return. She had to return. Probably in the potty. I was feeling pretty happy and kinda cocky that I'd fooled everyone until I saw this HUGE, and I mean HUGE, man lumbering toward the chair, THEN it dawned on me . . . this chair didn't have gadgets! How could I have been so stupid. Stupidstupidstupid. I got outta there way-fast 'cause when he sat down so hard I knew it was going to fly out from underneath him and propel the object out over the yard, over the hedge, over the hill, into outer space. Didn't happen, (except in my mind) but that chair sure creaked loud.

I had to wind down. I was hurtin' bad for two reasons, first, it wasn't Sabrina's chair and second, I had lost good time. I was beatin' myself up big time. I didn't need to be slacking (once again) on the job. I was so nervous I'd be late again. I started pantin' fast. Shaking really hard—a pathetic nervous MESS until I decided that was not what I was about . . . I collected myself . . . I scanned the courtyard with laser focus: man,man,fatwoman, man,womanwithlittleboy, skinnywomanwithwoman and manwithatallman, young girlswithwoman . . . there! I'd seen a small red wheelchair filled with equipment behind it, and brown, flowing locks of beautiful hair—SABRINA—I'd finally found SABREEEEENA.

My heart was pounding as hard as my paws were, she was being pushed through the door into the Meditation room, going directly to the place where Seu Miguel was. I sailed across the cement walkway, whizzed my way through the human feet, upstairs, over the stage, down stairs, just in time to squeeze through the doors before they shut. I had to be careful because I was panting so hard people would hear me, so I tried hard not to open my mouth too wide, keep it shut. I stealthily managed my way directly to Sabrina's dangling hand and licked it exactly 2 times before I heard her say, Chico! Oh, God. Shhhhhh Sabrina, I thought. But then, I was just where I needed to be, I'd be okay, until I felt a large hand encircle my body—lifted up, up—whirled me around and tossed me out the door from whence I'd come.

MIGUEL SOUSA DA SILVA

Seu Miguel slipped into his crisp white shirt, pulled on his white gabardine slacks and stepped into his worn sandals—the uniform requested by the entity doctors. He had a haunting feeling today was going to be intense. Something lurked in the back of his mind, pulling tight the muscles in his neck like a vise-grip. Would this be the day the police would arrive? Armando would be holding back the crowds and sending out his scouts and would not start the session until he was satisfied the corrupted officials were not anywhere on the premises.

As SeuMiguel left the house and walked across The Moradia de Dom José de Barros's lawn, feeling the dew moisten his toes through the gaps in his sandals, his nervousness left. He remembered last night, when he had been introduced to a small paraplegic child in a coma, and her family, who had just flown in from America—such a sad case, such a beautiful little girl. He almost wished that he could remain conscious so he could observe this healing. However, when he lent his body for the entities to use, he had no recall when he claimed it back for his own. This was the downside to his work—not remembering.

He could sense the scorch of the day ahead as he walked into the early morning light in the courtyard and then into the cooling shade of the waiting area. Being here before the people who were starting to congregate just outside The Moradia de Dom José de Barros's walls came in was a refreshing time for Seu Miguel to observe and appreciate all that had been created for him. He leisurely took the steps up, up, one by one, onto the stage where he would be addressing everyone before going into trance.

He looked out over the waiting benches. Everything was neatly in place. Armando had done a great job. The video cameras stood silently waiting for their photographers to arrive—their jobs were to record everything during the healing session so Seu Miguel could review them. It was always amazing for Seu Miguel to watch himself afterward, implementing surgical impossibilities one after another—miracles everyone called them—and he always looked forward to this at the end of the day.

As Seu Miguel and the staff viewed the footage, there was always a small feeling of disappointment that hid in the back in their minds because video cameras hadn't been able to capture the Otherside. Except for—look at that, did you see it? a rare flash of light that looked like a temporary camera malfunction. Now, with the digital video camera, an orb or two would fly through the picture but it would be so quick that the eye wouldn't see it unless the image was slowed down during reviewing. Also, if an observer knew what they were looking for—Look! Look to the right, up there in corner . . . another one next to it, see it, over there, right there!—an orb, or a number of orbs could be seen hovering for a few minutes then instantly disappear—even misty outlines of the Entity doctors sometimes could be seen. God in heaven, that's them, that's them walking through the picture! That was always an exciting moment for Seu Miguel and the crew. Their discussion would focus on the possibility of technology eventually advancing so much that indeed the Otherside could and would be vividly recorded. Seu Miguel secretly included this wish in his evening prayers.

Armando came running in. There were police all over the parking lot, what should he do?

Talk to them—ask them why they've come.

I did. They said that they want to arrest you.

Why this time?

Someone complained.

Who? . . . No . . . ask them in after my lawyer arrives—

I'm having trouble getting—

Do the best you can. Have Martim stall them . . .

How?

How . . . how—here's how . . . no, I've changed my mind. Don't stall them. Have the official in charge come in, as a guest of honor. Tell him that I want him to see everything for himself. Invite him to sit right next to me as I work.

Armando wiped his brow with the back of his hand. Do you think that's wise?

Tell him . . . I have nothing to hide. I have not had time to prepare any deception, not that I would . . . no, you find a better way of wording it.

I'll tell him but I don't think it's going to deter him at all.

I can't be arrested, I have too much work, too many people . . . Then he stopped, pulled into a idea, I don't know why I haven't thought of this before, make sure two video cameras are shooting in case there's trouble, then we'll have it all on tape.

Don't worry I'll handle it. You just get ready.

I will. I will . . . SeuMiguel watched Armando leave. Would this be the best way to deal with the police? It was relatively easy with doctors, as they knew what to look for. But a diligent doubter has an agenda, and agendas always bend the truth to fit their inexorable judgment. Maybe he had made a mistake.

Seu Miguel walked around the waiting area looking at the fading photos displayed on the newly whitewashed clay walls. They had captured everything on a common 33-millimeter camera, wasn't this enough proof? The most impressive were the pictures blotted out by the Entities' flashes of light, bleaching a large portion of the picture and obscuring parts of the patients' image. In his favorite picture, the patient was sitting, while he in entity, was doing surgery on the woman. His eyes in the photo were peering upward, seemingly looking at nothing. Seu Miguel would give anything to know what the entities were seeing through his eyeballs. He smiled knowing that would be a perpetual mystery because the entities never shared anything with him—the lowly mere man that he was.

Seu Miguel sat down on one of the benches putting his head in his hands. It was this lowly mere man, not the Entities, who went to jail . . . repeatedly. It was he, who would be beaten.

He put himself in the minds of the people who waited for him to arrive, into their anticipation, their hope, their fears. These were the people that appreciated and respected his work. They made him brave. He had known poverty—intimately—as a youth. He knew disease—and how it devastated the poor.

There were those, however, who hated, feared, or were jealous of his work. The larger than life-size photo—the one that showed him helping a very old woman to walk—brought on a chill of dark memories. Not too long ago, someone had copied the photo, superimposing a young, naked woman over the old one. It ran it in the newspaper with a fictitious, scathing story: Seu Miguel dos Milagres has been caught molesting this innocent, young lady and this was the undeniable proof. He had been thrown in jail because of it. That day Armando had called all voluntary mediators together in the big hall and asked them to pray to the Entity Doctors and the Master

Entities: King Soloman, Buddha, Radah and Krishna, Mohamed, Isaac Ben Halevi, Abraham, Saint Rita of Cascia, and their greatest amigo Jesus the Christ and any others they could think to call—they wanted help to find a way to get him released from jail. Armando spoke the prayer saying, This is a call to the deepest Loving we can find when situations like this happen to our Seu Miguel dos Milagres. Peace be still in every soul's heart. Amen.

The people had meditated for hours—turning into days—while Martim contacted past patients all over the world via the Internet asking them to pray with the same intention. Within the week, Seu Miguel's lawyers were able to find the young woman and ask her the truth about what had happened. She confessed that she was very poor and was prostituting herself to support her family. Some men had approached her offering her *muito dinheiro* to pose nude for a photo. The fee had helped her take care of her family for months. She was appalled when she found her body plastered all over the newspapers, for she had great respect for Seu Miguel and had taken her son to see him on occasion. She was always appreciative he charged no fee when the medical doctors would not help her without paying.

She agreed to publicly tell her story and clear everything up.

Seu Miguel was released but was reprimanded and warned that the authorities would continue to watch him 24-7. One day he <u>would</u> slip-up and the next time he was incarcerated, they would surely deposit the damn key in the nearest river.

Was Seu Miguel a risk to medical professionals because he charged no fee and was able to do what they were not? Was it because he was just a bricklayer, an owner of a mine and a tailor—a man who held no credentials and knew nothing about surgery?

He was just an ordinary man who smoked and drank and loved all women—especially his wife. He'd never professed himself to be a guru or a spiritual leader, only a spiritual servant, giving permission to etheric doctors to animate his body to do their work.

Though he knew he was always in danger, nothing could stop him from being dedicated and committed—and, yes, protected by the omnipresence of the Otherside.

* * *

Where was Armando? What had happened?

He glanced at his watch and saw it was time to head for his office and meditate—the people would be finding their seats now. Hopefully, Armando was able to do his job with no problems.

Once inside, he sank into his overstuffed leather chair and with a few deep breaths he was able to let the relaxation pour over his body . . .

* * *

Seu Miguel, we're ready for you to lead The Lord's Prayer. Armando's voice came through the door.

Come in here.

Yes, sir.

Well . . . ?

Armando took a deep breath and sighed. I couldn't convince them, they're stationed throughout the room, people are very nervous.

Seu Miguel stood, feeling lightheaded, but knowing that was surely an indication that he was about to leave and give over his body. Well, we'll proceed as normal; the entities will find a way to deal with it.

Martim and Armando took their positions on each side of Seu Miguel and led him from the room in case he lost his balance and fell. They never knew just when the entity doctors would enter his body, and sometimes when Seu Miguel left, there was a period of imbalance until the entities could establish their domain. It was rare, but Armando and Martim were always there to support him, just in case. And this was such an occasion, for Seu Miguel indeed did stumble—the entities had decided they themselves would be leading The Lord's Prayer today: the room's energy had to be raised to the maximum, and specific instructions to the meditators had to be given, not to mention a special message to the dubious law enforcement officers.

When Miguel Sousa da Silva's spirit left and floated to the side of the stage, he was met by a dozen protective light beings and taken to a space in a dimension where he would wait in safety. On the Otherside, Seu Miguel's spirit had to be just as careful. There were energies there too—dis-incarnate spirits who would take advantage of his soul if he were careless and not mindful of creating a vehicle of the highest frequency of light to surround him. These dark spirits were capable of creating immense havoc in the life of a medium, sending out their Aka cords of light with barbed ends that could lodge themselves in the energy field of the unsuspecting—enabling them to feed their victim negative, destructive thoughts that could prove fatal to that spirit and to others he came in contact with. Seu Miguel's earthly weaknesses put him at risk. However, because of the fine work he did, his guides and teachers on the Otherside had managed to band together a great arsenal of Archangels to stand by in constant vigil.

ABE

Sitting in the diverse audience, Abe suddenly felt like he'd been trapped. Everything appeared so plebeian to him. What was this hogwash he was watching? There were little TVs on the walls in the waiting area where hundreds of people could view videos of Seu Miguel doing surgery on people, fully clothed, standing on their feet with their eyes closed, their shirts pulled up to where the incisions were being made and not one of them was feeling a knife going through their stomachs. Wonder how much Seu Miguel and his cronies paid these people to fake all this? Hell that was easy: Brazil keeps their people in great poverty so they can control them, everyone knows that. All this had to be propaganda to get people to believe. Anyone with a background in medicine would and should be insulted to the core. Which he was.

Abe scratched his head, it suddenly itched. Anger rose up through him and enough to want to stand up and yell Charlatans!. He would have phoned the police if his cell phone had gotten reception here. No wonder they have The Moradia de Dom José de Barros here in a third world country so far away from civilization. Fine setup. But not smart enough for a healthy, intelligent person with a sense of scrutiny. No Abe, he thought to himself, if you were really smart you'd be very quiet, go along with everything, make notes, look for mistakes that would finally expose the real truth of this corrupt organization. Then you could call the police the first time you had a chance. Hell, call the FBI . . . or just who do you call in another country?

He had to admit this was new territory for him—espionage. Oh, poor Lillian. She'll be devastated. All these people will. Heck, what about me? What about the shit-load of money I dropped on this little excursion?

Everyone came here with such hope. But it's got to be done. People will have to live with the fact that no one has a white steed galloping into their lives to save them. No such thing. The only thing Abe hadn't yet figured out was why Seu Miguel was not charging for his work. Maybe he was using guilt. He must be receiving large donations from churches or corrupt organizations. Something wasn't right. Look at the walls covered with pictures of Seu Miguel and the Pope, Seu Miguel and the Dalai Lama, Seu Miguel and famous celebrities from Europe and South America, hell even Russia. Fakes, probably. But, if they were real . . .

Abe was going to have to toss that around for a while. Meanwhile, he'd play along with all of this hoo-hah and then he'd find an ingenious way of lowering the boom. He'd call Bob—pump him for information. He knows more than he's letting on. After all, he's in Rio right now.

LILLIAN, ABE AND SABRINA

Armando opened the door and smiled down at the child tucked deep in the gadgetry that surrounded her. Come this way, he said, smiling at Lillian and Abe as they pushed the equipment-float through the room. On both sides, six rows deep, people praying and meditating sat dressed in white. Lillian felt embarrassed by how out of place Abe looked in his green Boston Celtics T-shirt. Armando had asked everyone in the orientation meeting the night before to wear white as the entities had said that any other color confused their energy work. The only color allowed in the room other than white and the paintings on the walls were the waist-high blue walls. The entities had instructed on this as well.

Lillian couldn't help herself from fighting tears—tears of fright and tears brought on by being in such intensely moving energy. She didn't think of herself as being sensitive at all, so when she was sensing all these new feelings flowing through her body she could hardly get her breath and had to lean on Sabrina's wheelchair so she wouldn't fall. Even though Lillian felt uncomfortable in the new environment, she couldn't help but be touched by such devotion to the healing of desperate people. She knew they had been sitting for hours since 8 AM, it was hot, and it wasn't exactly comfortable on steel chairs and benches. This indeed seemed like a church of some kind, but she couldn't figure out which. There were pictures of Jesus putting a long arm around bearded men dressed in the white coats of a doctor. This must be the painting of the disembodied doctors that worked their magic through Seu Miguel. She had to admit if she hadn't brought her daughter here as the last chance to heal, she'd have judged the place to be full of crazy people doing crazy things and would have turned on her heels with indignation and left in a huff. She was amazed at how humble she felt, amazed at how loved she was by complete strangers, and how nearly everyone in the room felt like her family, a family of oneness with love.

She looked at her brother and knew by the hardness in his eyes he wasn't experiencing the same blissful feelings. She'd never seen his face so dark and rigid . . . not even when he was under work pressure. She almost couldn't recognize her brother, he'd changed so . . . why?

SEU MIGUEL

Seu Miguel was helped to the stage, as the audience grew hushed. From Seu Miguel's body came a voice—deeper, stronger than Seu Miguel's—Dr. José Lacerda de Adão Santos *(Dou-tor shJos-ae Laser-da Ja-dow Sant-tus)* a famous Brazilian doctor who had died only recently after establishing Matria de Energia *(Ma-tree-a de Ener-shjeee-a)* a mediumistic rescue work, in a Spiritist Hospital in Porto Alegre. A visitor—this doctor wasn't normally an entity who worked through Seu Miguel, but today his special talents would be needed.

Speaking from the Otherside through Seu Miguel, the doctor said, Dear Souls, thank you for your help. You are always crucial to the work we do, and for this we are always grateful. First, we would like the experienced meditators to be seated in the first and third meditation rooms. It is essential that you do not—repeat—do not open your eyes at any time during this session. To do so, will not only dissipate the energy but you may expose yourselves to the antics of dark entities that I and the other doctors are dislodging from the patient. These entities may have been connected to the body being healed for many lifetimes and have contributed to the weakening of the body by controlling their thoughts and actions.

People of all ages and races took their places in the meditation rooms—many had traveled from remote countries, others from Brazilian cities, or the next town or even from across the road. Some were there for the first time to be healed while others had become residents in Paramanguaia so they could volunteer their time every day.

Seu Miguel was helped to sit in his leather chair (a replica of the one in his office) in the third and largest meditation room. Beside him, on a table covered with white linen, stood a statue of St Francis of Assisi and a foot-high clear quartz crystal Point—a thing of great beauty holding rainbows of intense colors within its hexagonal structure. This particular crystal was found in the depths of Seu Miguel's own mine and was selected by the entities as a tool to help them do their work. Behind Seu Miguel's head hung a painting of the first Doctor in Entity, Dom José de Barros, dotted with orbs of golden light while holding a turquoise healing triangle, and above his head he was surrounded by the blue, cloaked arms of Jesus with his enormously kind eyes. To Seu Miguel's left, hung a glowing portrait of St. Rita, the patron saint of the destitute, and to his right, portraits of the entity doctors when they were incarnate.

Seu Miguel's possessed voice continued, A very young child has come here today, she has a nonfunctioning body that has chosen to remain in coma state for many years. We will help her to rebuild her vehicle so that she may be able to use it again. Please bring her here now.

Armando rolled Sabrina in her wheelchair, followed by Lillian and Abe. Abe and Lillian were directed to stand on either side of Sabrina while Seu Miguel rose and started snapping and clapping around Sabrina's body.

We are clearing the entities that are attached to her now, he said, and then his voice sped up so quickly that the words were not understandable. More clapping and snapping while his voice rose in what sounded like a command, snap, clap, clap—these entities will leave their habitation in this body NOW! . . .

Sabrina's eyes closed, her body went limp and her body started shaking. Lillian gasped and had to be held up by an assistant — what was happening to her daughter? Even Abe was ashen grey and fighting to stay on his feet. Armando and Martim had rushed to each side of Sabrina and were holding her through the convulsions until at last she was calm and sitting up straight on her own—then her eyes opened again.

The doctor entity completed his directive, And return to where they have originated—with the purest of Light, the purest of vibration—merging once again in God's Perfect Realm. (More clapping,) SO BE IT. IT IS SO! (CLAP!)

Seu Miguel's body returned to his chair. When seated, he suddenly grew limp—Dr. José Lacerda de Adão had left. Just as suddenly, another voice boomed through, and Seu Miguel's eyes, possessed by another Doctor, fiercely searched the meditation room. Where is our resident healing dog? Who is stopping him from being here? He is to be here, this is a command.

Armando and Martim quickly left the room. A shock-wave of intense energy ran through the room, the meditators moved in their seats, they wanted to open their eyes but knew they could not. Some of the meditators were professional clairvoyants who could see into the Otherworld in their mind's eye—they were able to observe the vivid, wild colors that were exploding like fireworks on stage, radiating from an extremely tall figure—from their past experience they knew this entity was the ancient King Solomon. Whispers and gasps ran through the crowd ... It's him . . . King Solomon.

XICO

The door opened and there stood Armando, hands on his hips. I knew I was in trouble—so I ran—fast. I knew if he caught me there would be no way that I'd get in to be with Sabrina.

Someone catch that dog! he yelled. Just as I was making my get-away, another man magically reached out and I flew right into his hand—his other hand grabbed onto my collar and I knew I was a goner. The collar was always the ultimate trap and there wasn't much a little body of mine could do from that point on—but I squirmed and squirmed until I couldn't squirm anymore. The man's voice was saying, stopitstopitshhhhhhishyou'realright you'realright but I couldn't hear a word 'cause I was way too busy. The more I squirmed the tighter I was being pinned in these huge man arms, tight up against his belly, and I knew right then and there I was not going anywhere from there.

Finally, I gave up. I had to. I was slobbering and panting so hard my heart was going to pop. I had to calm down! It would be temporary, believe me, until I could figure out something else. But to my surprise as I looked up, the man was smiling down at me. And it was Martim's arms I was in. Oh, fitzbingbong was I ever in trouble now! How could the Powers-That-Be allow this to happen to me? I was a hero back at the pond. I was loved at the Moradia. I was a dignitary, a prince of light on a souls mission, and how was I being treated? Like shebit! Sabrina was with Seu Miguel right now, where I was supposed to be. I managed a little tired try at escape but to my surprise, Martim (Mart-cheem) and Armando were very happy to see me. They petted and ooogled me... What the fiztbingbong was up? I was finally being carried through the meditation door! Yes, it was true ... I was to be with Sabrina at last. All-lay-looo-yah!

SABRINA

Lillian sat trembling in her chair—Abe finally had to be lowered to a seat as well. Martim entered the room carrying Xico in his arms. Like a quick transfusion of energy had occurred, Xico bounced out of Martim's arms and landed on the f loor—running. He sprinted for Sabrina and jumped up on her lap—kiss-licking all over her face. He was with his true love at last. He had accomplished the first step of his task. He knew a lot more was to come and *I'm ready as hezzop!*

Sabrina laughed and cuddled Xico in her arms. She was so happy to see him. And a blanket of warmness was encircling her in a strange way—like little fingers were touching and pinching her softly all over, inside and out. She was becoming groggy, sounds were warping, distorted, but she remained vaguely aware of everything around her. Xico—as though he had been commanded from another place—curled up in her lap and immediately went to sleep. Sabrina and Xico were wheeled closer to Seu Miguel. He released some of the tubes in her body that were connected to the chair's equipment—and none of the alarms went off.

Abe became gradually aware of a funny sensation—something like what he remembered feeling during an electrical storm he had witnessed during his childhood. He was on the edge of his seat, ready to spring to action—this was all making him very uncomfortable.

Armando, as directed, leaned Sabrina forward in her seat and held her forehead while a female staff member lifted her t-shirt to expose her spine. Seu Miguel, looking out into space, made incisions—in the exact areas that Abe had been treating, *how in the hell did he know to do that without x-rays? What is he using as a scalpel?* Abe couldn't quite make it out, but he did see hat it looked as though . . . *strange . . . it looks like he's using . . . what is that? A blue laser beam?!* Abe realized he was sweating profusely as he witnessed only tiny drops of blood where Seu Miguel worked, and yet, Sabrina showed no signs of pain. *Was it sleight of hand?*

Looking up at Abe as though he had heard him thinking, Seu Miguel's entity said, Doctor, will you please come forward for a closer inspection?

Abe stood and was directed to take a key position, one that a supervising doctor would take in a normal operating room, and was encouraged to touch the wounds. He was impressed with the precision—then suddenly shrank back—he had just broken a cardinal rule and perpetrated an open wound without scrubbed hands in a sterile glove.

Seu Miguel smiled and the Spirit Doctor spoke through him, There has never been an infection reported in all the 40 years we have been working through Seu Miguel. When the doctor and the patient are enveloped in the highest frequency possible, there is no possibility for disease or infection to exist any longer because, as you know, they are in the lower frequencies.

Next, Seu Miguel reached for his steel tray—holding needles, thread and a knife—and took a vial of water. He poured this Holy Water over the incisions while muttering a prayer in what sounded like an ancient language, then blotted them dry with a soft cloth. When Seu Miguel was finished the incisions were entirely healed. Abe was astounded, his mouth hanging open. He took a deep breath and wiped his forehead in amazement.

As the nurse pulled Sabrina's shirt down, Armando returned her to her sitting position. She woozily smiled up at Abe and then over to Lillian while petting her little Xico who was now wide awake, panting and holding his body up against her.

Seu Miguel looked up at Abe, Now . . . is there anything we can do for you, doctor?

Abe could hardly get his words out, No, no, I'm fine. I'm just here for my niece.

Are you sure?

Abe smiled graciously, Yes, sir. I'm fine.

You are a doctor, no?

No . . . no, I mean, yes . . . I'm a retired surgeon at the University of Virginia, heading up the Spinal Care Investigation Division.

Welcome. Thank you for coming. We appreciate your presence.

You're welcome.

And you know you have a weak heart, no?

How did you know?

We can see clearly—a severe blockage on the right coronary artery—may we help you with it?

Abe's mind raced, *they can see?* he thought. *What do they take me for, some kind of sucker?* You can see? asked Abe. W here I come from, we have x-rays and MRI's.

Yes, but where we come from, we can see all from different levels not perceived in the physical. And we can help you from different levels as well.

Oh man what a bunch of bunk! This nut is not going to lay a hand on me, not now, not ever. No, thank you, he said to Seu Miguel, I'm perfectly fine. Dr. Gettes has been keeping a close eye on it... *I'm taking my medication, I should be fine,* he reminded himself and felt better.

Seu Miguel frowned and turned back to the delicate Sabrina. She was hugging Xico and smiling from her heart. She was, for the first time, glad to be back in her body, free from pain. Seu Miguel beckoned with a flat hand for Lillian to stand and join them. Tears were flowing down Lillian's cheeks, making it hard for her to see.

Looking at Abe and Lillian he said, You will both stay with this child for three days. We are going to put her back into a coma while we rebuild her body. You must promise to stay with her continuously, 24 hours a day. You will meditate, think good thoughts, see your child whole and happy again, yes? You two may take turns with her, but she will need someone by her side at all times, do you understand?

Lillian nodded. Abe did not. *Meditate? I don't know the first thing about meditating...* he thought.

Seu Miguel continued, Xico, our resident medium healer, will be accompanying you. He will sleep close to her spine so you must keep her on her side at all times. Don't worry about having to move them to keep their bodies exercised, feeding them, or giving them water. There will be no need for them to relieve themselves. Xico will be serving as the medium, in the place of Seu Miguel. He will be our bridge to the physical, holding our energy in place, so it is essential that he remain close to the spine, is that understood?

Lillian nodded, Abe did not.

Turning to Armando, Seu Miguel said, Please take Sabrina to the coma room. Work will start immediately.

As Armando pushed Sabrina and Xico in her chair toward a door at the end of the room behind Seu Miguel, Lillian and Abe followed. Behind them, they could hear Seu Miguel's voice change once again, calling Martim to bring him the next patient.

THE ETHERIC COMA

That first day for Lillian and Abe was very uncomfortable. Abe had been given a white shirt so that there would be no interference—the green energy was too heavy to be around Sabrina.

Sabrina lay on her side on a cot, Xico close by her, while Abe and Lillian settled into their chairs beside them—eyes closed for meditation. There was another family on the other side of the room, a Brazilian boy younger than Sabrina flanked by his grandmother and mother. Scattered in various places in the room were people who would come in to meditate, but leave when they wanted.

Flavia entered to check on everyone—she helped Seu Miguel with the patients, as did Martim. Her fresh white starched nurse's smock smelled of sunshine as she brought a pitcher of holy water for them to drink, and in a soft voice explained where they could find the bathroom. She pointed to a blanket-covered cot in back of the room where they could take a nap while spelling the other, and to the covered veranda that overlooked the garden just outside the door where they would find hot bowls of the soup the entities had blessed. It contained all the nourishment they would need at any time of the day, she explained, and they would be surprised that it would fill them nicely. She or someone would always be close by should they want anything and, with that, she left as quietly as she had come.

Lillian took to meditation like a fish to water. She closed her eyes and asked Grandmère to join her, wherever she was, and felt her presence off to her right shoulder. She smiled as tears welled up. Memories of happy times she and Grandmère had shared played behind her closed eyes like a grand movie, one after another. There they were in a magnificent otherworldly garden together playing with Sabrina, watching her running and skipping and laughing and so happy. Meditation was great, Lillian thought. She could do this for three days easily.

For Abe it was quite different, he had never meditated before and never wanted to. He had always thought of people that did as freaks—weirdos. He moved in his seat and let out a deep guttural *humph*. He wanted to help Sabrina, he really did . . . but he had no idea that he'd be asked to meditate . . . *meditate! . . . how in the hell will that ever help Sabrina*? He hadn't a clue. He had given his word to Seu Miguel . . . but had he? No dammit, he hadn't. Hell, he *had* made all the arrangements for their flight, the medical equipment, brushed up on all the emergency procedures and how to trouble-shoot any problems with the equipment. It hadn't been easy—he was so much older now and things didn't come as quickly as in med school. It had cost him thousands of dollars to pull this trip off—he even had to cash in some of his favorite stocks, which was painful . . .

Damn, his back ached, his right hip was hurting. He squinted at Lillian beside him, she looked fine, *how does she do it? Can't talk to her to find out* . . . he was suddenly very hungry and thirsty. He opened his eyes and looked around the room: Lillian, over there a meditator, the small boy across the room, his family bowed in prayer, their lips moving as fast as their fingers were f lying over their rosary beads. They had religion—they knew how to do that. Abe had played hookey from Hebrew school more than he had attended. He'd hated going to synagogue, it had made him as uncomfortable as he felt now. When he was really little, he'd fidgeted so much his mother had slapped his little hands and shhhhhed him. She'd riffled through her pocket book and found a pencil and torn out checks from her checkbook so he could draw on the back of them. Even then it didn't work for too long; he'd draw airplanes dropping bombs and of course they had to have sound effects to go with them . . . *ewwwwwroooooommmmm skiiiiish! pow- pow-pow!* Then . . . the very best noise he could do . . . *chukkkkkkkkkkk!!!* He could make the *best* explosion sounds—ever—so true to life—he just *knew*—even though they didn't watch TV or go to movies.

What he'd give for a pencil and paper right now. Taking in a deep breath, he let it out and didn't fight the need to get up.

He touched the shoulder of his sister to get her attention and motioned that he was going to the bathroom. Once he was outside, he felt an immense sense of relief. He relished the feeling of warmth from the sun and fresh air.

He knew at that moment he would not be able to return to that room—ever, ever, never. NO.

He headed down the dirt road that led to the main street—six blocks long, referred to as town—found a pay telephone way, way back in a little room at the one and only Internet Café that served the same kind of boring vegetarian food as did the Pousada . . .

He called Bob.

FLAVIA AND LILLIAN

Lillian felt a soft nudge on her shoulder and looked up. Flavia was beaming down at her. She looked at her watch . . . she had been at it for six hours! How had she done it?

Looking around, where was Abe? She didn't remember him coming back. What had happened?

I'm sorry, she said, I need to go find out if anything has happened to my brother, then I'll be right back. Would you be so kind as to take over for me?

Flavia smiled and motioned to one of the volunteers meditating in the back of the room. The woman silently took Lillian's seat, smiled at her with a look of don't worry everything's fine, and went directly back to her meditation.

Lillian asked Flavia to accompany her to her Pousada room—she was very concerned and afraid of what she might find. When they got there, she found a note from Abe:

Dear Sis,

I've gone to Rio. Wade has a very important meeting we have to make before the conference. So sorry. Will call you when I know for sure my return date. Hope you will be able to find someone to hold vigil while I'm gone.

Your bro, Abe

My bro Abe, she said, wadding up the note. Just like him to . . . she burst into tears, What am I going to do?

Fernando took her into her arms and just let her cry. Don't worry, we women can all team up and help you through this.

I'm just so angry!

Flavia nodded and led her out of the room. Let's get you something to eat; I just happen to know the cook here.

FLAVIA'S KITCHEN

The kitchen, empty of staff, was quiet in the lull before the evening meal. Everything was arranged neatly: large cutting, chopping, and preparing areas, pots and pans hung over the stove range—everything organized.

Flavia moved gracefully to the refrigerator and brought out an enormous piece of chocolate cake.

Happens a lot with men . . . they're not so good at what women do best—be mothers—willing to do anything for our children no matter what it is.

She pulled out a shiny professional cake knife and drew it neatly through the cake, lifting the moist pieces onto a thick pottery plate. God forbid, if they had to give birth, we wouldn't have children on this Earth, would we? said Flavia smiling, pushing the platter toward her.

Lillian laughed, snorting through her nose, plugged up from heavy crying.

God forbid . . . Flavia repeated and laughed and handed her a paper napkin to blow into. Lillian watched her as she took two forks from a large drawer. Flavia was such a beauty, her dark skin so smooth, there didn't seem to be one worry line on her face. Lillian admired her poise and grace—the unique dignity Latin women possessed. It must be that their culture gives women a position of worth, she thought, unlike our own culture's history of repressing the strength of women.

Flavia scooted a chair over beside Lillian, pulling the cake platter between them and handing her a fork.

I mean, Abe has done so much for us already, Lillian said, taking the fork from Flavia and sinking it deep into the chocolate.

That's true, so we'll just think the best right now, right? Flavia held her bite up to be appreciated before slipping it into her mouth and closing her eyes for the deep, sensual experience.

Yep . . . the only thing we can do . . . but I feel so . . . so . . . so . . . Lillian stopped and poked at the cake.

Betrayed?

Betrayed and abandoned . . . she fell into tears again, feeling embarrassed by this new outburst.

Flavia drew close to Lillian, putting an arm around her and said softly, A long-standing issue for you, yes?

A very long-standing issue. Is it written all over me for everyone to see? Lillian Fleur is a big, fat, fraidy cat. She stabbed at the cake and then sat back and folded her arms across herself.

I don't know, what is this . . . fat, big cat?

Me, that's who. Me. I'm afraid of everything.

Name one thing.

That . . . I can't do this anymore . . . that I can't do this anymore . . . by myself.

Lillian. . . you have to understand when people come here, even if they don't think they're here for healing for themselves . . . they are here for healing. They've come here to be healed because there is an issue that has overcome them, to the extent that it has turned into a physical or mental problem and most of the time . . . it is absolutely subconscious.

Subconscious?

Yes, we aren't even aware what it is that's creating our problems. Whether it comes in a form of sickness or just a weakness in the mind, it doesn't matter. Those are symptoms. The problem wants to be known and dealt with.

So you mean, abandonment is my issue . . . and my weakness?

Think about it . . .

Well, yeah, my father and mother abandoned me, my husband was never there to help me with the children—with anything. Grandmère . . . Grandmère . . . oh, god . . I abandoned her!

Please be gentle on yourself here, Lillian. This is a very special place, Paramanguaia. Under it is quartz bedrock ten miles deep. Seu Miguel's entity doctors chose this location because the energy here is immense. And the energy intensifies everything. You can't miss your deepest fears here, because they become tremendously present.

She finished her piece of cake and pushed the platter toward Lillian. Lillian finally took a bite. It was heavenly—just what she needed.

You know when I think about it . . . when I first got here I thought I wasn't going to be able to walk a straight line. I kept running into doors like I was drunk. I thought I was coming down with something.

That's what most people report when they first arrive.

Taking another bite, she spoke with her mouth full. You sure it wasn't jet lag?

Partly . . . but you've felt jet lag before . . . was it like that?

No . . . I don't remember feeling that I was getting an intense headache or being so damn irritable. I thought I was going to scream like I do with jet-lag. Suddenly she craved something to wash down the rich cake. Do you have some milk?

Oh! Forgive me, and with that Flavia was up, flying to the refrigerator and within seconds, producing an old fashioned bottle full of rich milk.

Ohmygosh, I haven't seen a bottle like that since I was a kid. Lillian watched her pour the thick, creamy fluid into a glass and pass it to her.

Then drinking her milk straight from the bottle, Flavia said, We get them from the local farmer every day, bright and early. She wiped away her milk mustache. Lillian fell in love with her at that very minute; Flavia had a magical way of making her feel like she was a long-lost sister.

Where were we? Oh yeah, how does quartz work with healing the body, do you know? asked Lillian.

Just as she had taught her children, she repeated the lessons for Lillian. Take a tiny quartz crystal, it is used to power clocks and the like, right? Likewise, quartz affects the machinery of our body. Patting her arm, she continued, This physical body is an electrical machine, if you hold your hand inches from the skin you can feel the energy. Here, let me show you.

Flavia held her hand over Lillian's arm and hand, moving it back and forth without touching her skin, and yes, she felt as if Flavia was touching her hand though she was at least an inch away. Lillian shook her hands because it tickled.

Flavia continued explaining, The ten mile thick quartz bedrock accelerates the velocity or the vibration in our body . . . and brain. Therefore, everything is exaggerated here. Even what you think. When stuff comes up from your past, it comes up big . . . so that we can see it . . . feel it . . . and heal it.

Lillian's mind was swimming, she wondered if it was a chocolate rush or too much information at once to comprehend—but it was so fascinating to her, she wanted to know more.

Flavia went on, In order to heal, we have to go through all these dark places in ourselves so that we can see them for what they are—then be able to release them—bless them, forgive them, then release them. Then we can know that the healing is complete and the darkness never to return.

The information was ringing bells . . . I know you're right.

It's hard work. But so rewarding when you realize there really is no such thing as being a victim.

A pang of unexpected anger hit her hard. What about Sabrina if there is no such thing as a victim? What did she ever do that has to be forgiven . . . and released? She's just an innocent little girl.

I don't know what your beliefs are—but if a soul comes here more than once it makes sense to me that we bring with us lessons that need to be healed from a past life and sometimes it can be what is called Karma . . .

Karma. Oh man, where is this leading—Karma. Lillian was becoming uncomfortable.

Yes, we come back to help people we love learn a lesson so that they can grow and evolve to a higher understanding.

So you think Sabrina . . . is helping me . . . to grow?

Definitely, because she loves you so much . . . but I'm also feeling there is something more. I just have this feeling, I don't know how I know this but there is something going on between Xico and her.

Chico, the dog? As much as she liked Flavia, she had suddenly tromped over a very well-drawn line . . . *a dog had something to do with my daughter . . . that sounds crazy, maybe this woman is crazy. I need to go.*

Flavia felt the shift and tried to soften what she had told her. Lillian, it's just a feeling I'm having . . . there is really so much we mortals don't know about what life is all about.

Lillian looked into the space within her, where she knew there were no answers, only questions, and felt that old familiar rage. Yet now, as the shock of what Flavia was saying had passed—strangely; she was feeling a great peace taking its place. She could no longer decipher what it was she was thinking anymore . . . maybe she shouldn't even try to . . . figure it out . . . since she had arrived in Brazil her whole belief system had flipped completely upside down. And suddenly, she had become aware she was feeling so very, very exhausted.

She let out a deep yawn.

Get some sleep, Lillian. Tomorrow will be an even bigger day than today.

XICO

I knew the minute I snuggled next to Sabrina in the coma room and fell asleep and started dreaming, I could expect The Voice to start yammering in my ear about what it was I was to do from that point on. Nope . . . floated around in lah lah land waiting, no Voice. Then WHAM The Moradia de Dom José de Barros' roof opened right up over my head and all these gossamer angels appeared and lifted Sabrina's light body right out of her broken body and transported her up up up through the ether and out of the Moradia.

Where are you taking her? I yelled, thinking I'd get an answer—not!

Nope, she was nearly out of sight. My teeth were chattering so hard together

I knew I had to . . . had to . . . what?

V-V-OICE, where the heEEEZzop . . . are YOU?

Xico, you need to go with Sabrina. Get going!

But it wasn't easy for me as I lifted off . . . I was forgetting to relax and everything was going hoooeeeey—I was forgetting all my lessons and I was only remembering my old habit of being confused and unfocused—ho-boy—tense, I was ssoooooo tense . . . while being churned around and around in a whirlpool of intense electricity.

Xico, what are you doing?

The Voice seemed baffled but all I could answer was, I d-d-d-dunno . . . I h-h-h-had t-t-to do something . . . so I ran and j-j-j—jumped—that's what I always d-d-d-ooo.

Just relax! Let go of holding on. Let go!

Letgoletgoletgo, I said to myself over and over. Until sssszzzzzzziiiish zzzziiiing I was swishing through atmospheres, one after the other, FAP-FAP-

FAP, with the power of one of those jets I saw in the evening Brazilian sky—tail and all.

Yikes. How do I stop myself?

Think stop.

Think stop???

Think STOP!

I did. And I did. I was looking around wondering just where I was. So easy . . .whew, I'm thinkin'.

Yes! Easy. What you think is what you create. Haven't you gotten that yet, son? After all the study we've been through?

I forget . . . I whined. But there in the mist—a huge building was coming into view. Was I coming toward it or was it coming toward me?

It's so confusing over here, I swear.

Thank God you have Me.

You got that right, bud. I was watching two grandiose doors open wide while I floated right through into an enormous round room. It all looked so familiar.

We've been here before . . .

You got that right, bud.

This is where you took me when I was in-between-lives and I had to review what a squizzel-poop I'd been as a dolphin, before I could choose my next life, huh?

You got that right, bud.

Well, I can see some of my fuppywap has rubbed off on you . . . bud. Congrats on your new sense of humor.

Thanks, I've been working on it.

Then like the sun rising in my mind, I realized, hey, I was here to save a little girl from becoming a cripple—why the hezzop was I just do-dee-dah joking around? I focused. That's it! We're at the The Hall of Records. Find her chart, we'll find Sabrina and Eeeoo.

Over here, Xico. It's over here, *The Voice had been on the job the whole time, joking or not.*

A scroll flew out and unrolled itself right before my eyes. I didn't bother reading it, I knew what I needed to know would be at the end—

SABRINA

WHUMMMMMMMWHUMMMMMWHUMM...

CRASHHHH. The SQUEALING of metal on metal. The CRUNCHING and spinning across the icy road until the little car thudded heavily into the snow bank. In the distance, a cacophony of metal, banging against trees, trees and rocks, and the smashing sounds seemed to dim in the night as the monster truck erratically banged down the mountain side and finally jolted to rest at the bottom with a hisssss and a final explosion that spewed a glowing fire in the pines.

POP SWHISH. The loudest quiet . . . and quiet . . . and quiet.

Nothing moving.

A small voice called out, Monmmy! Dadd-deee! Mommmeee . . .

Sabrina, only eight years old, stood outside her limp body crumpled in the backseat. She was calling to Lillian, to Ben—her mommy and daddy. Over and over she was calling as she was by their sides in the front seat petting their frozen faces with her fingers.

She remembered: She'd drawn her daddy a picture of them skiing together . . . She had been yelling at her daddy from the back seat to turn around and look! See? See, Daddy? See what I drew? Daddy? Daddy?

Lillian had turned around from the passenger seat and had looked at it and said, Ben, this is so sweet, and had smiled at her. Sabrina had felt so proud that she had to make him see it, now, at that moment, Daddy, look!

It was her fault! She knew it. If she hadn't made him look, he'd be . . . alive. And mommy wouldn't be so alone. And Grandmère wouldn't have cried every day. It was Sabrina's fault! She had to be punished. She had decided: she too would die, even if she was alive and her father wasn't. She hated herself so much she made herself re-live it—and re-live it.

WHUMMMMMMWHUMMMMMWHUMM... CRASHHHH. The SQUEALING of metal on metal. The CRUNCHING and wrapping and spinning across icy road . . . THUD . . . metal, banging . . . rocks, trees, the sounds dimming... then a small voice breaks a slow silence, Mommy! Dadddeee! Mommmeedadddeeemommee daddee . . .

XICO

I heard Eeeoo's voice calling, SHE'S OVER HERE. SHE'S OVER HERE, ZEEEP!

Eeeoo? Where are you? I was panicking, because after that all I could hear was—

WHUMMM-CRASHHH-SQUEEEECHHHHHH . . . metal on metal.

Then I saw her—eight-year-old Sabrina, with the blizzard whishing all around her—watching the accident over and over and over . . . crying, Dadd-deee! I shot over as close as I could to Sabrina but the velocity of the storm seemed to be keeping me at a distance.

SABRINA! SABRINA, STOP IT! I yelled as loud as I could.

She stopped and looked around, her reddened eyes landed on me—a little white and brown spotted dog trying to run in the wind toward her. She'd seen me before . . . in her dreams. As soon as she focused on me, the storm ceased. I ran straight over to her as fast as I could. She crouched down and started petting me, her hot tears landing on my face. I was so relieved she could hear me—she understood every word I was saying.

Your daddy's here and he wants me to tell you it wasn't your fault.

I thought I was telling a fib. I'd thought I'd made it up to stop her from crying but to my amazement there he was . . . Her daddy had her in his arms—hugging her, letting her cry, shhhhhhhing her, telling her, It's not your fault, pumpkin. I hope you understand . . .

He held her up so he could look in her eyes, O sweet, sweet Sabrina, I wish you could have known, I was done with my Earth life. It was the time for me to leave and go Home. It had nothing to do with you making me do anything. It wasn't your fault sweetheart. Please believe me. Please . . .

The winter, the road, the smashed up debris lying all over, the blood, the horror, all vanished—POOOF—and there we were back in the round room with the gold light all around us. Grandmère appeared and Sabrina ran to her and threw herself in her arms. Grandmère stroked her hair and smiled over at Benjamin.

A Scroll suddenly materialized and unrolled itself right before us. It sure was a relief to see it wasn't mine. Nope, Benjamin Bir Fleur was written there, at the top, in swirly writing. It said something about him needing to transcend to the Otherside in order to do other important work and there it was, in writing, how he was to transition—in a car accident.

Ben stroked his daughter's hair and spoke softly, So you see, Sabby my sweet, I never wanted you to think it was your fault. This was written long before the accident, so how could it have possibly ever been your fault?

Sabrina stopped crying and looked deep into her father's eyes . . . and smiled sadly.

Are you alright, baby? Do you understand? She nodded and they hugged hard.

Er . . . excuse me sir, I just want to say I'm very sorry Mr. Fleur, I said—I too had guilt I needed to release.

Whatever for? Ben asked.

Well, all this time, sir, Eeeoo and I thought Sabrina was with you and that she was alright.

Eeeoo?

That's who is taking care of your daughter's comatose body while she was gone.

Ben looked incredulous, and let out a deep breath.

I looked over at the little girl and said, Sabrina? Hey girl, after you were wrapped in a cocoon of Love for quite a while, and you were feeling better, you told Eeeoo you wanted to go find your father—to be with him—and you wanted Eeeoo to take care of your body so you could do that. And that's where we thought you were, being taken care of by your father. Otherwise we would have been very worried.

She looked up at me with eyes that could melt the meanest heart, I'm sorry, she said. I really was looking for my daddy, this was the only place I knew to look . . .

The Voice whispered in my ear, ***Don't worry, Son. She couldn't go to the Light where her dad was, because of her guilt. Her Guardian Angels tried to get her to look to the Light but she had decided to go right to the accident and because of her grief she got stuck there.***

What you think, you create?

And, her chart hasn't been completed yet, either.

Because her body is still alive?

Because she still has more she wants to learn in this lifetime.

I think I understand . . . but . . . I'll get back to you on that. Though I was a titch confused, I was feeling much better—until I remembered Eeeoo. She was back in Sabrina's body and the Spirit Doctors were coming to heal it. If Sabrina wasn't back in her Earth body in time she could lose out on the healing.

I frantically looked at Ben and said, We have to get Sabrina back to her body before it's too late . . .

He hoisted his daughter in his arms, I'll come with you, he said.

* * *

FAP-FAP-FAP there we were back in Habitação da Cura (Habit-a-cow da Ku-da) the spirit hospital that floated over The Moradia de Dom José de Barros down on Earth—we could see Eeeoo hovering over Sabrina's body with Lillian in meditation by her side, and there was me still curled up next to her.

* * *

FAP-FAP-FAP—I was in a grass field somewhere, lots of sun, lots of laughter . . . laughter? Where the hezzop am I now?

Rodrigues, get the ball!

I turned around and I was about to be trampled by a herd of children. I yapped like mad! A ball as big as me, was only inches away. I leaped for the ball, snapping at it. I heard a squeak as I bit down, reminding me of the ball I had just been in and how it, too, had squeaked on my teeth. Next thing, without thinking, I was running right along with the kids, heh-heh-heh-heh, it felt so good to run again heh-heh-heh-heh run faster, I knew I could run faster,and faster and faster—a kid's foot was nearly in my face heh-heh-heh-heh, I swerved, I leaped—I was safe. Uh oh, the herd had turned around, coming toward me, heh-heh-heh-heh okayokay, I'm fast, I wheel around in a split second, kept up with them, I'm having so much fun feeling my heart heh-heh-heh-heh pounding, taking in deeps gulps of fresh air, every muscle moving in—the—rhythm—I—love—and—miss—so—much. Wasn't long before I realized what this was . . . Brazilian soccer. Played it a billion times with Mariana Vitória and Rafael in the fields, across from the Posada. Whooooooo I'm looooving it so much—but like a dummydog—I didn't get that, dikdik, I was in someone's fitzbing dream until the game was heh-heh-heh-heh over. Then duh . . . yeah.

Kids were slapping each other and running at each other and jumping on each other and there I was heh-heh-heh-heh-ing like crazy trying to get my breath. Rodrigues? Sergeant Rodrigues? . . . Was I in Rodrigues's dream? When he was a kid, maybe? I looked over and there are the parents and who do I see? Sergeant Rodrigues himself—uniform and all.

Bira! he calls out, and this kid runs up to him and jumps in his arms. Is this Rodrigues's kid? I thought he was blind.

Then I got it.

I was in Bira Rodrigues's dream. Handicappers do that all the time. They have dreams about being normal.

***Excellent deduction**, The Voice comes through as deep and resonant as always.*

Hey pal, what am I doing here? Thought I was supposed to be with Sabrina?

No son, she's just fine for the moment. However, if we don't get Seu Miguel out of jail by tomorrow, Sabrina is going to have big problems.

Like what? My heart was flippin' around.

Ahhh, this information is not for you to know—

Well, thanks for the votta confidence, just what is it I am supposed to know?

I was really peezonked! How dare he hold back information like that. My Eeeoo's life is on the line and . . .

Calm down. Here's what you need to do. As you know, this is only a dream, but you must persuade the boy to ask his father to take him to see Seu Miguel.

But Seu Miguel's in the jail.

Precisely.

Oh! I get it, I squeaked, and I was off like lightning on a rainy day, a dead-run straight for Bira.

Heh-a-heh-a-heh-a-heh Bira! Heh-a-heh-a-heh-a-heh Bira!

The kid turned around and came running to meet me like we were old friends—dreams are like that. I rolled around with him in the grass for a while, got him to laugh like crazy before I laid it on him,

Hey, in your real life . . . heh-a-heh-a-heh-a-heh . . . do you wanna see like everyone else?

Yeah, I do.

Well, I'm Xico. I'm a magic dog.

Really?

I know someone who can heal your eyes so you can be like all the other kids.

Really?

Now you gotta promise me something. You can't tell your dad about me or what I'm telling you—do you promise?

Why can't I tell him?

Because, Bira, he doesn't believe. You have to believe, in order for magic to happen.

Why?

Because if you don't believe, you stop the energy you need to have for miracles to happen, get it?

Yeah, sometimes grown-ups get scared a lot, huh?

You got that right, bud. I had to chuckle 'cause I knew The Voice was listening.

So here's what you do . . . just ask him to take you to work with him tomorrow. Be very persistent. Make sure he does, because if he doesn't the magic energy can go away. Okay, can you do that?

We'll, I don't know. He's never taken me to work with him before. Do you want to be able to see?

I knew I was being a little rough on him but there was a lot at stake. You're a smart kid, you'll figure out a way. Right?

I gotta. He looked a little stressed but hopeful.

Then, when you get to his jail where he works, you must go see a prisoner there called Seu Miguel.

Seu Miguel?

Seu Miguel dos Milagres, he'll be the one who will heal you.

How will Seu Miguel know?

I'll tell him you're coming and that you want to be able to see like other kids.

You will?

I'm magic remember? Do you believe?

I gotta.

Now, when you wake up, go in and tell your Dad you have to go to work with him.

I'll tell him it's a school project . . .

Brilliant, that's the stuff!

Okay! he said, then he picked me up and gave me a big hug, I love you, Xico.

Wow, I suddenly broke out in tears, no way could I hold them back. Nobody but Eeeoo had ever said that to me before. He had tears falling from his eyes, too, so I licked the hezzop out of his face. He put me down and said goodbye and asked me to meet him the next night in his dreams and he'd tell me what happened. I told him that the next time he saw me, it wouldn't be a dream but it would be real life. His eyes lit up and as I watched him walk back to his father who was talking with other parents, I said a little doggie prayer—after all, it was a dream.

* * *

FAP-FAP-FAP, I was in the Habitação da Cura again. Sabrina was in tears—her father had her standing before him and was talking quietly to her.

What'd I miss? I asked The Voice.

She doesn't want to leave him.

I don't get it . . .

She thinks if she goes back into her body she won't be with him ever again.

Yeah, and she's just found him . . . give the kid a break. Eeooo will do fine staying in Sabrina's body back on Earth.

But that's not what's written—

What? So Eeeoo . . . I . . . she . . . we . . . ?

Sabrina has so much yet to learn and Lillian needs her.

Lillian has her no matter what! I spit.

No, it's important that the original Sabrina takes her body back, they still have karma to work out.

Karma? What kind of karma?

In their last life together, Sabrina was Lillian's mother. She was a child who had to take care of Lillian all the time by herself. She felt her life was ruined, so she abandoned her by putting her in a home and virtually forgot about her.

Wow, heavy.

Now Sabrina has to learn about being taken care of. Because Lillian knows what that feels like, it's very important to her that she be there for her no matter what and teach Sabrina the error of her ways.

Fascinating—this human stuff.

Well, it's all just a game in the holistic scheme of things. What you think is what you create.

So? They create games, these humans?

Very, very creative game players. But what comes of it, is knowledge. And they all take what they've learned and throw it in the mix and together

they soon realize once they've come to the Otherside, they are actually One—a much stronger and wiser One with the Source, where they first came from.

Well that's all beautiful and all but . . .

Son . . . you have forgotten already? You know that Eeeoo and you are already One don't you*?*

Suddenly I was stopped in my tracks. Right there and then I felt a hugely extraordinarily tremendous . . . Peace. If the original Sabrina came back to her body, Eeeoo and I would be okay, because we were already okay. Now that felt like the truth. I was ready to let whatever happened—happen. I also was learning. I was learning to heal—I had to accept what was. Dikdik, I was getting to be a pretty smart cookie for a dog.

Get back to work, kid, *The Voice said and pushed me lovingly on my way. Somehow, when a soul comes into enlightenment, a hundred other souls transcend, too.*

SARGENTO FERNANDO OSVALDO RODRIGUES, BIRA AND SEU MIGUEL

Daddy, I wanna know all about where you work. Show me everything, will you? I wanna feel it.

Sargento Rodrigues took his son around the desks where he did paper work then to the area where the bars separated the staff from the inmates.

Bira, this is the jail where we put people who have broken the law.

The keys clanged against the metal as Sargento Rodrigues opened the gate to the cells, then slammed it shut with an equal racket. He'd watched his son take in the noises, his thoughts playing all over his face.

The tap-tap-tap had awoken Seu Miguel, he'd sat up with a start, rubbed his head when he saw it was Sargento Rodrigues holding the hand of a blind boy as they approached his cell.

Rodrigues? Is that your son, come to visit?

Yes, this is my Bira.

Trata-se de Seu Miguel dos Milagres? Bira had asked, holding out his little hand for Seu Miguel to shake.

Sargento Rodrigues reacted by pulling his son back, then it had dawned on him, How do you know about Seu Miguel, son?

Oh, Xico told me about him in a dream. Bira couldn't lie to his father any longer.

Xico?

Seu Miguel smiled at Sargento Rodrigues through the bars. Xico is a little dog who helps me at The House of Dom José de Barros.

Martim's Xico?

Yes, Daddy. Xico said Seu Miguel would help me to see.

Is that so? He squinted at Seu Miguel.

Yes, would you please let him. Please? I'd like to be able to play soccer like Carlos.

Carlos is Bira's best friend at school, Sargento Rodrigues explained. He keeps telling Bira that he will be a great soccer player some day.

An' I wanna, Daddy. Can I?

Sargento Rodrigues upper lip started to quiver and he blinked back the moisture accumulating in his eyes. He ran his hand across his brow then said to Seu Miguel, What do you need to do?

Bring him closer . . . Seu Miguel said, kneeling, as he reached through the bars. He put his hands on the youngster's eyes and began saying the Lord's Prayer out loud. Sargento Rodrigues bowed his head and joined Seu Miguel in the prayer. Then Seu Miguel asked the Spirit Doctors to come forth and do what was necessary.

Sargento Rodrigues couldn't keep his eyes closed for this. He watched Seu Miguel tremble slightly and his eyes close. But when he opened them again they were a deep, dark brown instead of the bright blue he'd just seen a few seconds ago. He was able to handle all of this until his son started shaking and breathing hard.

Don't worry, whispered Seu Miguel, Bira's little body is getting used to the new frequencies of eyesight. He's never had this in this body before.

Sargento Rodrigues didn't understand what Seu Miguel meant but he felt less frightened as he watched Seu Miguel pulling something off of his son's body. He couldn't see what it was at all but the way he was moving his arms it looked as if there were strings of some sort—Seu Miguel was ripping them off and throwing them to the floor—then returning his hand to Bira's eyes and holding them there.

The disease has been removed, Seu Miguel whispered again.

Sargento Rodrigues took a deep breath and let it out slowly, he could feel a slight headache coming on—all this was way out of his belief system.

Seu Miguel finally took his hands from Bira's eyes and smiled, What do you see, young man? Bira blinked his eyes rapidly, trying to focus, he dropped his stick—it fell to the ground. I don't know, I don't know . . . because I've never seen it before. He put his hand out to touch all over Seu Miguel's face, his face all aglow. But there is . . . this is a . . .

A man? Seu Miguel asked, smiling kindly.

I think. Yes. It looks like what I've felt.

Seu Miguel asked him, And can you find your father?

Sargento Rodrigues had stepped back out of the way to test his son earlier on, while he had been talking to Seu Miguel.

Bira turned around and walked directly over to where Sargento Rodrigues was, looking straight into his eyes. When he arrived, he grabbed onto his father and started sobbing, I . . . I . . . I can see, Daddy. I can see you!

Sargento Rodrigues knelt down and pulled his son into his arms, hugging and rocking him—joining in with his sobs.

SEU MIGUEL

Seu Miguel walked through the throngs of meditators filling the hall and like stars popping out at night—one-by-one, then two, four and five—they raised their heads, smiling, so happy to see Seu Miguel released and back with them. Their prayers had been answered. They all stood while clapping their hands and shouting, Welcome back, Seu Miguel!

Seu Miguel raised his hands for silence, and said, It's been a hard week and I thank you all for what you have given for this moment to happen. This is absolute proof that prayer is all-powerful over adversity. No one needs revenge. God has it all figured out. We just have to honor that Knowing at all times. Thank you. Thank you all.

As he lowered his hands, *a wh-o-o-o-o-o! who-o-o-o-o-ooo!* was heard coming from the Coma Room.

Xico! Everyone laughed.

Bring Xico and the young lady to me, if you will. We'll get right to work, said Seu Miguel as he took his place in the big leather chair and prepared for the entity doctors to take their place over his body.

* * *

The coma room was in a hubbub. Xico had suddenly awakened and heralded Seu Miguel's return with a howl. Lillian had been shaken out of her half-sleep-meditation and Flavia had to prepare her for what was to come. He's here. Seu Miguel's here.

Lillian gasped when she saw Sabrina's eyes flicker open.

Flavia exclaimed, Sabrina's awake! Oh . . . She lifted Xico from the cot in order to sit Sabrina up.

Xico shook his little body furiously trying to get used to being back on the physical plane. It felt heavy and sore—not the lightness and freedom he'd been flashing around in, on the Otherside.

Sabrina was looking around, not smiling, looking like a young child awakened and not yet knowing exactly where she was. With the help of the other women in the coma room, Lillian and Flavia helped carry Sabrina from the cot into her wheel chair. There was no need to connect her equipment and tubes, Sabrina was sitting up on her own, looking around and breathing with no help.

Martim, all lit up with joy, came into the room to help. Seu Miguel's ready. Let's rock and roll as they say in the US, yes? He gave a great big hug to Lillian, This is it. This is what you've been working so hard for. Let's all go see Seu Miguel, yes?

C'mon, Xico, they all said in unison and laughed together, following Martim as they filed out of the room.

XICO

Seu Miguel was finally back. Well, since I'd been in a dream, I didn't really need any more sleep, so I'd met the sunrise with a good ol' fashion howl. There I was, sitting up beside the Sabrina who-o-o-o-who-o-o-o-o-o-ing away. I didn't care what anyone thought, I was happier than I'd ever been in my life. My spontaneous Wh-o-o-o—oo, was met with an ocean of laughter. The original Sabrina was back in her body at last, her eyes were open and she was lookin' around. Eeeo was right there beside me,—back in her glowing orb body—pretty as ever, floatin' around. It was a day to celebrate and everyone was there to do just that.

I followed them to the hall and made my way over to where they were parking Sabrina. I looked over at that ever-serious Armando, wondering, what does it take to make him smile? But nobody was tossing this pup out this time—I was one of the gang at last. It felt like I had been given the best dog bone in the whole-wide-world.

I looked around—at Sabrina, at Flavia, Lillian, Martim, Seu Miguel—and I felt like they were my family . . . that, and of course, Eeeoo floating all over the room, drinkin' in all the Love. Even when the Spirit doctors, Dom José de Barros, Dr. Enesto Espirito dos Mean and Dr. Alvaro de Alvares came in the room, flashing in their columns of Light—even they felt like my family.

I was hap-hap-happy like I've never been before. If this was all a game we each created, then I was in. I loved all of it.

But if you think I was happy then—the next thing I knew I was even happier!

The Entities had stood Sabrina on her feet! She was standing! Then they started walking with her, holding her up, getting her to move her legs. Sabrina had this look of sublime exhilaration on her face as she walked down the hall, everyone laughing and cheering her on. She was back in the world, back in her body, wrapped in Love and she was, in turn, loving every moment of it.

So much so, that when the doctors let go of her, she just kept walking on her own.

I looked over at Lillian, her hands up to her face, tears streaming down, unable to move. Was she in fear that this wonderful dream would all just vanish? I could see how much she loved her daughter, and now that she was finally really with her again, how much it meant to her. At that point, I have to say, I fell in love with the wonderful Lillian. I admired her courage and her perseverance, and I was so not into my selfishness any longer that I actually realized—she had what I wanted—to know how to love someone unconditionally—no matter what, no matter how. Sabrina was walking and talking—look at that. A miracle.

And it took every one of us in this room to make it happen.

All of a sudden I could feel another shift. Everything felt so much lighter, so much easier. I realized if I kept making these shifts I would eventually be as light as I was on the Otherside. I realized it truly could be possible if I kept working hard at it—watching my thoughts—

For everything you think, you create . . .

I know . . . I know, and yes, I loved The Voice, too, even if he was a royal pain in the patoooshki.

LILLIAN

Waiting outside the Pousada, Lillian watched as the children—Rafael, Mariana Vitória, Bira and Julio, so full of energy, with little voices rising in excitement—pushed Sabrina all around in her wheelchair with Xico on her lap. They had her rolling here and there and every-which-way: back, swing around, go forward, then they would tear down the street as fast as they could, then lean back on their dust raising, skidding feet to stop her vehicle then whip it around and push it all the way back up the street and all the while explaining in those eager voices how much fun it will be when she can do wheelies in this thing and they would show her how to get it going just so fast before holding one wheel in place while the other would go into a skid. She could practice it and get it down real well. Sabrina said, by the time I get that strong I will be walking and I will never want to see a wheelchair again in my whole life.

Lillian laughed to herself watching the children. She hadn't felt so good in such a long time. They were all waiting outside the Pousada for the taxi to pick them up and take them down to the waterfall—the healing waters would do magic for her, make her stronger, Seu Miguel had said. And you too, Lillian, he had added, you need to go.

It was Tadeu, she was sure, who would arrive with his taxi. He was always the driver at the Pousada and she really liked going places with him. He was like family to the Mosques's, helping out all around the grounds, doing errands and fix-ups with Martim, and laughing in his distinct way. "It was so . . . melodious" was a kind description Lillian had heard Flavia use for his chuckle-snort-guffaw combo.

When the taxi arrived, Lillian was disappointed to see an unfamiliar man get out and introduce himself as Roberto. He was a young handsome fellow, with dark hair and dark eyes and was extremely attentive to Sabrina: setting her and Xico in the front seat and folding her wheelchair and stowing it in the trunk before packing the other kids into the back seat with jokes that set them screaming with laughter before he, with a little Latin flirting, helped Lillian into the front seat next to her daughter.

Roberto pulled out cautiously and happily rambled on about how this was his first day on the job and he was new to the company and how absolutely dedicated he was to being the best driver she would ever . . . ever happen upon, from this day forward.

Did he know Tadeu?

Oh, not yet, but Tadeu had been busy with Martim this weekend, and when he gets back he would certainly introduce himself. But now, he was there for her and the children in anyway possible—and with the good looks and the flirting—Lillian was sure he had inherited his Brazilian machismo from his ancient Portuguese ancestors. What a character, this Roberto was.

FLAVIA

After the healing, the kitchen buzzed with preparations: pots and pans were clanking, the refrigerator doors were slamming, wooden spoons were turning over thick cake batter in crockery bowls, and the cooks were speaking of the amazing miracle that had happened just that morning at The Moradia Dom de José de Barros. Many miracles had happened there, it was an everyday event in Paramanguaia, but the one this morning had a special energy that needed to be talked about. Everyone agreed their hearts had been possessed by that little girl—Sabrina, was that her name? Yes, Sabrina. Even though she had been comatose, she had woken up when she saw Xico. That was amazing. But then they all had agreed, lowering their voices, that they had all seen an eerie glow emanating from her small body when she had finally been animated with the Spirit—and then had stood and walked all around the room by herself. And that little one was just exploding with this vibrant immense personality, yes what a special child . . . ahhhh, it really made their hearts sing to be present at such an occasion. And because Flavia was so moved and overjoyed, she had called for this special dinner to be assembled in honor of the occasion—a special party for Sabrina.

All the guests from surrounding Pousadas had been invited. Mariana Vitória and Rafael and Martim were in charge of making sure that everyone who wanted to share in the celebration of a child being reborn into her body was invited. It would be a great sendoff for the rest of her life wouldn't it? Mariana Vitória had said.

Yes, everyone agreed.

The activity in the kitchen filled with the magical energy of everyone working together in a musical rhythm, in tune with what might even be called—divine.

LILLIAN

Roberto was carrying Sabrina piggyback down the steep pathway to the magical waters of the waterfall—all fresh with negative ions—while the kids followed behind Lillian. Bira asked, Do they hike in America?

Oh, yes, I think so.

You're from US, no? Julio asked.

No, North America—Canada, Lillian replied.

That's clear on the Otherside of the whole world, said Rafael.

Just about, she answered.

Eager to help her out, they told her how to be careful when hiking and how not to get those black, hairy, fuzzy caterpillars on their clothes or skin, because oh boy, do they sting and itch, and each told a dramatic story of when it happened to them.

Roberto gently lifted Sabrina from his shoulders, removed her flip-flops and placed her in the dancing pool of water at the bottom of the Blessed Waterfall. The others all pulled off the clothes that covered their swimming suits, waded to the liquid curtain of healing water and squealed with delight as they ducked their heads under and let the water pour over their bodies. When they scurried out of the pool—their hair tight to their heads—Roberto calmed them by telling a story about the magical butterflies that live in this forest.

It is said the *Fulnio Indianos* created these butterflies out of magic and if they were all very quiet and called out to the butterflies in their thoughts, they would come. So they sat on the rocks with their feet in the water and became very, very quiet and thought about the butterflies and looked around so that they could see them coming and sure enough after a short time, one, then two and three came flying through the forest toward the group.

They were awed by the large, deep turquoise-blue butterflies—bigger than anyone had ever seen.

One of the butterflies actually landed on Lillian, and instantly she understood why she was there at that moment in time—the healing wasn't just for Sabrina but it was for her, too. She would remember this moment with the magical butterflies for the rest of her life and the power of the waterfall washing over her and filling her with such exhilaration. She knew that she was never alone, there was always something to call on and it was very powerful—an Unconditional Love—she was experiencing it right then and there . . . and yes, she could forgive Abraham one day . . . and maybe even herself.

The kids remained quiet after the butterflies left—their eyes and hearts large with wonder—and Roberto helped them, one by one, to step out of the pool. When Roberto saw Xico licking Sabrina's withered legs, he said something to Lillian that set her heart right.

He said, I've heard Xico is a healing dog. Look at what he's doing. I know Xico knows how to heal your daughter. Xico is Sabrina's angel from heaven.

An electric excitement ran through Lillian's body—she knew at that moment everything would be all right for Sabrina. Gratitude welled up from the center of her being and she was at peace—at last.

Her prayer was that she would never forget this.

SABRINA

Laughter filled the Pousada courtyard as guest after guest brought presents and food for the little girl-of-honor and her party. Mariana Vitória and Rafael and Julio and Bira and Hernandes all ran around Sabrina in her wheelchair, laughing and playing games. She knew it was too soon to join in, but Sabrina daydreamed about her new life, filled with Hide and Seek, Hopscotch, Cat's Cradle—and by the end of the party she would learn some new Brazilian games!

FLAVIA AND LILLIAN

Flavia and Lillian sat in the hammock, swinging, watching the children at play. Rafael was teaching Sabrina how to get Xico to do that whirly trick where it looks like he was chasing his tail a mile a minute.

Heh-a-heh-a-heh—it's a trick alright. If I stare at my tail and never take my eyes off of it, I can go round and round forever if I want —works every time—when do I stop? Listen to those kids laughing. I may do this 'till I drop. Heh-heh-heh

Lillian said, Seu Miguel told me that we need to stay a few more weeks, maybe a month, so Sabrina can be fully healed before we leave.

Well, you know we would love for you to stay.

And Abe will be back and maybe, who knows, after he sees Sabrina's progress, he'll . . . oh, I can't get my hopes up, can I?

XICO

No . . . I was feeblewabbled. Where was the spunk I felt? I think it had gotten up and taken walk somewhere without me . . . left me with . . . sighing and whining—even my desire to bark was all capooted, and if I had a whole tail it would have been stuck down between my legs refusing to wag. See, I hadn't heard from Eeooo since she's left Sabrina's body and flew off in her orb body. The pain of missing my lover was beyond excruciating. And . . . The Voice was off doing HIS thing, whatever the heezop that was. I was feeblewabbled.

I tried a happy face though, didn't want to put a damper on the celebrating. Whooooo! Look at me spinning and spinning around. Wheee what a party. I'm the life of it. Look at me. But I was getting so dizzy trying to put on this show that I was not surrrre I could stop spinning. But stop I did—yep I did—almost mid- air even though my body kept going heh-heh-heh Whizzz whooozzzch. I sensed something was very wrong in that moment <u>*and*</u> *as soon as I was back on all fours I knew something was very, VERY wrong . The energy was different: it was wheeeeeezzzie before, but now it had changed to wo-o-o-o-oooooommmmmm. My ears and nose were paying intense attention to the front door. Someone was on the Otherside with a wonky, heavy energy and they were gonna ruin this party—big time.*

Suddenly I had a purpose. I was running to the door and barking like hezzop, had to let everybody know.

Xico, stop it. Stop barking!

Are Mariana Vitória and Rafael mad at me? Don't you guys remember the last time? All those Lizards? Hezzop no! Can't stop. You feel it? There's something right outside the door . . . grrrrrrrrrrr!!!!!!!! Sabrina, no one's going to fibblefabble your party up. Not if I have anything to do with it. Who-o-o-o-o-o-who-o-o-o-o-. Out of the side of my eye I could see someone was headed toward the front door, No, Tadeu!, Don't open that door whatever you do!. I ran over and got a good hold of his pant leg—one of my best clamp-block bites—it will never come undone. Grrrrrr, I gave him my best mean growl—to tell him to stop . . . oh wait! He's hitting at me—ouch ouch ouch—stop, that hurts! Grrrrrr I'm doing this for you. What are these humans? Stupid?

I'm barking harder now. Stop it. Don't. I'm saving everyone here. Tadeu you stupid, stupid man.

Get your dog to let go of my pant leg, kids. Now!

Tadeu was livid. He kicked at me, spinning me around, I let out a yelp 'cause dikdik, the whole side of my head was in pain and I could see nothing but stars as I fell the ground—but I was back up on my feet before anyone could know—and shook my body from top to bottom. I was good to go, I don't let somebody kicking me keep me down. Rafael and Mariana Vitória didn't hear or see what happened 'cause they were too busy playing with all their friends so when I got up I heard, I'm a baaaad dog—go away.

I give up. I give up! I was just trying save their butts from what is out there and this is all the thanks I get? Okay, let them find out for themselves HOW STUPID—HOW ASININE they are TO OPEN THAT DOOR!

I sat my little sore butt down right there and watched them open the door and let in . . . oh man, how can you!? Oh forget it. I don't even want to see this. I suppose there's going to be a thousand lizards—a diksnik lizard blizzard—but I'm gone 'cause lizards just suck in my book and guess who will have to be up all night trying to get rid of them Who? Well, it wasn't me. Nope. Nix. Nada.

Okay, I'm leaving. Here I go. I'm leaving. You'll miss me when I'm gone .....I'm gone now. Bye.

And I crossed the courtyard with my stub between my legs and my head hung low and went through the kitchen and outside through the back door with no intention of returning if nobody cared. Now my feeblewabble was really flivilflompted.

BOB

Yes sir? Tadeu said to the man standing on the Otherside of the open door. A man whose carefully styled sun-streaked hair and tanned skin made him look distinguished and important. He was dressed in big city clothes: a fine Brazilian shirt and designer jeans and smooth deerskin shoes that looked more like a glove for the foot than a shoe.

From across the yard came Lillian, waving as she ran toward this man yelling, Bob! Bob! What are you doing here?

And the man waved back, but he had no smile.

Lillian pointed over at where Sabrina was out of her wheelchair pushing it to help her to stand up and stiffly walking it around with Xico and the kids and said, Bob! Good news, look at Sabrina—

And when she reached him, Bob commented, That's great, Lillian! What a miracle, I'm so happy for you and Sabrina. He gave her a hug and a kiss on the cheek and she could sense his sadness.

And she's walking and talking . . . what's wrong?

He spoke very softly, Lillian, can we talk outside, sweetheart?

Thinking to herself, *Sweetheart? Bob has never called me sweetheart, what is going on?* as she followed him outside to the sitting area and the large shade trees looking out onto the dirt street running in front of the Pousada.

Where's Abe? She asked when she was standing right in front of him, looking into his sad eyes.

Where's Abraham? She repeated breathlessly.

Tears fell from Bob's eyes. He cleared his throat. Abe . . . Abe keeled over . . . he had a heart attack . . . The man wiped away his tears like they embarrassed him.

Oh God, Lillian said, He's dead . . . isn't he?

He nodded, avoiding her eyes.

Lillian sank down onto a bench—her face white, her hand holding her heart with both hands so that it wouldn't jump out of her chest.

When? She asked.

He sat beside her, I'm so sorry, Lillian, I tried to—

When!

Softly he said, Yesterday... clearing his throat so he could get it out, Late . we had been at a party last night and he was drinking and he started feeling—

She slapped him.

He grabbed his cheek, looking surprised.

A party? He was not supposed to be at a party. He was supposed to be at a very important meeting! One you set up! And anger raged through her. He . . . was. . supposed to be only at . . . very important . . . meetings . . .

I'm so sorry, Lillian, he whispered, so very sorry.

Her eyes were red and filling with glistening tears as she looked straight into Bob's eyes, trying to gather herself. No. He was supposed to be here, helping me and little Sabri . . . oh god . . .

And finally her words failed completely.

Bob sat beside her and tried to take her in his arms but she fought him away.

He tried to say, Please, I know how hard this—But she wouldn't have it. Hundreds of questions pounded into Lillian's mind one after the other. Questions without any damn answers.

What am I going to tell Sabrina? She's so sensitive. She could put herself back in a coma.

Probably best not to tell her anything right now, Lillian.

She doesn't even know Grandmère is dead, because she was still in a coma when it happened.

I had no idea . . .

Bob stayed by her side on the bench, saying no more, while the jovial party inside could be heard going on without them. She didn't move for fear she'd fall part—everything would dislocate and disengage and she would be on the ground—a big amorphous blob of nothing. But then she sat up straight—and decided to be strong.

Are you okay?

Yes, she said, calmly—wiping the tears from her face.

Bob offered her a Kleenex. She took it and blew her nose thinking, *I must be strong for Sabrina, this is her happy time. I will not ruin her happy time.* How was she going to do that? *Just one thing at a time,* she thought. Get one thing done before she went to the next. She stared at the walls and she looked around, just looking, nothing registered. She sighed deeply and stood up, Yeah, that's what I'll do—one thing at a time, she said out loud, mostly to herself.

Looking at the ground, Bob spoke, Lillian, I can't stay. I just wanted to let you know in person so you wouldn't hear about this any other way.

Thank you, I appreciate that, I really do.

Abe's jet is waiting in Brasilia and I'll be flying back to Rio to get his body. I can take Sabrina's equipment in the van with me now—she most likely isn't going to need it for the trip back home. I'll meet you at the airport hotel tonight when I return from Rio. I suggest you pack everything now and leave as soon as possible.

No, I can't, she said firmly. Sabrina needs to be here for maybe a month for completion of her healing.

Bob let out a heavy breath, I'm sorry this had to happen but I'm afraid we have no choice. You'll need to meet with authorities in Brasilia to fill out papers for transport of the body out of the country. Then you'll need to be with the body when it's admitted into the States.

You can't?

I'm not family. It's a foreign country—so many things can go wrong working with the authorities.

Oh God . . .

There was a long pause before Bob spoke. It's a good thing we have Abe's private jet. Please go pack, Lillian. I've arranged for you and Sabrina to stay in a hotel until morning—we have a very early flight back. He held her for a long time before he summoned Tadeu and got into the taxi.

She stood as the taxi moved slowly down the road, feeling very lightheaded. She walked to the door—and started shaking hard. She could feel the beginning of a terrible scream. She covered her mouth with her hand desperately holding the scream back—she turned back and ran out the door and tore down the street, trying to get away as fast and far as she could.

She ran out into an empty field and hid behind a collapsed wall of an abandoned house where no one was, except a contented cow tethered on a jute rope where he could eat the field's grass until his master would come for him at night.

And it was there, where she let go that scream and that deep guttural crying that she couldn't stop from happening no matter how much she tried. She was in Paramanguia, the place of deep healing. It felt as though this was a long needed emotional vomiting.

Which it was.

THE DEPARTURE

Mommy, I've looked everywhere for Xico, said little Rafael. Sabrina will be upset if he's not here to say goodbye, and his cool black eyes looked so concerned.

Flavia wiped her hands, wet from dishwashing. He'll show up, you know nothing gets past Xico.

Rafael and Mariana Vitória ran out of the kitchen and off into the main yard yelling, Xico, Xico*!* Come Xico, Sabrina is leaving, while Sabrina was being pushed in her wheelchair out of the front gate to the waiting taxi. Roberto was busy loading all the luggage and Lillian pacing back and forth making sure they didn't forget anything.

Flavia and Martim and five or six people came out to wish her a safe trip and for everything to work out, and they were so sorry, and they wished them the best, and Flavia reminded her not to forget the directions to where Abe's jet was that Bob had left her.

Sabrina was telling Roberto how she was looking forward to seeing Grandmère and telling her all about the wonderful things that had happened to her here and about Xico . . . and where was Xico?

Flavia stepped forward to give Lillian a hug and noticed how wet Lillian was with perspiration and that her smile of appreciation had a nervous twitch to it. You be well. We'll keep in touch, right? she said.

Lillian kissed her right cheek then her left and said, Of course. And thank you for all you've done for us, I may not be showing how much I appreciate it but I really do—

Mommy, I have to say goodbye to Chico, mommy. Tears were now running down Sabrina's cheek, so Martim squatted down, lifting her chin gently to look into her eyes. Dear Sabrina, he said, Xico would be here if he could but he has very important work to do. He has so much healing to do and that's probably where he is right now. Just like he was there for you all the time every minute, he now has to be there for the next person that needs him so much. You know he is a very famous dog with a mission, don't you? Sometimes when you have an important job, you can't be there for people you really, really love all the time. You understand?

Sabrina stopped crying. She let out a shaky breath, her cheeks wet with tears.

Martim took out his handkerchief from his pocket and wiped her eyes, Better? He asked as Mariana Vitória and Rafael came running back, hot and wet and breathing hard from searching for that silly dog. Sorry, we couldn't find Xico, we looked everywhere, and then told her that they would miss her so much and they wanted her to come back soon.

Lillian was quiet. She suspected that would never happen, especially without Abe's influence and money. And if there were a will, it would probably have to be contested for years to come. She suspected he'd given it all to the medical University—that was how his mind worked—do for your family while you are alive and give to others for education after you're gone. *A noble thought but perhaps an ignorant deed,* Lillian thought to herself.

THE TAXI RIDE TO BARRA DO BURGES

As the taxi departed, Sabrina and Lillian waved back at their wonderful new and loving friends. Sabrina watched them grow smaller and smaller the further away from the Pousada they drove, and just as they rounded a corner and the Pousada was out of sight, Sabrina saw something through her tears, a wavy-hazy looking . . . dog. A dog that looked just like Xico walking along the side of the road.

Mommy! Mommy, there he is.

Roberto pull over. It's Chico! said Lillian.

Xico was indeed coming out from Pousada Coragão *(Po-sa-da Cord-a-sewmm),* Martim must have been right, Xico had been doing his healing work and now he was going home. They became concerned as they watched Xico, he didn't seem to see them or hear them . . . his head slung low and his back legs looked as though they were shaking from weakness.

* * *

Staying in flivilflompt and feeblewabble can be very dangerous. Yes. I have really sinned. I have. I had . . . a little sex—no . . . a lot—with different bitches and the next one that comes along I'm doing her, too, that'll show ol' Eeooo whom I don't hear anything from anymore cause she's too good and high and mighty and doesn't give a sheebit about me anymore. Boy, that pousada is never gonna see me around here any more—no more free healing work, no sireee. Just because I jumped up on the table and helped myself to a bunch of cold steaks that were just sittin' around, suddenly people thought they had to start screaming at me, smackin' my butt hard—but when they picked me up and virtually threw me out the door and didn't care that I landed on my head, not my feet, that was the clincher. Never again shall I grace them with my presence Truth is, I really hate this world, I hate people, people hate me . . . I'm gonna eat cockroaches and spit them at people . . . buncha no good ingrates . . .

Roberto pulled the taxi over to the side of the road, while Sabrina yelled for Xico. Lillian opened the door and Xico without hesitation jumped right in and started licking everyone in sight, turning around in circles on top of everyone, acting like he hadn't seen them for at least a year or two.

Sabrina held him in her arms and buried her face in his fur. Watching this, Lillian suddenly knew she needed this dog for Sabrina: she knew if Xico were there in her arms when she had to tell her the horrible truth, there was a good chance that Sabrina would not go back into her coma . . . was her prayer being answered? . . . was Xico the answer to all her problems?

Roberto started to whip the taxi around to go back to the Pousada.

No Roberto, lets keep driving. I'd like my daughter to be with Xico for as long as she can, then you can take him with you from Barra do Burges when you go back.

Okay with me, he said and pulled out on the highway headed northeast to Brasileia.

Okay, well I was pretty happy. I was going somewhere with Sabrina and I didn't care where. I was fed up with how I was being treated at that Pousada and I was tired of being taken for granted. I had busted my patootski trying to be a healing dog for everyone and what had it gotten me? Nothing but a headache and a butt ache from being smacked . . . heck I hated Lizards as much as the next guy. Lizards I wouldn't miss. And all the gook and darkness I had to wade through just to get to . . . more lizards. Ha. Those reptiles sure as hezzop wouldn't miss me, that's for sure.

No, this was good—going away. Being with people who loved me for just me . . . no ulterior motive. And talking of ulterior motive, I hadn't heard from The Voice in a long time so I take it, my job was over. Of course I haven't called on Him in a while either, but that's beside the point. I'm with Sabrina and . . . Eeooo's off somewhere and I'm sure she's happy without me . . . so . . . I'm happy and everybody's happy . . . I guess everything is in order . . .

I hope.

BARRA DO BURGES

There it was, just as before, the bustling Barra do Burges, a distinct contrast from slow-and-easy Paramanguaia.

The taxi pulled up at the Hotel del Brazil with its thousands of windows that faced other buildings with thousands of windows. Roberto got out and ran around to open the doors and get out the wheelchair and run to set it up and help Sabrina into the chair.

Lillian smiled at him as they walked the ramp up to the front door. You were right; I am impressed with your talents as the finest taxicab driver I have ever laid my eyes on.

Obrigado, senhora. I do my best.

There is something I'm going to request of you please, Roberto. What might that be?

I would like you to stay here tonight because I may need someone to take us around to do some shopping and to dinner.

That will be my pleasure.

And I don't think this Hotel will admit dogs. Do you have any idea where we can kennel Chico for the night?

Absolutamente! I know of a vet nearby who will have wonderful facilities. I will call on my cell and set it up *rapidamente*. There was something coming from Lillian that was making him very uncomfortable—but he was quick to dismiss it thinking, Nah, it must be because I haven't eaten all day, yeah, that's what he must be feeling. Hunger.

I'd like to go with you to this vet to see for myself, can we go after we have checked in? said Lillian.

Absolutamente, bonito Senhora. Your *desejo é meu comando*.

XICO AT THE VET'S OFFICE
BARRA DO BURGES

Where am I and why am I here?

I didn't like this place. Nope. I hate crates especially stinky crates and this one was smelll-lllly. If I had known the way out, I'da run right outta that foul place licki-spit! Growlin' and meeeeoooooowin goin' on . . . and there was some kinda jungle bird right in the next cage beside me. Have you ever been cooped up with a parrot squaaaaawking right in your ear? Reminds me of the sound of my toenail running down Rafael's balloon—Ergggggh—and it happened all night long. It was so bad my hackles stood straight up and saluted!

And if I listened real hard I could tell what they're saying. Every one of them was sayin', Help! Get me outta here! I wanna go home!

Me included.

Everything was making me very very nervous and I was shakin' like crazy—gugguggguggugg—then the Woo-oo-ooooo-oo went off!

Woo-oooooo-ooo—I couldn't help it!—Woo-oooooo-oooo-ooooo-oooo-ooo-oooo—I know it's a dog thing but I just couldn't access any of my dolphin savvy. I think it had all been over-ridden by my dog programming by then.

And just when I thought I'd calmed down a little and I'd be lookin' for some water to drink and there was none, then—Oh no!—There I'd go again—Woooo-oooooo-ooooo—I was trying to stop—Wooo-ooo-ooo-oooooooooo—I really was . . . and too, I'd be wishin' I could stop shakin' . . . but no can do.

Oh, someone's comin'—who's this? A lady in a white coat? Oh, I recognize her scent. Yeah, I remember she was there when Roberto and Lillian abandoned me, just dropped me off like some old chew toy.

Should I wag my tail and smile or grrrrr my teeth real hard? My plan was that I was goin' to try the wag and the smile routine I cooked up, the one Mariana Vitória and Rafael liked so much, yeah, my plan was to show my friendly side and maybe she'd fall for it just long enough for me to make my getaway. I don't know, though, she was dressed like one of those Entity spirit-doctors at the Moradia, but she had no sparkly light so she must have been some kind of Earth doctor . . . She was calling me Xico, acting pretty friendly and rubbing my ears—so I figured okay the happy technique was working . . . then she said she had a lot of paper work to do. I couldn't tell if she was talking to me or herself or someone else, but . . . I did need to pee! Bad! And I knew that could get me outside . . . so I wagged my tail and acted all nervous, like I did when I needed to tell Rafael to take me out . . .

But it didn't work. I was put back in my crate again.

Oh man! I'll try this—Whoooooooooooo-oooooooo-oooooooo—as loud as I can! I'm in pain here. Oh, thank gawd the Doc was finally coming out and walking over to me.

Yip yip yip—I was sayin'—Open this jailhouse door up, that's right—I was being let out of the still smelly crate—finally—and carried over and lowered to the floor.

And when, at last, I was on the floor . . . Yesss indeed, I was, wee-weein' like crazy all over it—heh heh heh heh—even while I was runnin' around everywhere—Can't catch me, heh heh heh, can't catch me—I'm telling her—and all the time trying to figure out where that friggin' door outta there was: joggin' to the right, the left, right, under chair . . . Look out! Now there was more than one of those white coat people—two—but that was perfectly okay, I could just as well outrun two as one—I used to be Zeeep. I've outrun sharks, for gawdsake—

Oops. Oh buggerz. They got me! Rats and buggerz! heh heh heh Yep, the gig was up. Okay you win, do with me what you want . . . I'm finished. I'm wiped out.

Okay, here we go.

They were liftin' me up-up-up onto this table—Ewww it's so cold—my toenails were makin' a real tickitickiticki racket on that chilly metal table—Oh it's makin' me feel real confident here—tickitickiticki-tickitickiticki I could hardly stand up heh heh heh—I'm tryin'. I'm tryin' to be a good boy here, but this is ridiculous . . . more tickitickiticki-tickitickiticki until—Okay, that works—The doc was running her hands all over my body,—Okay, feels good—and I was starting to calm down a little bit but <u>then</u> a little pokin' started goin' on—No no no that tickles—stopit—

Then—Hey, careful with the ears, they're real sensitive . . . now what's with the eyes? Lifting my eyelids? . . . lifting the lips . . . argg, whaddya tryin' to do, tickle my teeth now? Phoooewy rubber tastin' fingers were not my favorite . . . Yeah lady, that's my mouth, it don't open that big—argggggg—Down the throat you gotta be kiddin'!!!! Stopit stopit now!—Haaaack Haaaaack!—Whadda jerk! . . . Phoooey! I was coughin' and coughin' then I sneezed—hafffffiiiiiiiisht!—Then, I shook my head like about 10 to 20 times, my ears makin' that flap-flap-flap flap-flap-flap sound so she'd leave me alone for a while . . . Please!.

And she must have picked up on my frustration because she started petting me and talkin' really sweetly to me, sayin, 'Sorry little guy . . . So sorry.

Okay better, I started thinking, 'cause a nice rub was going on the tummy there and the lady was talkin' and' talkin' real nice—Okay a little pat on the butt, that's okay . . . more rubbin' ahhhh oh yeah, oh yeah—And just as I was letting my guard down, I swear, she'd snuck up on me once again and started with the private parts.—Hey! What in the heck are you pullin' my tail up for? Get . . . your . . . fingers . . . outta my butt! That's private! Nothin' goes up my butt, that's my rules. Look lady, you don't know me, I don't know you and just let's just keep it that way—I was tryin' to say and all that was coming out was some lame whistling sound—Stopit. Hey, oh shoot, that is friggin' cold, take it out . . . Take it out, NOW! Grrrrrrr Pull that cold thing out of my butt or I'm gonna have ta bite ya . . . . grrrrrrr any time now . . . TAKE IT OUT!

Good, now keep it out! Mortifyin'!—And I was flappin' my ears at least ten to twenty times like mad again.

Welp. Now I guess she knows me a whole lot better in a whole new way now hahahaha . . Gotta keep the jokin' goin' here so's I DON'T GET REALLY DEPRESSED.

Now jeeeeezzzz just what the hezzop is that? I was looking down the longest and skinniest point I've ever seen.—You're stickin' it where, lady? Oh no you're not! No!!!!!!!!!! not there . . . Whaaaaaaaaaa ouch, ouch, ouch, that thing stings like hezzop . . . what's goin' on? What's going' on here—I was getting real warm all over my body . . . oh, oh, I couldn't feel it anymore—I feel so tired all of a sudden . . . so tired . . . Excuse me, I gotta lay down, gotta lay down and take . . . . a little snooooze here . . . just a little . . . lit-tle—

And I didn't see Lillian come in and sign a bunch of papers and pay a bunch of money and say thank you and walk out with me in a smelly crate 'CAUSE I WAS FRIGGIN' ASLEEP.

ROBERTO

Roberto had a great breakfast of sweet Brazilian papaya and green melon and sausages and eggs and all kinds of pastries—a breakfast of Kings. The hotel room had been top-notch, too—oh, he was loving his new job as a taxi cab driver with all its perks.

He glanced at his watch; he was on time if he left now.

He smiled his best flirty smile at the lovely desk clerk and rested his cheek on his hand looking up at her with his big blue eyes. *Ola,* he said, *Doce um do bom dia.*

Doce um do bom dia, a você demasiado, she flirted back. How I can help you, she said in English.

He smiled bigger, you're not from here?

No, she said, her crimson cheeks setting off her white blond hair, I come from England.

Well, welcome.

Thank you.

I am meeting Lillian Fleur this morning, has she come down?

Oh, yes. She was down very early. At around five A M I believe. And you are . . . ?

Roberto . . . Roberto Canarieo, pleased to meet you.

Yes, Roberto she left you a note. She seemed in a bit of a hurry.

Roberto took the note and opened it.

Dear Roberto,

I am so sorry. I had to leave very early; I misunderstood the actual time we were supposed to leave. Luckily, Bob had already arranged for a Limo to take us to the airport.

Thank you so very much for everything you did for us: I am including cash for your fee. The vet bill and hotel bill have already been taken care of.

Thank you again, you are the best taxi cab driver I have ever had the pleasure of laying my eyes on. Stay healthy and happy.

Truly, Lillian and Sabrina

Roberto looked up from the note and asked, Was there a mention . . . anything about a dog?

No, no nothing about a dog.

I guess I need to go pick him up then. His blue eyes twinkling he added, He's a famous dog, you know. Xico is his name. Xico Rodriguez Juliando Mosques. Maybe he's the second or third or the fifth, I don't know. You heard of him?

Uh, no.

Ah too bad. He's very famous. And I'm his driver. Well . . . Okay. Anything else I can help you with? Oh, don't get me started.

She blushed and looked down at her paper work. Have a wonderful day, Roberto, she said.

Yeah, I come this way a lot, maybe . . . I . . .

I'm married.

Oh! Oh. Well, cheerio.

Cheerio.

As he walked toward the door, he removed his cell phone from his shirt pocket and thumb-punched the number of his vet friend.

Outside, he paused to speak into the phone, *Ola, Jauna, Como é você?* Just called to tell you I'm on my way to pick up Xico . . . He'd started down the large staircase and stopped,

What do you mean they came already and picked him up? . . . Aiiii! They're taking him to Canada? . . . What? . . . She . . . No, I can't believe this. Aiiee-yiy-yiy, how can this be? They paid the bill I hope . . . You helped them with the paperwork? What paperwork? It's illegal to take a dog out of the country isn't it? . . . It's not? But you don't understand, my friend, I was supposed to take that dog back to Paramanguaia, that was the deal . . .

He sat down on the step and put his head in his hand, No, they stole that dog, he was a very important dog . . . What? they said it was a gift? A gift? Who from, did they say? . . . They called the Mosques' last night? They said that? That doesn't sound right . . . Well, maybe they did give them the dog . . . But I don't get it, why wouldn't they tell me? . . . Yeah, maybe . . . But now I may lose my job because you didn't call me and let me know and now they're gone and

I'm the one that's screwed . . . I'm not yelling at you . . . No, I'm not . . . Yeah, thanks anyway, yeah, *Adeus*.

Roberto flipped his cell phone shut and sat looking across the lush green lawn and bushy trees and up at all the mirrored windows looking back at him like they were watching him, and he stared at nothing for the longest time. His eyes cleared and he could see, there, way down the street, was sitting the taxi that he'd brought them in and he was thinking how good he'd felt this morning and how bad he felt now.

Maybe he should just go back and not say anything about Xico at all, after all no one saw Xico get in his cab . . . he hoped . . . but maybe someone did . . . he hated telling a lie, he hadn't appreciated Lillian Fleur lying to him so he knew how it would feel to the Mosques' if he didn't tell the truth—but again if he just didn't say anything that wouldn't be a lie . . . maybe if someone asked him . . . then . . .

FLAVIA
2 MONTHS LATER
THE MORADIA SEU JOSE DE BARROS

Flavia moved slowly between the cots. The room was hot. The whirrrr of the three fans attached to the walls, pointed up to the ceiling, was mesmerizing—good for those who were sleeping—but making it hard for her to stay alert.

She had been sitting in the infirmary all day with the people who'd just had physical therapy. There was a little boy just Rafael's age with cancer and as she looked down at him, she felt so grateful her son was in good health, so grateful, but she couldn't help but wish Xico were there to help this poor little soul to heal.

She needed a break and found someone to spell her. She walked outside and stretched long and hard, closing her eyes to experience how good the sun felt on her face, and when she opened them she had to blink a few times to focus. She saw out in the courtyard, a line of pilgrims dressed all in white and standing in line to see Seu Miguel. The line went all the way down the walkway, a good city block long, to the sanctuary by the overlook where one could sit and meditate and look out over the rolling hills. It was there near the line of people, that she saw someone looking very familiar—someone she hadn't seen since Sabrina left and Xico had disappeared.

It was Roberto. And for some reason she was being drawn to walk over to him and strike up a conversation.

Hello Roberto, remember me? Flavia Mosques. How have you been?

He stood up and his face suddenly blushed. Hi, of course, how are you Flavia, long time since I've seen you. How are the children?

Well, they're obsessed with finding Xico, right now.

Why? Don't they know where he is?

No, it's been crazy-making with our family. Martim has been making the rounds asking everyone he sees, and now it's rubbed off on the kids because they're doing the same. Do you know anything about Xico, have you seen him in your travels around town?

I . . . I don't understand. I thought since Sabrina had to leave in the middle of the healing, I thought you had given Xico to Lillian to take to Canada so he could help finish Sabrina's cure. I thought you gave him as a gift. That's what they told the vet—

The vet . . . ?

Roberto looked down and kicked at the ground, then he looked up and told her the whole story and how guilty he had felt and how he was glad that he could finally lift all the bad feelings off his shoulders by telling her everything because he had always worried in the back of his mind that Lillian really <u>had</u> stolen Xico.

Flavia had to sit down and cross her arms—during his cathartic narrative—because Lillian had been her very good friend and now the betrayal was stabbing her hard in the stomach. All the amazing memories of Sabrina's day at The Moradia Dom de José de Barros with Seu Miguel's Entities and everyone working so hard to get Seu Miguel out of jail just so he could be there for her in the most perfect timing and how they had celebrated—and now the memories were turning meaningless and stale.

I'm very sorry. I should have come to you right away and told you everything.

Well, I'm glad we had this talk, now at least we know.

And she stood up and gave Roberto a hug and walked toward their Pousada thinking about how she was going to break this to Martim and, hardest of all, the kids.

She told them during dinner—and the children were devastated. Martim tried phoning Lillian and found her number was no longer hers, so all the next week he went around to all the Pousadas and got a list of everyone who had ever visited The Moradia de Dom José de Barros and started emailing everyone and asking if they would join in on the return of their Xico. He requested they write a letter or as many letters as they could, asking Lillian to relinquish the dog.

Meanwhile, Mariana Vitória and Rafael formed a plan of their own. They were appealing to the local children through posters they had made and hung all over school and when that was done they made more to tack up in shops and stores and anywhere they could find a pole or fence around town. After months of this and getting no response from Lillian, it was the kids that came up with the idea to go see Seu Miguel. After all he could get the Dali Lama or even The Pope in that Vatican way over in Paris or even Rome! That was <u>much</u> closer to Canada then Brazil was, right daddy?

But it was Martim who grabbed their idea and approached Seu Miguel, who indeed was willing to have his lawyer do some investigating.

The news from his lawyer was rather disappointing in the beginning— indeed Lillian had not broken any laws by taking a dog out of the country... except upon further examination, it surely was against the law to export or import stolen goods or animals from a foreign country. Now, the Mosques's had a good legal reason to lean on her and that was when Sargento Fernando Osvaldo Rodriques was contacted to put the pressure on her through the Canadian legal system.

Flavia watched all of this with reservations. Being a mother herself, she could understand Lillian's desperation—having to leave right in the middle of Sabrina's healing. She decided to attend to her prayers in a big way: setting a vision and a loving intention for the highest and best for all concerned. Prayer she knew had the most authentic and influential power.

XICO
MONTREAL, CANADA

Just look out there, would ya? It's blinky-blank cold! That's called snow that's comin' down all over everything—and sometimes this stuff comes down for days and even weeks and even months on end. I ain't lyin'. Nobody had heard of snow back in Paramanguaia and look at me I'm livin' in this body built for the tropics! Ooooooh it's been . . . soooo brrrrrrr-cooooold! And I'm just about getting used to my body doing this constant shake-a-shake-a—shake shake and I'm not talking about dancing either.

Lillian finally got me the cutest fur jacket though . . . can you imagine how embarrassing that was? A little skinny dog walking along with long, shaggy hair stickin' out right in the middle of him. And it was bright pink, too. Humiliating. But that's not as bad as . . . the red—are you ready for this?—<u>booties</u>. Yes, in order for this tropical dog to walk out in the snow without falling through or getting stuck—and freezing every one of my four pads not to mention the toenails that go with it—I had to wear little rubber <u>booties.</u>

Being cooped up all winter has just about pooped out my zippy drive. I've become a flat-liner. Or maybe just old—and it's only been a year. Don't get me wrong, The Voice came back and he and I and Sabrina and Lillian have been down at the hospital in the Recuperation Unit hangin' out working with sick and busted up kids. We been healing them and stuff like that and it's been great fun cause I get to be my crazy self and everybody loves it and I don't get smacked for being a bad dog or anything, so that's good, but Eeeoo hasn't been coming around as much—I think she had some forgiving work to do after my fall from her grace—or maybe it's just my guilt that keeps her away—I guess over on the

Otherside there is nothing but Love and Forgiveness so it's not her but Sabrina and I both miss her . . . I especially miss her.

Oh, Sabrina?

Been walkin' and talkin' and helpin' other kids keep their minds wide open to the angels that come around and help her with the healing. Little Sabrina's really great—no she's friggin' amazing—so much so, I'm startin' to feel my work here is done and I need to go back to Abadiania . . . yesterday would be soon enough.

I'm really missing my other family, Mariana Vitória and Rafael's laughter and kisses, Flavia and Martim and the weird food they serve, and yes, even Tadeu smackin' my butt . . . sigh . . . and Seu Miguel and all the wild things that go on down there in that crazy House of St. Jose' and I miss the spirit doctors and I even miss the lizards . . . .

But I guess, most of all, I miss myself. And I'm so tired of being called Chico—it's not Chico . . . it's Xico!

Eeeoo? . . . Voice? . . . Where are you? I'm tired of being lazy, now I want my old job back . . . and I wanna go home . . . are you listening out there?

Huh?

Hello?

. . .

Hellooooooo-Wooooo-ooooo-oooooooooooo-ooooooooo

MONTREAL, CANADA
THE LAST OF A HARD WINTER, 2004

A little dog sits on the back of the couch looking out the window into the cool dark-blue night outside. He howls now and then—looking this way and that, and the little girl with blond curly locks comes into the room and crawls over the couch cushions and puts her arms around the little dog and whispers in his fur. She carries him to her bed and he crawls in under the covers and curls up in a ball and the little girl snuggles up all around him and lays her little hand on his head and rubs his ears until they both go to sleep.

In the middle of the night when the house creaks and moans from the cold, a knocking is heard - a loud knocking - and a woman awakens from her sleep, confused. She puts on her cold chenille robe and her squeaky leather slippers and shuffles down the hall towards the front door. She enters the darkened front room with only a small lamp on in the window, and goes to the door, not wanting to turn on the porch light until she knows who might be there - the knocking is so loud. Yes, they'd gone to bed early, but no one comes knocking at night unless...

The woman moves quietly to the window and is careful to part the curtains just enough to see who's out there, and her body goes weak when she sees two very large men on the porch puffing out breath-smoke and dancing around to keep their circulation going. And waiting.

Oh God, what was she going to do—two men dressed in black and only she and her daughter and the dog are here. Then she catches sight of the car . . . down there . . . at the end of the driveway . . . their police car.

Another knock—louder and faster—but this time she can hear a muffled, Police! Open up we'd like to talk to you.

She goes to the door and with great trepidation she opens it a crack.

Yes? . . . she says.

Lillian Fleur? They say.

Yes . . .

Do you mind if we come in?

What is this about, officers? She finds a voice coming out of her that is strong and defiant—

May we enter and discuss our reason, it's very cold . . .

Her arms cross her body and she refuses to answer.

Madam Fleur, we have evidence that you are harboring a small dog stolen from Paramanguaia, Brazil.

I have no dog, officers, so if you'll excuse me . . . and she starts to close the door.

We've just interviewed your neighbors, ma'm, and they have verified that you indeed have a dog on your premises answering to the description we have on file—and they go on and on about breaking the law and penal code this and that and it all becomes such a blur after awhile—and so she says, Leave me alone! I have no dog, I don't know what you're talking about . . .

And when she can't think of anything more, she slams the door on the police and puts her body against it and notices that she can't breathe very well and she's shaking all over.

Lillian remembers that all year long she has been opening up her email inbox and seeing hundreds of messages . . . first, a few from Flavia, then Martim, then hundreds from all over the world—places and people she'd never even heard of or met—and some of them were kind and pleading, and others were threatening and cruel, and the ones from Mariana Vitória and Rafael were just simply heartbreaking and then came the children's e-mails from distant places telling of how Seu Miguel healed them and how he needed Xico back to help him with his work with children and would she please send him home?

Then the letters from Seu Miguel's lawyer came . . . and every day she was constantly erasing them all so Sabrina wouldn't find out . . . and every day she was haunted with the guilt which has taken over her life—and is now making it unbearable.

She can't send Xico home—no—Xico has been a godsend. He's helped her daughter to heal and when Lillian told Sabrina the truth about Grandmère and Abraham—it was Xico on her lap, licking her tears away.

But no, Sabrina is stronger now and happier because she is helping children heal with the help of Xico—now her life has a wonderful purpose.

But the policemen aren't going away and now Sabrina is awake and standing there looking up at her, her eyes wide and scared, and Xico is at the door barking at the space underneath and the warpy energy on the otherside.

Sabrina runs over and picks up Xico and turns to look up at her mother, and her eyes are wise and clear and she says to her, we have to take Xico back to Brazil mommy—let's take him home.

And she is right. Lillian couldn't live this life of lying any longer.

XICO COMES HOME

My return home was—spectacular—cheering and laughter and everybody's so happy to see me again. Mariana Vitória and Rafael and Flavia and Martim all welcomed Sabrina and Lillian back and showered them with forgiveness—and me? I was so elated. Everyone I loved was right there again in one big package—except Eeeooo—but the best of all . . . I was friggin' WARM again.

~EPILOGUE~

On January 2, 2006, I graduated from Earth.

And as I was ending my trip down the great tunnel leading into the Bright Light, Eeeooo was there with tears of Love in her eyes and in her heart and I cried out of sheer Joy because I finally had my sweet lover back—we were together again.

The Voice and Eeeoo took me to the Otherside where all the Doctor Entities and Light Beings and Legions of Angels I'd worked with in Paramanguaia greeted me in a celebration that made everything on Earth look faded and flat like in a dream. And as my life was played out on the hologram I was able to feel a warm a deep sense of accomplishment and self-worth beyond my wildest dreams. My life had been blessed and bless-ed, I was here emerged in Love. This was real—this was the Truth—and I was welcomed Home again.

And Eeeoo and me? We love each other up all the time, and go to concerts of Angels and fly over mountains of diamond blue and oceans of onyx purple and . . . ohhhhh an amazing thing happened—a large, blue turquoise butterfly suddenly appeared and flew all around us before disappearing into a whole fleet of butterfies flying in exquisite formation like that of a floating lace—what a sight that was—oh, how I love the magic and we sing all the time and we hear gorgeous music never even thought of existing yet, and the artists here are doing things they can't even begin to describe in any language and Eeeoo and I are dabbling with this intense desire to—paint—we love it so much.

So today we are in the Temple of Records because we have a very important appointment with The Voice who will be representing us to the Highest Council of The Great Spiritual Poobah up here. Yeah, it's a big deal. We're planning our next life together—maybe in Paris or New York or some place like that where we will learn how to paint and become . . . great artists. Human artists. Would you believe? And at our last gallery showing, we connected some amazing ideas we're dying to try out. Get it—dying? Just a little reincarnation joke I'm trying out . . . heh heh heh. And I'm thinking, maybe I'll try out a little standup comedy while I'm there, tell jokes about dolphins or dogs—or humans—that's always good for a hoot. But then I'd like to try out an instrument maybe an oboe or a fiddle or maybe . . . no no no—I wanna try . . . maybe cooking, yeah I could find out what it was like to have gourmet human food especially if we're in Paris, or . . . or we could take care of animals, Eeeooo would like that, you know kinda payback, but then . . . oh oh I'd love to learn dancing can you imagine Eeeooo and I doing the Tango we'd be so hot-hot-hot and oh by the way this is THE END it really is, so you can stop reading now if you wanna but I know Eeeooo and I could become famous Tango dancers from Argentina but I'd have to think about that because I have my heart set on New York or Paris like I said, but I'd love to move my body ew-ew like makin' love oh yeah I want to do a lot of that too . . . So dancing is good but . . . how about high jumping wooooo that'd be great, maybe try out for the Olympics . . . but that would take a lot of practice and I'd really like to try my hand at doing Sculptures, you know big ones like Michael An-gello did with that David fellow or maybe that might be too difficult right off so maybe I could do huge, cause I want to do huge, huge sculptures for high-rise buildings, modern, yeah, I could really design something great for the Guggenheim or how about a bridge somewhere and when I was done I'd throw pottery, just little pottery, nothing big, but then I've heard a lot about being a mom so that would mean I have to be the girl and Eeeoo would have to be the boy and I don't know we'll have to discuss it but I think it might work out because heck, I need to know about being female and having babies and stuff like that and she sure could sure learn about what it's like to have testosterone running your brain cause she never could understand when I went on my binges sexually . . . you know? It made sense to me but then I never could understand her moodiness so that would be good for me to learn, so I think this all could be good which makes me wonder why just two sexes? Why isn't there more than just two, I mean, it could get boring . . . maybe we'll invent something, maybe we'll be the first clones to . . .

PORTUGUESE NAMES AND THEIR PRONUNCIATIONS

Miguel Sousa da Silva *(Meeg-el Su-za da Seel-va)*
Seu Miguel Sousa da Silva *(See-u Meeg-el Su-za da Seel-va)*
Seu Miguel dos Milagres *(Meel-log-gres)*

Pousada Raiar do Sol *(Po-sa-da Hi-yar-jch do Sole)*
Pousada Coragão *(Po-sa-da Cord-a-sewmm)*

Hospital de Bela Aurora *(Hose-peet-tal dee Bel-woo Ad-roar-da)*
Habitação da Cura *(Habit-a-cow da Ku-da)*

Inely *(E-nel-lee)*
Martim *(Mar-cheem)*

Moradia de Dom José de Barros *(Mod-o-shee dee Dome shJo-say day Ba-hoose)*
Dom José de Barros *(shJo-say day Ba-hoose)*

Dr. José Lacerda de Adão Santos *(Dou-tor shJos-ae La-ser-da day Ja-dow San-toos)*
Matria de Energia *(Ma-tree-a de Ener-shjeee-a)*

Barra do Burges, Mato Grosso, Brazil *(Baha do Bushz-ee, My-you Groz-zah, Bra-zeel)*
Paramanguaia *(Para-mon-gee-a)*

Tupani, Mato Grosso do Norte *(To-pan-ee Mau-do Groz-zah du Nort)*
Porto Alegre *(Porto A-leg-grey)*
Brasileia (*Bra-zil-ee-a)*

ABOUT THE AUTHOR

Cher Slater-Barlevi, MA is an Artist, Writer and Spiritual Counselor with a passion for lifting consciousness on this planet.

Her background is in the arts as a graduate of Art Center College of Design getting her BA, cum laude, in Illustration. She's illustrated children's books, tabletop books, magazine editorials and education books. She also illustrates and writes her own children's books under the name of *Gramma Nanna Banana*.

She has worked 40 years in show business: working both sides of the camera—as an actress in film and theater and featured in hundreds of commercials. She has experience heading both Hair, Makeup, and Wardrobe Departments for film, TV and commercials. During that time she also worked as a model and stylist for photographers.

Her passion as a writer started while working in Hollywood as a screenwriter for 12 years. While attending UCLA and Media Bistro, she was able to work on her dream—to write a novel about healing. For over 40 years she has worked at developing her talents as a Medium: doing readings and using her art for channeling large "SOUL" paintings having to do with images and messages she receives, to help to move people's lives forward. She also does art with a message for people's pets to help in the healing process, whether it has to do with a pet's health, the owner's healing or after a pet's passing.

After earning her Master's at the University of Santa Monica in August, 2011, she has worked with the graduate volunteers from the Freedom to Choose Prison Project. She also loves working with people, helping them to find the "Kid Within®"" through her retreats and seminars: sharing her insights into the immense value of having "Fun" and "Play" in their life.

Visit www.dogofgod.com